Cookstrips

The first cookbook I ever owned – rather than took off my mum's or my nan's kitchen shelf – was a unique object. I still have it. A second-hand, hardback edition of the *Action Cookbook* by Len Deighton. It was the 1970s, so it had a piece of parsley on the front cover, but it was jammed down the barrel of a Smith and Wesson Model 40 Centennial revolver.

In 1962 Deighton had written the incredibly successful espionage novel *The Ipcress File*, which in 1965 was made into a film starring Michael Caine as Harry Palmer, the working-class spy with a laconic line in chat and a way with the pots and pans.

In 1962 Deighton was also the Food Correspondent for the *Observer* where he created 'Cookstrips'. These were, I suppose on one level, 'cartoon recipes'. He'd trained as a graphic designer and illustrator and said that rather than take his treasured cookbooks into the kitchen to get messed up, he'd draw a kind of visual representation of the recipe instead.

I was at art college myself when I first saw the Cookstrips. To me, they were something completely different. Recipe books back then were aimed solely at women and if they weren't joylessly practical, were about a middle-class, aspirational scene of dinner parties and 'entertaining'. They didn't speak to me on any level.

The Cookstrips did. I felt, immediately, that they were the most brilliant form of communication I'd ever seen. So innovative, so clear and so minimal. I became obsessed. I had no idea back then that I'd ever make a living writing about food. But if I had, I'd have wanted to do it like Deighton.

There's a shot at the beginning of *The Ipcress File* film, when Harry Palmer is moving around his flat making coffee for breakfast. I already had the same percolator and grinder as my hero, but I noticed there was a Cookstrip pinned to a pillar in his kitchen. It was a tiny detail – Deighton was on set throughout the shoot and there are lots of quirky little references – but this was special. I had to have that Cookstrip on my wall…

(Continued inside the back cover...)

ULTIMATE STEAK SANDWICH

1. CUT

Flank Steak

into thick FINGERS

dried oregano
chilli flakes
garlic

EVOO 25%
RED WINE 75%

MARINATE

SLICE white onion

glug balsamic vinegar

2.

GRILL bread (one side only) **PRESS DOWN** to crisp

DRY & SEAR the steak

HOT & DRY

LOWER heat **ADD** (drained) onions

@ 54°C (129°F) core temp **REMOVE** steak to rest

COOKSTRIPS

3. POUR marinade
into the hot pan
REDUCE it to a syrup!

4. BUILD then NAIL on the lid

DIJON
SAUCE
ONION
STEAK
LETTUCE
DIJON

BREAD

BREAD

DIJON → DON'T SKIMP

Steak

Steak

———

Tim Hayward

Photography by Sam Folan

quadrille

Contents

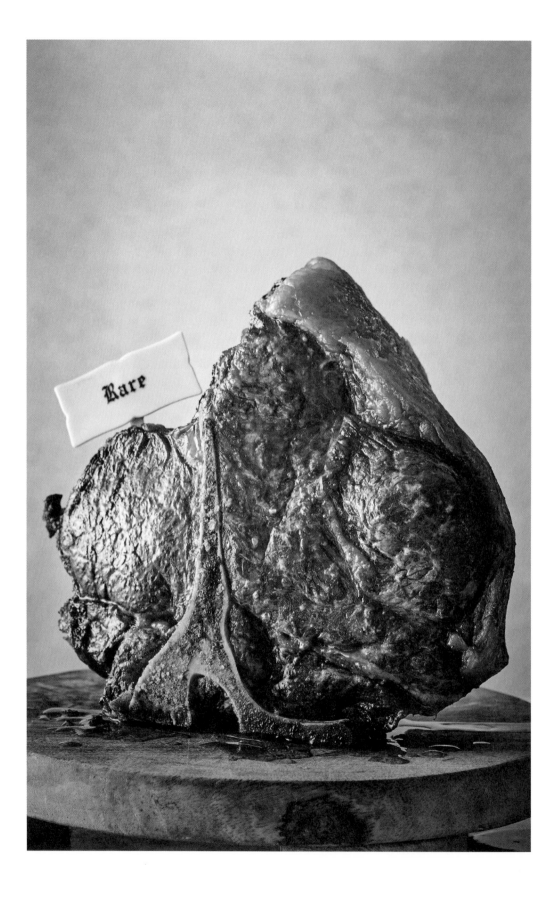

Steak

Steak is unlike any other food. It's a single lump of protein, usually from a cow, that's prepared in the simplest way possible. It should be the most un-complicated thing on the menu, but instead we've turned it into one of the most complex, symbolic and status-riddled foods in the Western canon. We have steak houses and steak restaurants, we go out for steak dinners and the butcher leads us to the expensive end of the counter to select 'a nice piece of steak'. Most foods have recipes – steak has rules. And people want to argue them.

Most food we order off a menu with a simple pointing finger, but steak requires that we, the customer, should tell the cook how we want it. When was the last time you ordered aubergine and were asked how you wanted it cooked? Animals are bred specifically for their steaks; states, nations and entire cultures define them-selves through steak.

So is it time to demystify the steak? Absolutely not! That would take all the fun out of it. Instead, let's become Steak Geeks. Let's find out how to choose them, cook them and serve them. Let's find everything that's ever been written about steak, bring it into one place and celebrate it. Let's cook together and learn. Let's have deep and involved conversations with our butchers, brief waiters with confident assurance, and tell chefs exactly what we want and why. This book contains everything you need to do just that.

Tartare with Elliott

Not long after starting on this book, a food-loving friend and I got our families together for dinner. These events are always a long, boozy sprawl, but they'd told me that their son Elliott, a brilliant and intense young man, had developed a fondness, bordering on the obsessional, for steak tartare.

It seemed an odd choice for him. An unashamedly old-fashioned, old bloke dish, but it's also delightful and I felt he should be encouraged. It would be kind of fun, I thought, if 14-year-old Elliott could make tartare as a starter for our dinner, in the old-fashioned way … table-side.

I love cooking with young people. I love their excitement in the creative mess, discovering the joy of making actual, physical stuff and presenting it to people, the delight in making them happy. There's selfish glee too, to be taken in passing on knowledge. But I also know that cooking in front of people can be a challenge. If we were going to do this, I had to make sure it was researched properly and organized to the last micron. So with about a month to go, I hit the books, started talking to experts, seeking ingredients, trialling and testing as I dived into my own happy place; the glorious maelstrom of mad arcana surrounding a single dish.

The commonest legend of tartare is that it was invented by the nomadic horsemen who ranged over what is now the Russian Steppe around the thirteenth century, under the command (at least for a while) of Ghengis Khan. These ferocious warriors, so the origin myth goes, would take the best meat from animals they'd slaughtered on cattle raids and hang it under their saddles for the ride back to camp. The heat of the horse's body, the salt of its sweat and the vigorous massaging of the saddle on a long, hard ride, tenderized and flavoured the fresh meat so the rider could tear into it, raw, when he got home around teatime. Rubbish, of course.

Actually, there are recipes for highly seasoned raw meat preparations all over the world. *Larb*, *carne cruda*, *kibbeh nayyeh*, *çiğ köfte*, *yukhoe, kifto*, many of which stretch back further than the Tartars. There are traditions amongst hunting cultures across the globe of eating some portion of the animal raw immediately after death. We have evidence of human ancestors hunting before we have evidence of fire.

Wild meat would have been tougher than the stuff we've grown used to today, so the only way to improve its texture before eating would have been to pound it with rocks. Human dentition is partially adapted to holding and tearing meat, so pounding would always have been a way to make meat that the family had hunted accessible to those too young, too old or too sick to rip into a steak. The idea of grinding steak to make something nourishing, health giving and healing was sunk into our psyches. In fact, pounding raw steak and administering it, almost as a medicine, so far predates any kind of recipe or cultural tradition that it feels like a deeper human behaviour.

Auguste Escoffier's recipe for Steak à la Tartare, is admirably short and basically runs, as almost most all his recipes do, as a variation on something else. His Steak Tartare recipe, one of the earliest written, was a derivative of Beefsteack à l'Américaine, served 'without the raw egg' and with tartare sauce on the side.[1]

---

[1] A mayonnaise-style emulsion sauce made with tarragon, chopped cornichons and capers. Now almost solely served with fish.

Beefsteack à l'Américaine is Escoffier's recipe for raw ground meat with capers, chopped onion and chopped parsley on the side and a raw egg on top. This was a quirky, off-menu item, jazzing up the raw mince that some American customers were ordering because of their own health regimes. Think of it as the green salad and egg-white omelette of its day. If Gwyneth Paltrow had gone to the Paris Ritz in 1898, she would doubtless have pushed the menu listlessly aside and whispered, 'Do you think Auguste could whip me up a Beefsteack à l'Américaine.'

The Américaine/American connection was important. Partly in adding another laden branch to the story – partly in giving me the bones of an ingredients list. If our steak tartare was going to be authentic, it must at least contain Escoffier's…

Capers
Chopped onion
Chopped parsley
And a raw egg on top

We know that the consumption of raw meat for health had taken off early in the US. Dr James H. Salisbury was a champion of a meat-centric diet and a surgeon during the American Civil War. He recommended his low carbohydrate 'Salisbury Diet' for weight loss and also believed that a regime of coffee and finely chopped beefsteak could cure diarrhoea in soldiers. He felt that a balanced diet should contain less than a third of starchy or vegetable foods and prescribed a Salisbury steak (see page 298) three times per day.[2]

There had long been an appreciation that prize fighters and jockeys could benefit from a protein heavy diet, which could indeed help with building muscle while avoiding carbs and fat. Boxers traditionally ate beefsteaks to build strength while training for a fight, an idea that seems to appear in many cultures. In 1929, M.F.K. Fisher, then living in Dijon, wrote:

'Down on the place d'Armes near Racouchot's, there was a restaurant … the Pré Aux Clercs … [that] made very good grilled rare steaks with watercress, which at that time were beginning to be in great vogue in the big cities among the younger generation … les sportifs … but were dismissed with impatient disgust by older gourmands raised in the intricate traditions of fine sauces and culinary disguise. It was like the Chateaubriant at the other end of the town, also known mostly for its steak and watercress and french fries.'

But it's not until the 1950s when steak tartare appears simultaneously on the menus of high-class restaurants in New York, London and Paris.

It's useful here to understand something of the workings of a grand restaurant when steak tartare was at its peak. Unlike the restaurants of today, they were almost never named after a chef. It's notable that for all his later fame, Escoffier never had his own name over the door. The chef was there to run the kitchen, but the restaurant – the 'room' – was run by the maître d'. It was the maître d' whose favour was courted, whose name was exchanged between enthusiastic diners, who managed the quality of the clientele upon whom the reputation of the place really depended. And it was the maître d' who could often be bought with a suitably cash-loaded handshake.

In fact, the entire structure of front-of-house ran on the customer's discretionary gratuities. A fat tip to the maître d' might be distributed, or just trousered along with his salary. The waiting staff, all lifelong professionals, often worked for no pay whatsoever, relying on tips, which in the best rooms, could be huge. In the best restaurants, the waiters paid a percentage of their tips back to the maître d' (if they wanted to keep their jobs), a percentage to the wine 'captain' and smaller handouts to the various under-waiters and runners who flocked around the table, creating the performance of service.[3]

---

[2] I should say that even 150 years later, I instinctively concur with every one of the good doctor's tenets … except maybe the one about soldiers and diarrhoea.

[3] Even today, when the balance between proper pay and discretionary tips is much more sensible, there's a kind of folk memory in the hospitality industry that a 'poor tipper' is directly depriving the server, in person, and is thus contemptible to the very core of their soul.

This balance of back and front-of-house seems odd to us today, but it's the driving logic behind many of the restaurant practices of the time. Table-side 'theatre' got bigger tips and that meant more money distributed around the crew. Whipping a giant silver cover off a dish with a flourish was worth a few extra pence. A waiter involved in the actual production of the food was worth even more and, best of all – in the days before sprinkler systems and smoke alarms – anything that involved setting fire to dinner was worth big handfuls of folding money.

It is the tip structure, then, that gave us the gueridon: the chariot or cart that could be wheeled to the table as a conveniently portable stage for the performance. Sometimes it was used to bring a cheese selection, sometimes to haul over the huge, steaming 'joint' to be carved. This not only bumped up the tips, which the floor staff loved, but also created a kind of feeding frenzy in the room. You couldn't really sit, sharing a modest bowl of soup with your date if the next table was enjoying a three-ring circus of ritual, fire and meat. Some dishes from the gueridon might not have been objectively the hautest of cuisine, but the whole 'we'll have what they're having' dynamic made them the most popular and lucrative items on the menu. At its best, the gueridon gave us the table-side steak dishes – Diane, Monkey Gland, Carpetbagger, all the panoply of performative dining – and lemon sole, dissected perfectly before your eyes, Fettucine Alfredo whipped up in a wheel of Parmesan, crêpes suzette and, of course, steak tartare.

Mixing those ingredients table-side was a sure-fire tip winner. The raw meat option wasn't an invalid food any more, it even had a sexy little edge of danger.[4] You had to be a serious player to go for the tartare and the punters loved it.

There was no question. This was going to be a public performance, and Elliott was going to need some gear…

A big stainless steel bowl
Spoons to move ingredients
Big forks for mixing
And a cart

…He was definitely going to need a cart

Setting up the gueridon for service requires understanding of one of the most important principles of restaurant life: the vital mise-en-place. If you look for a strict translation, it means 'establishment', conveying the idea of everything being in its correct place. In fact, a very literal translation would be 'put-in-place'. But in 'kitchen French' the 'mise' signifies much more. It's the nature of work in a commercial kitchen that cooks might only spend a few hours in the utter firefight of service – the hours when the public are in the dining room – but they'll spend many more, while the restaurant is quiet, preparing ingredients, side dishes, and constituent parts of mains. This is the 'prep'. A cook who thinks ahead will do as much prep as possible, so there is less to do in service. 'Mise' is how the prepped stuff is lined up, ready to go, without having to think, when the first ticket chatters off the printer.

When a waiter wheels the gueridon to the side of the table, the mise is entirely ready. Everything portioned, weighed out, ready to roll, so the ritual of finishing the dish can run on greased rails. Getting the mise straight was going to be vital for our starter.

But I've long believed that the mise does something else for the food in a restaurant. Often, particularly in places like diners or steakhouses,

---

[4] I always love it when I order the tartare and the waiter asks, 'You are aware, sir, that's raw?' I used to be a little insulted that they maybe thought I was such a hopeless rube that I didn't know the whole damn story, chapter and verse, but then I did an interview with an old maître d' who'd spent years serving tableside in some of the world's best restaurants. 'If we stopped asking,' he said, 'people would be so unhappy. Of course the person who ordered it knows that the meat is raw… that's why they ordered it. The point of asking is so everyone else at the table is clearly informed that a tartare is raw meat, and that the diner is a wild and fearless culinary adventurer.' I loved it. I loved it so much I nearly tipped him.

people who are maybe not full-on master chefs stare, every day, at the same organized line of ingredients. Only a hack with no soul would not experiment. I don't believe anyone invented the chilli burger any more than I believe that a cook, with burger patties and a big pot of chilli on his line for two different dishes, wouldn't at some time combine the two. Same is true of the French dip sandwich, the Philly cheesesteak, and Steak Diane. Having spent far too much of my youth as a line cook in diners, steakhouses, seafood shacks, and every level of general low-end hash-slinging, I can honestly say that, despite feverish claims and spurious origin myths, 99% of the menu of every one of these joints developed from the mise and not from the genius of an individual. 100% creativity, 0% attributable to individuals or establishments. I can see why restaurants and indeed diners would want to attribute Tournedos Rossini to the personal tastes of a genius chef or a celebrity diner – that's just competent marketing – but knowing what a chef would have had in his mise in a French restaurant in 1890, I just don't buy that it had a whole lot to do with Rossini (see page 179).

But this does go some way to explaining some of the more 'out there' ingredients that crop up in a tartare. It would have been a poor restaurant that didn't have a few anchovies left over, and a poor chef that didn't wonder whether they'd perk up the tartare as well as they did other dishes. There was always hot red pepper in some form. If not fresh chopped, then dried and flaked, and if that didn't work, Tabasco could be had by negotiation with the bartender. Worcestershire sauce would be back there too, a clever substitute for fresh chillies and anchovies all in one splosh. Mustard went with beef … sure, why not. Hell, if your clientele were more straight-out rich than necessarily classy, you'd probably do well adding a glug of ketchup. Yes! They'd go for that, and the sweet/sour element would really help things along. There is no original 'master' recipe for steak tartare. It's a kind of living meme, grown and iterated from countless repetitions. Not a protected classic, defended and protected through aeons but of a function of a kind of service Darwinism. Elliott probably wouldn't

need a written recipe, but he was certainly going to need a few more ingredients. Let's add…

Worcestershire Sauce
Mustard (Dijon or English… we'll decide later)
A single anchovy… not essential with the
Worcestershire there, but key to the theatre
Tabasco
Ketchup?[5]

I'm lining up the ingredients in this list and suddenly something lights up in my head. Maybe it was the ketchup thing … but I remember someone asking me to write a piece about the sauce in a Big Mac. What was it? What was the combination of ingredients in that pink unction that transubstantiated an utterly flavourless meat-puck-and-bun combination into the best-selling food on the planet? It took weeks of searching, stalking food nerds and borderline loon obsessives online, reading endless food blogs about experiments in professional kitchens and dorm rooms to discover that the 'special sauce' in a Big Mac, though an incredibly well-guarded industrial secret, was in fact derived from 'Chop Sauce', a standard in American burger bars in the 1950s, composed, unsurprisingly, of everything in the mise-en-place, stirred into mayonnaise.

That's right. Chopped onions, chopped pickles, mustard, Worcestershire, hot sauce … hang on. Is this ringing any bells?

It was only last year that I sat reviewing the new restaurant of a promising young chef on the English south coast. Every item on his menu was clever, challenging, innovative, creatively brilliant, but the one that jumped out at me was a starter of 'Steak Tartare with Big Mac Sauce'. I know the guy's work: he knows his food history and his way with flavour combinations is intuitive and inspired. The recipe had sprung fully formed in his mind … and I think I can see why.

As the day of the dinner approached, it was time to get the meat, and this is not a case of dropping into a supermarket and picking up a dispiriting pod of prime mince. There were lots of considerations.

---

[5] No. I just can't. I'm sorry, but that feels too far to push it.

People have issues with raw meat and they're not wrong. All manner of pathogens are usually killed by the heat of cooking. If we're honest, one of the main reasons we cook meat at all is to make it 'safe'. There are questions around the safe serving of raw meat and I don't take lightly the idea of helping a young person poison his family, so it was going to be important to understand the full risks. Almost all the pathogens that meat can carry are bacteria that develop and reproduce in a very specific set of circumstances. These tiny organisms need a certain window of temperature, they need a certain degree of moisture, they dislike salt and they need air to breathe.

Think, for a minute, about the 'rules' we apply to storing meat. We refrigerate it. That's because bacteria can't reproduce below 5°C (41°F). We cook it because bacteria are killed by exposure to temperatures over 65°C (149°F).[6] We wrap it tightly to exclude air so the little buggers can't breathe and if we really want to preserve meat without refrigeration, we salt it or dry it.

Healthy meat doesn't have bacteria in it at the point the animal is killed. Bacteria are deposited on the surface during butchering and processing and, without wishing to get too graphic, the slaughter (and initial butchery processes are pretty messy). There's a lot of dirt on the outside of a live cow and there's a lot of fecal matter about when you cut up a dead one. The possibilities for cross-infection are endless, but even then, away from the surface of the meat, away from the air, bacteria can't take a hold. A steak that's so rare it's raw in the centre will have no home for bacteria within and will have had its surface entirely sterilized by searing. Perfectly, totally clean.

But this leaves us with the problem of mincing.

Unlike a steak, with a tight airless interior and a limited surface area to sterilize, mince has, by its very structure, a vast surface area. In even a small

weight of mince a ridiculously large proportion of the meat is exposed to the air and, as a lot of cheap mince is actually ground at the same plants where animals are slaughtered and 'processed', you can see why there are very strong regulations around serving raw mince in restaurants.

In French *boucheries*, they have things better organized. You choose the lump of meat you want from the counter and the butcher feeds it through a mincing machine which, by law, extrudes past a powerful UV-C light – which also kills bacteria. No, I'd have to chop the meat myself, as close to the moment of preparation as possible. So I went to my butcher and spent a happy hour discussing the piece we wanted. I know Dan well. In fact, I know him the way everyone who cooks should know their butcher. I know he cares deeply about food, about animal welfare and his trade. He's shown me round his spotless fridges, and he has a cutting room in which I'd happily consent to be operated on. A relationship like that and subsequently an ability to trust the full supply route of your ingredients is possibly the single most important factor in any food hygiene.

We could choose fillet steak. The easy option. A pure fatless single muscle with a soft texture but very subtle flavouring. That would be easy to chop up, but it would require heavier seasoning. We could go for rump, also a single muscle, with more pronounced flavour but a tougher chew. That would require much finer chopping. It would be good to have a decent fat content – but that would have to be well distributed intra-muscular fat, not big ugly lumps. Hmmmm. Wagyu? Incredibly expensive, good when raw but, I would argue, rather missing the point.

We settled on a grass-fed Hereford sirloin. Dan knew a lot about the animal and showed me how one end of the 'strip' had better marbling than the other. It was a lot to think about. Loads of variables and each of them affecting the way we might think about handling and seasoning the meat when the

---

[6] Trainee cooks are taught the mantra "sixty five to stay alive" because bacteria are killed by even short exposures at that level. There is in fact a graph by which you can calculate other time and temperature combinations that are similarly lethal – this graph illustrates the process of pasteurisation. Products can be safely pasteurised at lower temperatures if held there for longer periods. At searing temperatures – like the flat surface of a hot pan on which you lay a steak – the process is instantaneous.

time came to serve. I thought we'd made a good decision on the fat content, but it would be good to be able to increase that. Don't the Italians bump up the rich smoothness of their tartares with olive oil? I made a mental note to add it to the list…

Extra virgin olive oil

I drove home with the wrapped steak on the passenger seat. I'd spent so much time getting to know it, I couldn't consign it to the boot. It should ride up front with me.

When I got the steak home, I dried it off carefully with kitchen roll, then powdered it generously with Maldon salt. That would make things uncomfortable for any surface bacteria, plus it would add to the flavour. I wrapped it loosely with butcher's paper. That protects the meat but also allows air to move around it. Fridges are incredibly desiccating environments and a night stored like this would allow the steak to dry out, losing a small percentage of its weight as water evaporated and, along with the salt, subtly curing the meat and concentrating flavours. As I patted it gently and closed the fridge door, the distant memory of putting my baby daughter into her cot passed disturbingly through my mind.

The day arrived. I'd quietly transferred the meat to the freezer 20 minutes before it was time to assemble which hardened it a little, so it was easier to slice wafer thin. After that, it was simple to cut twice, at 90° angles, to reduce the meat to regular dice with minimum exposure to the air. Come to think of it, it probably remained safely below 5°C (41°F) anyway.[7]

As drinks were being served to the guests, Elliott and I convened over the cart. OK, I admit, many years ago, I spotted a mid-century Scandinavian gueridon cart in a junk shop and leapt at it. The woman behind the counter with acquisitively beady eyes spun me some yarn about a cocktail wagon, but I could see the big ring-shaped burn mark where one too many waiters had been overenthusiastic when flambéing the crêpes. I can't remember what I paid for it, but it was a steal. I love the way it has a box on one side with holes in it for bottles of brandy, Worcestershire sauce, and little cups of chopped stuff. We talked through the order of things. He saw the mise, set up in order from left to right, adjusted a couple of things … I must have been in thousands of briefings with cooks, but Elliott … hell, he *got it*. He kind of read the ingredients the way he'd placed them … left to right. I don't know, is this how they play video games? He could see how it followed … no, *explained* the recipe. And then, when everyone had been seated, he wheeled the trolley over as if born to the job and began a deft assembly.

You can find a full recipe later on in the book (see page 160), but Elliott didn't need it. He'd seen it done and, of course, the process was intuitive. The anchovies have to be broken up against the side of the bowl with the fork. The mustard goes in early, like emulsifying a mayo. Once the meat has gone in, the egg yolks are smoothly combined. That stuff is all organization and then later, muscle memory. This was proof positive of the *Power of the Mise*. But cooking isn't just about technique, it's also about taste.

Any young cook must develop their taste, understand and trust it, and a dish like tartare, where distinct and powerfully flavoured components are gently tweaked, adjusted and brought into balance, is all about tasting as you go. Elliott got that straight away … you don't need a measurement for salt or lemon juice, you need a tongue and an opinion. It was unbelievably good to watch him tasting and judging, stirring and adjusting. He scooped the meat into rough quenelles on to toast points and served it to warm applause.

We'd decided months before that it would be a good idea to write something about steak. We talked about it being comprehensive, accessible, about the relevance of steak in the modern diet. We'd also considered sustainability arguments,

---

[7] Once you've reduced the meat to thin slices you can put it back into the freezer for another 5 minutes. It will stiffen very quickly, making cutting even easier. I use latex gloves while prepping too.

the ever noisier frenzy around lab-grown meat and the rising cost in a crashing economy. I'd had several false starts and hadn't quite found the way in. As I cleaned down the kitchen at the end of the evening, I realized the problem had resolved itself. Going back to first principles, researching in order that Elliott could cook, I realized that steak isn't an ingredient or a recipe. It's a symbol, a cultural icon, a cluster of dreams, preconceptions, traditions and prejudices. I'd loved digging out the history of it. I loved how it taught me so much about the hospitality industry I work in. To the weird places the journey had taken me. It reminded me how I love teaching and telling stories. Suddenly, the scope of the book expanded massively, but the objective narrowed. You can't consume a steak – not even when cooking with young people or sharing it informally with friends – without understanding its social, historical, and cultural implications, the whole life of the creature that produced it, the techniques of butchers and cooks.

Steak has a uniquely complex life and history.

And Elliott's tartare showed me that what steak really deserved was its own story. The whole story.

What Even Is a Steak?

Before things get too involved, we need to define terms. What even *is* a steak? Take a look on your phone and you'll see that steak has an emoji. Foie gras doesn't get an emoji. There's no neat little cartoony image for seitan or tofu. Nope, a steak is a thing. The *OED* defines steak thus:

> Steak *noun* [mass noun]
> High-quality beef taken from the hindquarters of the animal, typically cut into thick slices that are cooked by grilling or frying.

It then lists some unconvincing secondary definitions that include a large slice or tranche of fish and the cubed and stewed stuff in a steak pie – neither of which you'd get any chef to agree with.

The word steak originates in Middle English, 'from Old Norse steik; related to steikja, "roast on a spit", and stikna, "be roasted"'. These definitions would quite possibly classify a doner kebab and a leg of lamb as steak, which is obviously absurd.

So, perhaps the first challenge in this book is to try to understand where 'steak' fits in the taxonomy of human consumption. Taxonomy is that branch of science concerned with classification. It's what gives us the ability to distinguish flora from fauna, then fish from insects, then a round fish from a flat fish, then a cod from a pollack. We should be safe in starting our definition with the assertion that steak is beef. Menu writers occasionally refer to a pork steak or a cauliflower steak, but that should really be in inverted commas. It's a reference to the protein being a single slab and cooked on a grill, *like* a steak.

We could say that steak comes from a group of muscles along the spine of the cow and towards the rear. That's where the big, clearly distinct and long-worked muscles that hold up the animal are located. As pieces of meat, they take well to being sliced across the grain to create the classic steak cuts. Large roundfish like tuna, shark and some of the cod family have the musculature and scale to make similar cuts. But in creatures like sheep, pigs and chickens, the same muscle groups are never large enough (even in very large specimens) to cut a decent single-serving slice.[8]

Of course, this logic is immediately subverted by talking to a butcher. Flank is a popular steak that comes from much lower down the animal, in the wall of the abdomen. Its fibres run longitudinally.

Weirder still are the cuts often referred to as 'secret' or 'butcher's' steaks. These are cuts from other places in the carcass that are tender, full of flavour and work well in any traditional steak recipe. They are often hard to find – there are only two 'spiders' or 'tri-tips' on any carcass – and sell cheaply. They're called butcher's steaks because, rather than trying to explain them to customers (or indeed lose profit by selling them as cheap and brilliant substitutes for traditional 'prestige' cuts), butchers would traditionally take them home to enjoy with their families.

---

[8] Take the 'rib eye' out of a lamb chop and you're looking at a pretty mean serving. The most popular part of the chicken is the breast, a huge muscle that operates the wings. The muscles around the spine are tiny so there's nothing to take a 'steak' from.

Physiologically, these are almost the opposite of our definition of steak, but they cook like a steak and land on the plate as a substantial tranche of grilled beef. Are they steaks? Hell yes.

For me, though, steak is much more than a description of a cut of meat, a line on a menu or a cooking method. It has come to symbolize something much more specific and much deeper. Steak means things.

When I was growing up, having steak was an incredibly special occasion. Mum would get some steaks out of the freezer and cook them with far more ceremony than Sunday lunch, high tea with my nan or even my birthday cake ever received. It was done 'for Dad', to celebrate something important or significant he'd done. The meat came from Iceland (the frozen food supermarket) and was the shape, size and texture of a slipper sole. It was grey, gristly, mean and any juices it may have contained bled out within seconds of hitting the pan. These days, you or I wouldn't put something like that in a stock and it certainly wasn't the most delicious piece of meat we ate in that kitchen by a very long way. A 'steak dinner' worked, though, even when the steak was nigh-on inedible. The steak itself was almost unimportant, but the ritual was everything. That's powerful magic.

In 2002, DJ Tom Birdsey of WFNX, a radio station in Boston, pronounced 14 March to be National Steak and Blowjob Day, as 'payback' for Valentine's Day. It was a stupid, sexist gag (please don't bother searching for it online, it only gets worse) but rather predictably, the idea became a worldwide phenomenon, spawning websites, memes, comment in mainstream media and becoming 'popular' across North America, Australia, Europe and New Zealand. It's obviously not worth analysing how deeply stupid and offensive the idea is, but it is worth asking: why did they pick steak?

Until comparatively recently in the UK (when our tastes suddenly became more cosmopolitan and sophisticated), there would always be a steak on the menu. It's a weird thought. A country pub serving food would have a steak above the shepherd's pie as an aspirational 'most expensive' item. Indian or Chinese restaurants would have a steak as a safety option for customers who couldn't handle the exoticism of their regular menu. Italian trattorias kept a steak on the list for punters who didn't like garlic and even the top-notch, Frenchified places would have a steak-based classic as a safe order, often with tableside flambéing for extra impact and added tips. My grandfathers, neither of them adventurous trenchermen, could have gone into a different restaurant every Saturday night of their lives and grumpily announced, 'I'll have the steak and chips.' It's strange that steak simultaneously signalled luxury, expense and extravagance at the same time as being the rock-bottom safe place for a generation increasingly bewildered by progress.

Steak is also one of the few types of food that's spawned its own genre of restaurant: the steakhouse. Wherever you live, the chances are that the most universally popular restaurant will be the steakhouse. Think about it: steak has its own house. If you believe your local church is the house of god, then that's quite the statement. Not only is steak a socially and culturally significant ritual, there's a building set aside in your community where you can gather to worship.

When you picture a steakhouse, all the stereotypes of a top-quality restaurant come to mind. Dark wood, brass and mirrors. A long, expensive wine list, waiters, glassware and napery. Pretty much the ideal surroundings of traditional 'fine dining' and yet, for all that fantastic front-of-house theatre and set dressing, the kitchen operation is a far simpler model.

A steakhouse kitchen isn't centred around a chef-de-cuisine standing at a range. It revolves around grill cooks and fire. Though there may be tweaks and twists, the menu is not an expression of the chef's personal creativity and vision, but the craftsman-like perfection of time-tested classics. Everything is made quickly and precisely, to order.

The difference between craft and art is that art ought never to repeat itself while craft ought always to repeat itself.

— Jonathan Meades

Nothing in that system changes much through the years, it just gets better refined and better practised (and, arguably, made with better ingredients). Steakhouses can be expensive … but steak is expensive, too. You're not paying for a celebrity to put his 'twist' on your steak. In fact, you should pray that the person on the grill is actually sixty-five years old, with bust knees, flat feet and a truly toxic attitude – but with fifty years of experience turning five cuts of steak into twenty classic dishes, each served rare, medium-rare, medium, medium-well or ruined.

And from the craft derives the canon. The menu of steak dishes that have been refined by grill cooks and steak lovers over generations was forged in steakhouses, diners and, to a lesser extent, home kitchens.

Steak is not just a cut of meat, it's more than a set of recipes, it's bigger than a tradition of cooking and it's certainly an enduring element of culture. It might even be a species-wide behaviour.

Why Do We Love Steak?

Steak was always a good idea. Just think about it for a bit. Imagine you and a few members of your wandering family unit or small tribe of hunter-gatherers have just killed something. An aurochs, let's say. You're looking at around a tonne of animal and there's no way you can carry it back to camp,[9] so it doesn't take you too long, hacking with rudimentary stone tools, to find the big muscles. Once you've got these main pieces home, it's time to cook them. Cutting them into slices across the

muscle into chunks that can be spit-roasted on a stick over the fire is a kind of natural progression. Some kind of 'steak' is the most natural and logical way to turn prey into dinner.

Archaeology has revealed enormous human ingenuity in hunting. Spears, arrows, daggers, pits, fire to terrify and snares to catch all helped us bring home a variety of prey. We had a particular advantage over cattle, however, because of their natural herding behaviours. There's evidence of human groups collaborating to drive herds of animals over cliffs and precipices, and of fences made of stakes or brush to funnel animals into a concentrated area to be killed. Some of these hunting practices – because they required the humans to plan, to collaborate, to understand animal behaviour and logically act upon it – are also regarded as the first evidence of humans engaging in social behaviour, reasoning and communication.

It's therefore not unreasonable to posit that we've had steak as long as we've been us … and that's powerful stuff.

It's easy to see, then, how steak became such a potent symbol of power. There were skills required for gathering – memory, intelligence, perception, dexterity – but prowess in hunting was usually rooted in physical strength, endurance and courage. The biggest, strongest, fastest and most aggressive humans would be the best hunters, and they'd be able to take the prime cuts before the rest was shared.[10]

We could spend our time trying to find scientific proof to back up the idea that eating red meat improves strength, power and mental development. To prove that it made collective sense for the tribe to willingly feed up their hunters so that everyone could collectively benefit from their skills. But the

---

[9] Researching a book on knives I discovered a whole sub-discipline of 'field butchery' amongst modern hunters. I'd realized that people were going deeper and deeper into the wilds to shoot things but I'd never considered that, after 4 days on snowshoes, tracking an elk, you've got to get the thing back out. Deer stalkers in the Highlands might use a pony to carry the beast off the hill, but extreme hunters have to carry enough gear in a backpack to haul the carcass into a tree, bleed and gut it, then take out the best pieces of meat to carry back. The problem of getting it home is ever present when we kill creatures larger than ourselves.

[10] Asshole Theory™: There is ample historical evidence that 'alpha' humans, entrusted with control of a commodity will garner the largest share for themselves. Our history and politics have been entirely formed by this truth. It therefore seems incontrovertible that almost as long as there have been assholes, they have been keeping most of the best steak for themselves.

Asshole Theory means we don't need to bother. After a few generations of the hunters reserving the best meat, it became deeply embedded in our belief structure. Steak, physical strength and social power were utterly intertwined from the very beginning.

Even as a child, I remember wondering how our little tribe would benefit from increasing my father's strength and potency when he routinely got the biggest lump of meat at Sunday dinner. This presumption never made much sense, but somehow we're stuck with it.

Sometimes, our belief in the power of steak has come near to the magical. For centuries, people who trained boxers, toreadors and even cyclists fed their charges steak to 'fortify' them. Like a modern performance-enhancing drug, it so assured superior strength that it was almost cheating.

Once the idea that steak could strengthen was established as a collective belief, it gained quasi-medical power. Steak could be fed to those who were weak, to the injured, convalescents and even, in modest quantities, to women in childbirth.

Such immeasurably powerful magic, of course, meant that beefsteak became more prestigious, more desirable and, inevitably, more expensive.

But how did steak become so gendered? In some cultures around the world, women consume raw meat, blood or liver in recipes specifically intended to replace the blood lost through menstruation, demonstrating a belief that it is women who need their strength and endurance enhanced and their recovery hastened. In most of the Anglosphere, though, the patriarchy seems to have conspired to keep steak for itself.

Perhaps a suitable place to start our enquiry would be with the Sublime Society of Beef Steaks. This was one of the most famous theatrical 'beefsteak clubs' in England in the mid-eighteenth century. It was founded in 1776 by John Rich, a theatrical producer and manager of the Covent Garden Theatre, George Lambert, his head scene painter and a significant landscape artist, and William

Hogarth. The club is said to have met in the large painting bay above the theatre to grill steaks on a gridiron and to 'sing patriotic songs'. Over time, it became a kind of Bohemian gentleman's club.

Patriotism was the key cause behind the creation of these beefsteak clubs. Popular theatre was a breeding ground for anti-French feeling during the period. Not only was there political unrest between the two nations, but there was a strong feeling among actors, writers and impresarios that popular taste was being 'weakened' by a kind of cultural invasion of European music and drama. The theatre was the place where English 'liberty' was best expressed and 'patriotic' themes became hugely popular with audiences. Perhaps unsurprisingly, these feelings continued to run high after the curtain had come down.

The best thing about the Sublime Society was the accuracy and comprehensiveness of their record keeping. There were only ever supposed to be twenty-four members, all of whom are carefully recorded. It was a combination of actors, dancers, painters and, at one point, even the Prince of Wales and his brother. Items from the club's collection display their special member's medallion, with the words 'Beef and Liberty' engraved around a representation of the club's treasured gridiron.[11]

Next, let's head to New York at the turn of the twentieth century, when steak eating had already grown into an expression of pioneer individualism and masculinity.[12]

The city had dozens of steakhouses that prided themselves on being representations of wide-open American democracy. There was no fussy classist etiquette about these places. Any man who had made an honest dollar could visit, a docker next to a shop owner and a porter next to a railway

---

[11] The medallion made for a quite spectacular tattoo, how could I not? Particularly as I'd named my daughter Liberty a few years before. A later incarnation of the club had its own premises with a dining room, a well-appointed kitchen and its own professional chef, but food was still passed through a connecting door designed to look like the gridiron. More on that gridiron on page 162…
[12] Grimes, William, *Appetite City* (North Point Press, 2009)

WHAT EVEN IS A STEAK?

magnate. There was no racial or religious exclusion. All could come, rub manly shoulders and chow down on the best steaks. Just no women.

Pontin's Chophouse on Franklin Street was regarded as an excellent house. The beef was hung for several weeks and roasted over hickory wood, then served on thick slices of bread with a mug of ale and sticks of celery. The tone was deliberately classless, with diners seated on upturned crates and food run to the tables with no ceremony. High society men loved the informality and the frisson of excitement that came from eating with 'real' workers and soon began hiring bars and steakhouses to host private shindigs they called 'beefsteaks', themed around democratic manliness. They were strictly invitation only.

Soon, the steakhouses caught on. Reisenweber's on Columbus Circle set up a 'beefsteak garret', Healey's at 66th and Columbus opened a 'beefsteak dungeon' and a hall called 'The Morgue' on 58th Street became home to the Beef Steak Club. Steaks were grilled on sheet-iron stoves and members sat around three sides of the room on soapboxes. The steaks they ate were seasoned first with salt, then with pepper 'until no more salt' was visible. They were again grilled over hickory, then dipped in a bucket of melted butter before being sliced and arranged on bread. Celery and ale were still served alongside, and when the beef ran out, they passed round lamb chops.

In 1906, the merchant and yachtsman Sir Thomas Lipton (who was competing in the America's Cup) had a beefsteak thrown in his honour at Reisenweber's garret. He was given half a lager barrel to sit on, an upturned Champagne case as a table and waiters dressed as jolly matelots descended from the ceiling on ropes to deliver steaming rare steaks, ale and, almost certainly, celery.

Eventually, beefsteaks were re-democratized, with political and social clubs holding them in saloons and selling tickets to raise funds. Rotaries, fraternities, brotherhoods, unions, guilds and church groups held beefsteaks where, unencumbered by their womenfolk, they could carouse together with meat.

What is perhaps strangest to the modern observer is how consistently steak has been associated with classless, libertarian inclusivity and open bohemianism and yet has always excluded women.

This goes some way towards explaining how dining establishments had a kind of gendering forced upon them. The classic waiter's preconception of 'steak for the gentleman and the lemon sole for the lady' was a simple acknowledgement of a broadly understood social convention. Somehow, to not offer at least the possibility of steak to a man was public emasculation. To offer it to a woman would be a calculated insult.

By the 1920s, broader social change meant that women could no longer be kept out and the steakhouses cleaned up their act. Cocktails were introduced – seen as a feminizing influence – along with desserts and sides of vegetables. There was less focus on fire, sweat and howling and most places kitted themselves out with the trappings of high-class French restaurants and hotel dining rooms.

Steakhouses had changed forever. The glittering gilt and cut glass, the candles, and dark wood, the napery and the silverware of elegant dining became the mark of a steakhouse and almost by accident they transformed from barely policed boys' clubs to the popular face of fine dining.

Considered by many to be the first fine dining restaurant in the US, Delmonico's was opened in 1827 by two Swiss-Italian brothers, Giovanni and Pietro Delmonico. Originally running a bakery and café, the two brothers soon realized that they could better serve the growing and increasingly wealthy people of New York with something a little more upmarket. At their peak, they had five locations across the city. At one location, customers entered between two pillars 'brought from ancient Pompeii'. These were huge, ostentatious and luxurious dining rooms where no expense was spared to bring diners the very best of food, wine and service, on a par with and often exceeding the best restaurants in Europe's capitals.

There are thousands of contemporaneous accounts of meals and lots of news reports of society occasions and general goings-on to be found, but best of all is the book written by head chef Charles Ranhofer, titled *The Epicurean* (1894). It is a glorious thousand-page resource, still relevant today, and an amazing window into grand restaurant lore. It is certainly as important as Escoffier's later *Guide Culinaire* and, in many ways, more useful. Ranhofer provides detailed information on ingredients and techniques and many of his recipes, as befitted an American restaurant, were more democratic than 'haute'.

Among the dishes to which Delmonico's lays claim (thanks to Ranhofer) are chicken à la king, eggs Benedict, baked Alaska, lobster Newburg and the wedge salad – though these are all disputed. Personally, I'm far more impressed with the veal pie and beet fritters 'à la Dickens', which Ranhofer created for the great writer on one of his trips to New York. I mean … I'm sure Anna tolerated her Pavlova and Dame Nellie might have been honoured, if a little baffled, by her toast, but a veal pie and a sort of beetroot hash brown? That's pure contemporary London and Dickens would have loved it.

Delmonico's represents a unique time and place and history. It was New York, at the height of its wealth and glamour, drawing influences from the best of the culinary world, when steak was most desired as a symbol of status and America prided itself on creating the biggest and best of everything. Unsurprisingly, the restaurant did great steak. In fact, it was a kind of high-water mark of steak culture.

Today, you can buy a Delmonico steak from almost any butcher. It is a fitting heritage. The steak comes laden with prestige but in terms of definition it is a little light on precision. Butchers will routinely sell any thick, boneless steak from the rib eye to the sirloin as a 'Delmonico'. The key thing is the impressive size and thickness (usually over 5cm/2in). Fortunately, Ranhofer was precise, and his writing gives some revealing insights into steaks during his heyday. Here are excerpts from two of his recipes, the first for the Delmonico steak and the second for porterhouse.

(1375). Delmonico Sirloin Steak of Twelve Ounces, Plain. (Bifteck de Contrefilet Delmonico de Vingt Onces, Nature) Cut from a sirloin slices two inches in thickness; beat them to flatten them to an inch and a half thick, trim nicely; they should now weigh twenty ounces each…

(1362). Double Porterhouse Steak à la Sanford. (Bifteck d'Aloyau Double à la Sanford) …cut through all the thickness of a short loin a slice two and a quarter inches thick; it should weigh, after being trimmed, four pounds and a half…

I've tried trimming both from sides of modern beef and I reckon mine are weighing in at roughly three-quarters of the weight Ranhofer specifies. He must have had access to some pretty big cattle.

Ranhofer also offers some further information about women diners. Unlike the 'beefsteaks' that ran alongside it, Delmonico's welcomed and encouraged women from the very beginning and steak was available to them. But there are continual references throughout *The Epicurean* to different dishes being 'suitable' for men or women. Steak was still seen as unfeminine.

In 1923, the business passed out of the hands of the Delmonico brothers and others took on the successful name. Steak continued to feature as the most important item on the menu and the clientele became ever more glittering. Throughout the 1940s and 1950s film stars, politicians and socialites were photographed at Delmonico's and these images became the main inspiration for another two immigrant brothers, Italians Frank and Aldo Berni. However, this time it was not in the neon canyons of Manhattan, but the rather more sedate city of Bristol in England's West Country.

The Bernis were a restaurant family, part of a wave of Italian immigration from northern Italy to Wales that started in the late eighteenth century. Mostly settling in the South Wales Valleys, the Italians started cafés, ice cream parlours and temperance bars. Frank and Aldo were born in Bardi, Emilia-Romagna in the early 1900s and joined their

family in Wales after finishing their education in Italy. By the time they arrived in the UK, their father owned fifty cafés.

Frank and Aldo's first business was a café in Exeter, south-west England. After the Second World War, they bought more restaurants around the West Country and then, in 1954, they took over an old pub in a covered market in the centre of Bristol and began their own steakhouse. Rationing had only been lifted in 1953 and the public was ready for their offering – an Argentinian steak, chips (French fries), peas and a bread roll and butter, plus dessert or cheese, all for just 7 shillings and sixpence.

As with many of the most successful catering operations in the UK, the Berni Inn (as this rapidly expanding chain of restaurants was named) tapped into British class obsession. The food was good, uncomplicated and no one need be worried they were going to be humiliated by posh staff, but all the trappings of the restaurant experience were present. Berni Inns had thick carpets, dark wood walls, brasswork and cut glass. In some, the tables were lit by candles and there were tablecloths and enough assorted cutlery to make you feel important without getting lost.

By the time I was old enough to be taken to restaurants for family occasions, 'the Berni' was where we went. My mum and my little sister loved it. The menu, by now canonical, comprised prawn cocktail, steak and chips and Black Forest gateau to finish (see page 246).

The prices and types of steak on offer are interesting. When the first Berni Inns opened, a 'prime rump steak' was offered in the 7s. 6d. set menu, but a menu from a Sheffield Berni Inn in 1971 shows the prices in the new decimal currency as well:

> Prime Fillet Steak (when available)
> (Half pound approximate uncooked weight)
> 21/- or £1.05
>
> Prime Rump Steak
> (Half pound approximate uncooked weight)
> 16/- or 80p

> Prime Sirloin Steak
> (Half pound approximate uncooked weight)
> 15/3 or 76p[13]

Berni Inns gave a huge number of my generation their first taste of steak and their first experience of restaurants. But it was a strange cultural inversion. While French or Italian kids might have grown up regularly visiting restaurants intended for 'everyday' dining, our first trips were to restaurants that were also cheap, but which were laden with signifiers of luxury, including steaks.

Though it's painful to admit, throughout its history, steak has been co-opted by assholes, cornered by the strong and consumed by the powerful. Steak was for the rich. It wasn't for women. Today, at least on the face of it, we have erased many of the class and gender barriers that have haunted the steakhouse. Nobody is going to be turned away and people of any class, race or gender can share their interest in a dish that, despite everything, appeals to all of us equally. There is a long way to go, and we need to work at it. In my day job as a restaurant critic, I will walk out of any steakhouse that has no female customers or which is filled with baying financial types. I don't feel comfortable in that environment and I won't be able to enjoy myself. But it seems that evolution might help us, too.

In recent years, doctors have recorded an increase in 'steakhouse syndrome'.[14] This is a painful and undignified complaint arising from an undigested piece of steak that becomes lodged low in the oesophagus. It does not cause choking, but rather discomfort and an inability to continue eating, requiring medical intervention. It is said to occur

---

[13] It's a brilliant bit of menu design. They obviously didn't keep a large stock of the fillet, which probably had the smallest margin. The rump sits in the middle slot, where you feel you're treating yourself to a little extra luxury and you avoid looking cheap. It's the lowest cost cut to the restaurant but the percentage markup on the rump will be really quite comfortable. And the sirloin is down there to mop up the rest. Again, a slim margin, but giving everyone choice – and far fewer will be sold. It's quite spectacularly clever. No wonder the business expanded with incredible speed. They went public in 1962.
[14] Shikino, K. (2021) 'Steakhouse syndrome', Clinical Case Reports, Volume 9, Issue 6

when the patient follows regular eating patterns
– like going regularly to a favourite steakhouse –
but, as they age, their oesophageal wall naturally
thickens and hardens, they chew less strongly and
completely and they are less able to break down the
meat before swallowing. In their minds they are still
the bold, virile young hunters of meat, but their
physical ability to consume steak has decayed.
Steakhouse syndrome seems to disproportionately
affect those who drink, smoke and take little
exercise … but mainly it's older men.

Ani

mal

Cattle

When you go into your butcher and buy a pork chop, it's a fairly simple transaction. You know you're buying a piece of pig and you know where on the animal it came from. Steak, in spite of being such a simple-sounding monosyllable, is a much more complicated proposition. Sure, we know it came from a cow, but the position of the cut varies and with it the flavour and texture of the meat. To add to the joyous complexity of the situation, it also varies depending on the type of cow and how the animal was raised, 'finished', slaughtered, stored and butchered.

Some people like to think of meat as something they pick out of a chiller on a polystyrene tray, cleanly wrapped in plastic, bloodless and only theoretically connected to anything that moos. If we want to understand steak, though, we need its whole life story. And that means talking about cows.

Humans first domesticated cattle around 10,000 years ago in the Fertile Crescent. It would be hard to imagine a more useful creature. It supplied motive power for ploughs and carts, leather, fertilizer, milk and meat, all from one input: grass.

Ancient Cattle

Cattle have been around for many thousands of years, and it's fortunate that we have evidence of early ancestors in cave paintings. It's a fascinating thought that in the earliest visual representations we made of ourselves, we proudly included some bloody huge cows.

These proto-cattle were aurochs, the first species to evolve across Eurasia. We have both pictures and fossil remains of these magnificent megafauna, much taller than a man at the shoulder and with a massive rack of horns a couple of metres wide. These were aggressive beasts, and athletic, too, with longer legs than modern cattle. They were capable of fast, agile movement. and there was powerful fighting musculature around the neck and shoulders. Big specimens would have weighed little short of a tonne. These were not animals you looked after and tended, they were animals you feared, worshipped and occasionally ate.

It's hard to imagine now exactly how awe-inspiring the aurochs must have been. Remember, man never coexisted with dinosaurs so, as long as you kept away from bears, these were some of the largest and most terrifying creatures we might ever encounter in much of the northern hemisphere.

The aurochs gave us buffalo, water buffalo, bison, fighting bulls, draft oxen and yak, but also the many breeds of cattle we eventually domesticated. It's thought that the last aurochs died in 1627 in Poland.

The aurochs, perhaps predictably, fascinate cattle breeders, so there have been several efforts to claim ancient or isolated herds as direct descendants and one particularly misguided attempt at 'back breeding' in 1920 by Lutz Heck, a German zoologist and close friend of Herman Goering. Heck and his brother Heinz were the sons of the director of the Berlin Zoo and were thus uniquely equipped to follow their weird eugenic obsession. By crossbreeding cattle with surviving characteristics of the aurochs, they intended to bring them back. A demonstration of German scientific excellence, somehow symbolic of some kind of ancient genetic purity, the new aurochs were to be released into Goering's private hunting estates, coincidentally in the same forests in Poland where the last real aurochs had perished.

We know now, of course, that while crossbreeding could conceivably produce an auroch-like phenotype,[15] it couldn't reverse-engineer the original, extinct genotype.[16] The 'Heck cattle' produced by the breeding programme never really achieved much of a physical resemblance to the aurochs, but the crossbreeding of fighting bulls, strong draft animals[17] and various feral specimens from around the world did produce a historical curiosity that's still around in some small herds, not really adding much to the greater glory or utility of cattle breeding and bearing an extremely queasy history.[18]

Breeds

The idea of breeds is largely something we've superimposed onto cattle. There is very little in genetic terms that separates any breed of cattle from any other and each breed can reproduce with any other. By carving out a portion of the population and effectively inbreeding to select desirable characteristics, man has 'created' differentiation in a way he can control. Left alone, populations of cattle that were separated by physical limitations like seas or mountain ranges have naturally adapted to their environments, but we have focused the evolutionary change to meet our own needs.

Since man first domesticated cattle we've been 'improving' them. In different parts of the world,

slightly different basic breeds have been developed by humans and by the environment. Obvious types are Highland or Icelandic cattle, built low to the ground, hardy and hairy, but in Italy and Spain, for example, breeds like Rubia Gallega have been bred, possibly from bison, as draft animals. In Spain and the Basque region, bulls are bred for fighting, and in many parts of the world, animals have been brought on to create better meat and dairy. In particular, there is enormous myth surrounding Wagyu cattle from Kobe prefecture in Japan, which have been carefully bred and reared for maximum fat dispersal throughout the muscles. The Chianina cow in Tuscany is prized for its hard-worked and muscular flesh, too, while British Holsteins and Friesians are incredibly reliable milk producers at industrial levels.

Each type has different advantages in a steak. American beef cattle, bred in part from the original wild cattle of the plains, are fattened on grain to produce tender, buttery meat without expensive ageing. Wagyu cattle hardly move during their finishing stages and as a result produce meat so fatty and rich it need only be briefly cooked and should be eaten in tiny portions. A *bistecca Fiorentina* (a porterhouse steak from a gigantic Chianina with a long and active working life) is full of flavour and robust texture, whereas in Britain, you'll likely enjoy a steak from an ex-dairy animal, fed on grass, which, though tender, can require hanging to develop flavour. Bull beef is rarely eaten. As they attain sexual maturity, the meat takes on a pronounced flavour that's not particularly palatable. Bull meat sold in Spain, France and the Basque country is usually from immature males.

Although domesticated cattle of various sorts are distributed all over the world now, it was not until the mid-eighteenth century that farmers in England began the process of controlled selective breeding. The country was undergoing something of an agricultural revolution at the time, and Robert Bakewell was the agricultural scientist who established it as a practice.

Until this point, farmers and livestock owners had generally bred any cow with any available bull. The results were unpredictable, though over time some characteristics, particularly around diet or

---

[15] These are the characteristics that result from the interaction of the genoype with its environment.

[16] The complete genetic characteristics of an organism.

[17] 'Draft 'or occasionally 'draught' animals are used to drag or carry heavy loads. Think 'Cow = Tractor'.

[18] Owners of surviving specimens are predictably unwilling to talk about them. The only information that seems verifiable about them is that they are grumpy, violent, intractable and often show symptoms of what one might describe as mental derangement. All of which seems oddly appropriate.

environment, naturally became dominant in some geographical areas. Bakewell's system involved finding specimens with strong characteristics and breeding them with others to reinforce their strengths while culling the undesirables. Through selection and control, he was able to build protected 'bloodlines'.

Bakewell developed particular strains of pigs, sheep, horses and cattle for export to other countries and agriculturalists all over the world went on to develop their own breeding programmes.

Where beef was concerned, there was a particular need in Britain for quick-growing, fatty cattle to feed a population that was expanding rapidly during the Industrial Revolution. Bakewell himself began with Longhorn heifers from the north of England crossed with a Westmoreland bull, which created a large, strong, fast-growing cross called the Dishley Longhorn. Other breeders started with Shorthorn cattle, sometimes referred to as Celtics, which are native to the UK. They are large-framed, robust and with an established ability to thrive on British pasture in British weather.

These creatures were refined into various commercial breeds, many of which were exported to other parts of the Empire.[19] The first Shorthorn cow imported by settlers to Virginia in 1783 was a 'Durham', which was sold to them as a breed suitable for dairy, beef and draft. It's interesting that by this date, a group of people heading off to colonize another country could be sold the benefits of a breed like they might today be sold on the off-road capabilities of a four-wheel-drive expedition vehicle.

This is a key point in the history of our relationship with cattle as it represents the first example of standardization, in itself the first step towards commodification.

There are thousands of cattle breeds, each with their own characteristics, but here are just a few that are particularly useful to know about.

---

[19] Experiments among British agriculturalists were extremely successful in improving beef yield. In 1700, the average weight of a bull sold for slaughter in England was 168kg (370lb), but that rose to 381kg (840lb) by 1768.

Highland Cattle
Compact, short-legged and with long, shaggy coats, Highland cattle were among the first cows to be formalized into a breed in 1885. They had become immensely resilient to the weather of their homelands in Western Scotland and the Western Isles – in some places, herds regularly swam across the sea or lochs in search of better grazing. Because of this, they were exported all over the world to strengthen other breeds, contributing to herds in Canada, Australia, Argentina, the USA and Russia.

English Longhorn
The English Longhorn was a heavy draft animal when Bakewell first got his hands on one. Large and muscular, it was the obvious starting point for his breeding experiments. You won't find much English Longhorn in butchers today, but their characteristics have become part of many other breeds.

Aberdeen Angus
Angus, usually called Aberdeen Angus in the UK, was first recognized as a breed in 1835. The breed has many benefits. The animals are compact and build muscle fast. They're naturally 'polled' (hornless), as breeding stock they can reduce genetic tendencies towards difficult pregnancies, they marble well and they've got pretty much the coolest name in the business. The Scottishness of the name and heritage has always appealed both to cattle breeders and to end-purchasers of meat.

As they're such an old breed, Angus were also some of the first cattle to be exported with the aim of improving other national herds. The USA, Canada, Australia and Argentina took substantial populations of pure Angus cattle in the last part of the nineteenth century. There is now Aberdeen Angus, Black Angus, Red Angus and even different rules in different markets around what actually constitutes 'Aberdeen Angus'. In some places, artificial insemination with sperm from a half-Angus bull is enough to claim the status on a package. Pure Angus, when you can get it, can still be excellent beef, but globally it has become a somewhat debased brand.

Red Poll
Red Poll cattle resulted from a cross between Suffolk Dun and Norfolk Red, dairy and beef breeds respectively. Horns were slowly bred out

of the cross, resulting in a pleasant, small, tractable creature of dual use. They were exported in large numbers to the US and Australia, where they were seen as ideal for settlers. Red Poll was the first breed to be registered in the US.

Other British Breeds

Your butcher may well have access to purebred carcasses or talk to you about various crosses. I've certainly had Hereford, Ayrshire, South Devon, Belted Galloway, Dexter, Jersey and White Park in my kitchen. I keep a record and have tried and failed to find any useful breed preference. I'm sure there are good and bad eating beasts in every breed, but by the time I buy it, it's been chosen by farmer, slaughterman and butcher… all of whom know their job better than me. In general, we are developing a taste for animals that have lived longer so, in some cases, the best-tasting meat might actually come from a breed originally intended for dairy or draft. We should certainly not reject meat that's not necessarily a traditional 'beef' breed. I can't help feeling that, once again, a trusted relationship with your butcher is a surer guarantee of a good steak than going for any particular breed.

Holstein/Friesian

Holsteins, also known commonly as Friesians, are the black-and-white cows of children's books. They originated in Northern Europe and were bred for dairy production. One would not traditionally expect to be able to buy beef from these animals but, since interest has increased in older ex-dairy cattle, you may well be offered it.

Charolais

Charolais is the most common beef breed in France. Like the UK, France exported prize cattle to other countries and now Charolais are common in national herds the world over. One of the largest populations is in Mexico.

Limousin

Limousin is the second most popular breed in France. It was selectively bred from draft animals during a frenzy of agricultural research in the Limousin region during the mid-nineteenth century. Limousins have a genetic variation that makes them good at putting on muscle, though they perform poorly on a grass diet, requiring corn or silage.

Chianina

The Chianina is a breed from Val de Chiana in Central Italy, south of Florence. They are said to have first been raised by the Etruscans, who had a tradition of bullfighting, and are significant for being the world's largest breed. Some bulls can weigh up to 1,800kg (3,968lb) at slaughter, double the size of common beef breeds. They are still used as draft animals today. Their meat – hard-worked muscle – marbles poorly, but individual steaks can be vast.

Rubia Gallega

Also known as Galician Blonds, these pretty, cinnamon-coloured animals are a cross between native Portuguese breeds (Criollos) and Simmenthals, a Swiss/French dairy breed. They are reared across the Basque region for meat, usually fed on grass and slaughtered much later than other cattle.

Criollo

Criollo (or Creole) cattle are descended from Spanish stock that were imported to the US and Central and South America. These were introduced by the colonizing Spaniards who brought their own trusted local breeds, which then developed into huge herds, often allowed to roam wild over vast areas of natural grassland. There are Argentinian, Bolivian, Brazilian, Colombian, Cuban, Ecuadorean, Puerto Rican, Uruguayan and Venezuelan Criollos as named breeds, plus Chinampo, Pantaniero, Barroso, Tabapuan and dozens more, all varying subtly as they've been selectively bred for certain characteristics. They're all descended from the original Iberian stock, even though some breeds are now widely regarded as authentically North American. The Florida Cracker, Pineywoods and even the prized Texas Longhorn are all of Spanish lineage.

These cattle are long-legged, small and hardy with a large head and nose. They reproduce regularly and at a comparatively early age and naturally protect their calves. They are resilient against the parasites and bugs of the grasslands and, while it would be incorrect to say they 'thrive' on it, they certainly survive well on scrub (wild, high-protein grass). The great herds of the American West resulted from the reuniting of the breeds, brought by settlers from Europe, and driven South and West with the Criollos spreading north.

American Beef

In the US, as in the UK, beef is more than just a meat, it's regarded as somehow part of the country's nationality. A txuleton or a Fiorentina is a good steak, but the roast beef of old England symbolizes something powerful about independence and liberty. In the US, steak symbolizes the American Dream.

And that's fair. America was a land of unbelievably plentiful natural resources, and even before gold, coal and oil were ever exploited, the seemingly infinite grasslands could be turned into money through cattle ranching. The cowboys who controlled and moved the great herds, turning grass into beef for the workers in the growing cities, have long been seen as an emblem of American values. Unfortunately, it's an image that ignores the original occupants of the land and their symbiosis with the native buffalo, as well as the thousands of Mexican *vaqueros* who first drove cattle and the black cowboys who were paid awfully and worked under appalling conditions.

It's also not exactly proportionate with the truth, as it was only for a couple of decades that it made financial sense to drive the giant herds from the west, where they were plentiful, to the stockyards on the brand-new railroad network.[20]

Nevertheless, the cattle barons were a powerful political lobby and were able to influence government policy to favour their industry. Federal standards for beef were first introduced in 1927. This was the beginning of the US Department of Agriculture (USDA) grading system.

This was devised by Alvin H. Sanders, a powerful lobbyist and the editor of the trade organ, the *Breeder's Gazette*. The intention was that purpose-bred cattle fattened for meat should be promoted over wild-grazed cattle or those that were a bi-product of the equally powerful dairy industry.

The key was in the fattening. If the cattlemen could convince the American public that the 'marbling' characteristic of intensively reared and fattened cattle was the vital mark of quality, their product would be protected. If they could sell the idea that 'cut-with-a-spoon' tenderness was a greater benefit than strong flavour, then that was something they could improve and control, whereas old-style ranchers with wild-grazing tough Criollos could not.

Initially, and for the first thirty years of the system's existence, purebred cattle were the model, particularly the Hereford and Angus breeds. This was great for the cattlemen, but cut out smaller, independent ranching operations. The USDA grading system favoured cattlemen with deep pockets, expensive stock and organized facilities close to the railheads.

After assiduous and protracted lobbying, the Department of Agriculture were persuaded to offer free 'grading' at all the slaughterhouses they certified, based largely on marbling.[21] To this day, USDA 'prime' beef is described as 'young, fine-textured and highly marbled'.

---

[20] An estimated five million Criollo cattle were left in Texas when the Mexicans departed in 1865, a resource the ranchers were able to take advantage of. When we picture cowboys rounding up cattle, it's Texas Longhorns they're herding.

[21] It is believed that the connection between marbling and flavour was disproved within ten years by the department's own studies, yet marbling remains the key judgement criterion in grading today and almost any beef lover in the world will cheerfully assert that 'it's all in the marbling'.

USDA Grading Criteria

Juiciness: extremely dry (1) to extremely juicy (8) (Initial and sustained juiciness)

Tenderness: tough (1) to extremely tender (8) (Initial and sustained tenderness)

Cohesiveness

Springiness

Beef flavour

Flavour intensity: extremely bland to extremely intense

Overall beef mouthfeel: extremely non-beeflike mouthfeel to extremely beeflike

Off-flavour: none (1) to strong off-flavour (3)

Characterisation: sweet (1), acidic (2), sour (3), rancid (4), warmed-over (5)

Fungible Beef

Let's talk about the fungibility of beef. Fungible is defined as:

> "fungible" | ˈfʌn(d)ʒɪbl |
> "adjective" Law
> (of a product or commodity) replaceable by another identical item; mutually interchangeable.[22]
>
> DERIVATIVES
> fungibility | fʌn(d)ʒɪˈbɪlɪti | noun
>
> ORIGIN
> Mid-17th century: from medieval Latin *fungibilis*, from Latin *fungi* 'perform, enjoy', with the same sense as *fungi vice* 'serve in place of'.

The concept of fungibility is most easily demonstrated by this simple question: if I borrowed it, would it be weird if I returned a different version of the same thing? A £10 note, for example, is entirely fungible. You don't check the serial number if someone pays you back. In fact, fungibility is the basic principle on which all currency works. Your dog, on the other hand, is non-fungible. If I took your labradoodle out for a walk and brought you back a bull terrier, you would likely take issue.

Fungible things are easy to trade and, crucially, easy to create derivative from. If you have a commonly agreed price for a fungible commodity, you start being able to bet on whether that price will go up or down. Money can be made.

Things get really interesting when it comes to food, though. A cup of sugar is fungible, but your wedding cake is not. However, a tonne of corn is fungible and a salted pork belly is, too. The carcass of, say, a Longhorn steer, carefully reared on fine pasture and slaughtered in Texas, is in no way fungible. It's a beautifully unique and high-quality carcass. But an animal of almost any breed, put through a process of standardization and certification, becomes as freely tradeable as actual currency. You can then trade in USDA 'prime' beef in exchanges all over the country and trade in futures and other derivatives without ever taking possession of a piece of meat.

The good thing about commoditizing food is that, in some ways, it's like insurance for the farmers. They can get a price up front which, though low, is guaranteed, because a whole slew of people are using the value, rising and falling, to bet on.

The USDA system has done this for beef, which is great for the cattle industry and for the food processing industry and, arguably, for the American economy. What it ignores (because it has to) is the incredible quality variation in tasty, non-intensively reared meats.

Commodity beef is fungible. Because the USDA system establishes the accepted characteristics of meat, almost like the value of a currency, individual pieces of meat can enter the system from anywhere, be transported anywhere and sold against those criteria. In one sense, it's a gigantic exercise in quality control. In another, it makes practical traceability kind of impossible.

In the 1960s, US public taste turned against large amounts of visible fat, so 'prime' grading adapted to suit consumer taste (fat requirement reduced in 1965 and 1975), but the industry didn't change production methods, so animals are still intensively reared and slaughtered young.

It is particularly galling that there's a growing international consensus that 'beef is bad' both for our health and that of the planet, which is based on US hyper-industrialized beef rearing and the other countries that have followed its lead.

---

[22] Beef is by no means the world's only fungible commodity. Money is fungible – money that is raised for one purpose can easily be used for another.

Stomachs

A lot of animals can't eat grass. Those of us with a single stomach just can't process the stuff. Grass has some nutritive qualities, but they're pretty scant when measured against the enormous percentage of cellulose and fibre. Grass surrounds us, naturally occurring in many climates and locations, but we humans only have a single stomach and a comparatively short digestive tract. It takes us about eighteen hours to process food before passing it out, enough time to deal with meat but not complex dietary fibres. Cows process grass for us.

You likely learned at school that cattle have four stomachs – it's also sensible to consider it as a single stomach with four separate compartments. After being chewed and swallowed, a mouthful of grass will pass first into the rumen, which is the biggest section. It is a large bag that runs a surprisingly long way back through the creature's body and which is mostly responsible for the huge, barrel-shaped belly that cows have, gently swelling outwards between front and rear legs.[23]

The rumen constitutes about 85 per cent of the stomach's total capacity, up to 150 litres (40 gallons) depending on the size of the animal. Think of it as a holding chamber and a giant fermentation tank. It holds lumps of chewed grass that the cow is able to belch back up into its mouth to chew again.

This 'first stomach' contains an enormous quantity of live bacteria, which help to decompose and process cellulose and complex carbohydrates in the grass as it's repeatedly masticated. This might not be how we'd like to digest our own dinner, but this process of regurgitation and reprocessing is what's necessary to break down the grass and make nutrients available. If you're ever able to get close enough to cows to listen, the noise of this process is remarkable. The muscular churning sounds like a washing machine mixed with a backing track of quite heroic burbling flatulence. We all know that cattle produce methane gas, but it's not until you get up close that you realize at what a spectacular rate they do it.

The vast surface area of the rumen wall is where some of the first nutrients can be extracted, but there's much more work to do. Attached to the front part of the rumen is the second chamber, the much smaller reticulum, with a capacity of around 15 litres (4 gallons). The reticulum is functionally similar to the rumen in that it contains bacteria and can regurgitate into the mouth, but it seems to be where the cow collects any indigestible matter it has swallowed during grazing. Rocks, grit, small particles or anything that hasn't been properly broken up by the rumen end up here. The reticulum enables the cow to clear out the waste matter and separate it from the useful material: the beautifully named, cud.

The third area is the omasum, holding about 50 litres (13 gallons) and lined with thick folds of soft tissue that remove excess water, concentrating the nutrient-rich paste before it passes to the final area, the abomasum. This is sometimes called the 'true stomach' because it is the first one that, like our own, contains acid. It comprises less than 5 per cent of the whole four-part system, but by the time the grass reaches the abomasum it has been broken down to a point that a stomach much like our own can carry out the final processing before the matter is passed to the small intestine for the final stages of digestion. It's worth mentioning that there's a certain amount of waste gas and a pretty constant flow of brilliant fertilizer that comes out of the final processes but, in the context of this book, that's not particularly useful and I think we can leave it there.

See page 45 to understand how what cows eat impacts beef production.

---

[23] Looking at a cow from the side, the lungs are situated towards the front of the animal, mostly between the shoulders and front legs. The proportion of the body given over to food processing never fails to amaze me, but also reminds me of the happy consideration that all of this weighs an enormous amount. It's the musculature of the spine, supporting this huge weight while it does its work, that gives us steak.

USDA 'PRIME' T-BONE AND NY STRIP ON THE BONE, KEENS, NEW YORK, USA

New York feels like it should really be the world capital of steakhouses. Sure, Chicago is more the spiritual home of the cattle industry and maybe somewhere in Texas might put you closer to the origin of your meat, but there's something about New York. Sparks restaurant was the first I was taken to, years ago, when the bullet marks in the pavement outside were still fresh from the night Paul Castellano got whacked by four wiseguys in big overcoats on the orders of Sammy 'The Bull' Graziano. Yeah … I know. Even back then, it looked like somebody refreshed the bullet holes each month with a chisel … but hey, if you can't be cynical in New York…

Gallagher's has the 'grammable 'meat window' and Peter Luger is … well, it's Peter Luger, but these days, steak aficionados with a yen for nostalgia head to Keens in what used to be the raffish edges of the theatrical quarter, a brief stagger off Broadway, but is now Koreatown.

I don't envy many other writers, but I wish I could have been Damon Runyan just for the night I went because it would need his command of language and fevered imagination to create a more comprehensive portrait of old Manhattan than this. The place, let's be honest, is brown. I mean, there's some reddish carpet under there somewhere and the tablecloths are pretty damn white, but everything else comes off the colour chart between 'Nicotine Stain' and 'Family Pew'. It's rammed at 8pm on a Friday evening and the floor staff hip-swing between the tables in aprons and waistcoats like well-rehearsed hoofers at the end of a run.

I couldn't have sat for more than about eight seconds when the waiter shimmied in and offered me a drink (he didn't so much offer me a cocktail as triage me and decide I needed a martini. I agreed.) In one long minute he came back with it and, glory be, a long plate of pickles. Proper Jewish 'sour' pickles from a barrel somewhere. Half a gherkin, shards of raw carrot and celery. The whole arrangement was a good eight inches long and came with blue cheese dressing that was actually sharp. I inhaled the first pot, then asked the waiter to keep replenishing the little ramekins for the rest of the evening. I wanted to be sure there was some of it still around as I lashed into dessert.

I started with a 'Jumbo Lump Crab Cocktail' because, hell, it just sounded so right. Do crabs have knees? Knuckles? I don't know but some salty son of the sea upstate somewhere had rooted the meat out of the creature's interstices and they sat, mounded in a glass full of shredded iceberg, about the size of a modest Buick. It was terrific. A lot of good, high-quality protein and I've got to wonder what happens to the rest of the crab … but fortunately starters containing crustacea, bivalves or fish eggs don't actually impact on your overall eating capacity. This is a medically proven fact.

The T-bone yelled at me from the menu and I listened. It was, as I had hoped, 'USDA Prime', which was really what the entire trip was about. I ordered medium-rare and, though obviously tempted by a mountain of fries, I took instead a baked potato. Partly because I needed to know what an 'Idaho' actually tasted like, and partly because it would have been the original accompaniment to a steak around the time Keens first opened. Until recently, by the way, it was called Keens Chophouse. It was a term that had come over from England and describes an establishment that, unlike inns or taverns, specialises in 'chops' – not a piece of fillet on a bone. Chops weren't the pork or lamb pieces we use the term for today, but any big cut piece of meat. Chop was a kind of slangy expression for a cut. Keens, indeed, still has a house speciality of 'mutton chops' but, history be damned, recent new owners thought all this was too confusing and renamed it a 'Steakhouse'.

It looked staggering on the plate. A hefty lump, about 3cm (1½in) thick, with a good balance between fillet and sirloin. A really good balance. To be fair, in England I'd have called this a Porterhouse and if it was a bit thicker it would qualify as a Fiorentina.

I've always had a bit of a philosophical issue with the word 'perfect'. We bandy it about in food writing, the 'perfect sausage', the 'perfect martini', but the truth is, in something as subjective as food, the concept is meaningless. But then there's the T-bone at Keens, which, with some bewilderment, I can't avoid calling The Perfect American Steak. The qualifier is important. By the time I got out of a yellow cab and walked under the awning at Keens, I'd been researching the story of steak for nearly a decade. I knew the entire process by which the meat would reach my plate but, more importantly, I was immersed in the vast evolved cultural expectation of how steak was supposed to be.

Keens looks like it could have been designed for a Scorsese film. A 'set' that doesn't just employ every semiotic cue for a steakhouse but amplifies each of them to the maximum. A USDA Prime T-bone looks like a steak in a cartoon – because it is. The shape, the colour, the two fat lobes of meat and the creamy bone appeared in *The Flintstones* and *Tom and Jerry*, more often than not chased by a slavering hound. It's an animated icon. And the expectation goes further. We know what we want from a steak because we've heard it a million times: 'so tender'… 'you could cut it with a spoon' … 'a juicy steak' … 'melts in the mouth'. And it does.

They age their steaks at Keens. Not for any ridiculous period of time, but enough to build some complexity. There's no gristle, no connective tissue, the fat is trimmed to healthy proportions and it glistens on the plate. Cut in, and the juiciness is instantly apparent, glittering on the cut surface with-out running out onto the plate (it's too well rested for that). It's startlingly easy to cut and then bite through, and the fats from all that internal marbling flood the mouth and coat the tongue. It is glorious.

It is also very different to what I'm used to in the UK. The texture is astonishing but beefy flavours are mild. There's a marked distinction in flavour between the fillet and the sirloin sides too. The fillet is sweet; the sirloin has an irony tang. I try again, but it's difficult to believe the two sides are the same steak – the difference is huge.

It's a sizeable piece of meat so I set to it. It's not tough, so I don't tire of chewing and each mouthful satisfies everything I could expect. It also has the strange effect of sort of contextualizing everything around it. Like most Brits, I suppose, I see a clean cocktail like my martini as a pre-dinner drink, but here, its fierce cutting edge is a balancing foil for the rich fattiness of the meat. The pickles – salty, sour and sharp – suddenly make incredible sense and, once again, I'm smearing that honking blue

cheese dressing on everything. It's a remarkably coherent combination of food in an ideal setting. Everything feels so very 'extra'. Powerful flavours, oiled up and wrestling delightfully. Weirdly, only the creamed spinach seems out of place. A guilt-driven order that's been so de-vegetableized with heavy cream that it no longer serves its purpose.

I leave on a sparkling high. It was a superb meal and, damn, that might have been the best martini I've ever drunk. But there's a shadow. Something intangible troubled me.

The following night I move on to the Minetta Tavern. A more rackety and Bohemian set-up, a crush of people, but they find me a seat at the end of the gorgeous bar, set me up with another, if possible more spectacular, martini and I order, of course, "Dry-Aged Bone-In New York Strip"[24] – the cut so good they named it after the city, and if it can be said of meat, an 'iconic' steak.

I'd limbered up with a very creditable Soupe à l'Oignon so when the steak arrived, I was in full critical mode. We need, I decided, a new name for the first bites of American steak, the gush, the flow and the soul-deep satisfaction that comes from the meeting of a long-engrained need.

The New York strip (sirloin to Brits), is a homogeneously textured muscle. The fat layer is clear and separate. There are no weird angles, odd ends or niches where a different flavour might lurk. It's pure muscle lubricated by corn-fed intramuscular fat in an ideal serving size. And so, I realized, as I chewed on, we also need a name for the last 20 mouthfuls. The weird combination of satiation and inability to stop. That huge up-front, smack-in-the-mouth sensation doesn't modulate or attenuate. It's big, glossy and, yes, 'perfect' … and it doesn't let up.

God, I don't want to sound like a miserable Brit, but I know now what my weird, niggling reservation was about my Perfect American Steak. It was just that … it was perfect, and, to my bewilderment, I could only take so much of it.

---

[24] With, since you ask, champignons poêlées and pommes Anna.

Japanese Beef

One of the most sought-after steaks is Wagyu, shrouded in lore and mystery and incredibly expensive. Japan had very little history of meat-eating at all before the end of the nineteenth century, consuming mainly fish and vegetables along with occasional game or chicken. With little dairy tradition either, there wasn't a great deal of interest in cattle until Emperor Meiji, an enthusiastic Westernizer, began encouraging the eating of beef.

The *wa* of Wagyu translates as 'oneself', 'us' or 'ours', while *gyu* means 'cow'. Wagyu, then, just means 'our local cows'. Native Japanese stock was originally much like the small black Chinese breeds, used solely for draft, but when they began farming them in earnest, the Japanese carefully improved the national herd by importing animals to crossbreed. There are now four distinct breeds in Japan, identified and registered since 1944: the Japanese Black, Brown, Polled and Shorthorn. They are referred to collectively as Wagyu.

Japanese beef production was strongly influenced by US methods and as a consequence Wagyu is almost exclusively fed on grain and slaughtered young. The characteristics of Wagyu are effective-ly those of the best USDA-style American beef taken to its logical conclusion. Though the animals are not 'intensively' reared in feedlots, they are hyper-fed, their movement is limited and they are pampered through the process of growing. Japa-nese Wagyu is unlikely to be full of antibiotics.[25]

Kobe city in the Kensai region has gained a terrific reputation for rearing beef and it is from here that stories have spread about cattle being fed beer, massaged with sake and played Mozart. Although these stories are partially deft salesmanship, this level of care can produce exceptional levels of marbling (*shimofuri* in Japanese). The fat in animals reared this way has a lower melting point than normal and consequently behaves differently in both cooking and eating. It is so rich and any attempt to cook it at high, searing temperatures risks catastrophic loss of all that fat. As a result, most authentic Japanese preparations of Kobe beef have traditionally involved little cooking and portion sizes are usually small.

Kobe beef is protected by the Kobe Beef Market-ing and Distribution Promotion Association using a rigorous set of criteria for the animals and their rearing. Meat quality is strictly controlled. Wagyu, on the other hand, has become such a successful signifier of quality in beef that large herds have been created in other countries. UK, American and Australian Wagyu is now widely available. Be aware that unlike Kobe, Wagyu is not a trademark, just a group of breeds. The name Wagyu doesn't in itself offer particular reassurance around rearing or quality. The awful truth is that the name Wagyu is no longer a guarantee that your beef hasn't been reared in the most unpleasantly intensive way.

Like much Japanese food, Wagyu is astonishing and revelatory to the Western palate and perhaps that explains best my attitude to it. In Japanese restaurants I have eaten testicles, cod semen, raw whelk and sea cucumber, in unadorned and tiny servings (the better to appreciate their unique flavour or texture), and loved them all. The highest quality Wagyu steak, entirely raw and served in three postage-stamp-size slices, is utterly, brain-alteringly sublime. Unfortunately, when we attempt to serve it as we, now too often, do in Europe, the US and Australia, in the idiom of the 'Western steak' – inch-thick and seared – it tastes to me like a fatty, poorly textured corn-fed steak. In a way it's akin to taking a piece of sashimi grade sea bream fillet to a fish and chip shop, getting them to dip it in batter and then deep fry it with a portion of chips.

---

[25] Japan and the EU restrict the use of antibiotics in cattle rearing.

Korean Beef

Korea has a 5000-year-old tradition of cattle-rearing for farming, transportation and religious sacrifice, but it was particularly in the period of recovery after the Korean War that consumption of beef rocketed. It is not just that beef is now more available, but also that it has tremendous power as a symbol of free-market affluence after generations of oppression and want. Koreans have become some of the greatest beef enthusiasts on Earth. Like Japan, they have built a successful beef culture, with incredible speed, based on the twentieth-century US model.

There are four native Korean breeds: Hanwoo, Korean Brindle (*Chikso*), Korean Black (*Heugu*) and Jeju Black (*Jeju Heugu*). During the Second World War and the Korean War, the population of Hanwoo shrank to 400,000, but farmers rebuilt the national herd, focusing on beef cattle rather than draft cattle since the 1960s. Today, there are around 2.6 million Hanwoo in Korea.

Beef farming is heavily supported by the government as a key export and source of internal food security. Since 1983, the South Korean government has administrated the National Hanwoo Breeding System with a complex and rigorous grading and traceability system.[26] They also control semen distribution from a central herd of twenty approved prize bulls. The grading system, perhaps inevitably, favours high levels of marbling.

Argentinian Beef

A couple of decades ago, Argentina would have been the dream destination for a steak lover. The country has a huge tradition of meat eating and sociable eating and had a seemingly endless national herd of Criollo cattle, reared the old way (allowed to roam effectively wild on grassland and then rounded up for slaughter by gauchos and flung onto the grill). But the huge commercial pressure of international beef consumption has modernized the Argentinian industry in an incredibly short time. North America's appetite for beef is bottomless and ranchers have realized the power of feedlot rearing 'USDA-style' beef.

A few ranches are holding out, but what they're celebrating is a system that's far harder to market. Free-ranging herds of indeterminate breed are difficult to 'productize' in the same way as Aberdeen Angus or Hanwoo so, in many ways, it feels like romantic nostalgia to swim against the tide.

---

[26] Hanwoo beef is classified by five grades that include 1++, 1+, 1, 2, and 3, depending on the degree of marbling, meat colour, fat colour, firmness and maturity. An individual twelve-digit identification number is generated for every Hanwoo calf at birth with DNA identity testing to prevent false labelling of origin.

Age at Slaughter

Draft and dairy cattle only really begin their productive lives when they are physically and sexually mature. Mass production of beef, however, with its imperative to minimize costs, requires animals to have shorter lives, reducing the quantity of feed needed and handling costs, so they are slaughtered as close as possible to full growth, at the end of adolescence.

Today, the majority of beef for human consumption across the world comes from young animals, reared expressly for the purpose. You can make your own decision as to whether consumers have changed their tastes or whether there has been commercial and political pressure on them to do so, but whichever side you come out, beef is getting younger and leaner.

- In the USA today, beef animals are usually slaughtered at 14–16 months.

- Italy prefers animals slaughtered at 16–18 months, though Chianina are slaughtered at 22 months or older.

- In Japan, slaughter takes place at 24–36 months.

- Until the outbreaks of bovine spongiform encephalopathy (BSE) in the 1980s and 1990s, most UK and French beef came from older ex-dairy cattle with 36–48 months considered best. As BSE was more likely to affect older animals, EU regulations introduced penalties for slaughter past 30 months. Since these regulations were lifted, the UK reports that the majority of beef cattle are slaughtered between 24–36 months.[27]

Veal

'Only young beef that have never performed any labor can supply tender rump steaks.'

— Charles Ranhofer, *The Epicurean* (1894)

It is perhaps because of the ancient and deep-rooted belief that beef is a fortifying and 'strong' meat that there has always been a market for a more delicate, digestible and, well, less 'meaty' version. This alternative is veal – the meat of unweaned calves.

Calf meat is pale, delicate in flavour and high in collagen, so it's tender. Calves don't usually move far from their mothers and aren't used for draft work, so their muscles remain unworked. Exercise or a grass diet would darken their meat, so veal calves were traditionally kept off grass and fed on milk, or a milk substitute, until slaughter at 5–6 weeks. Unfortunately, this led to various barbaric forms of 'crated' rearing, in which animals were restrained from birth in cages, often in darkness, and rapidly fattened on whey or milk powder.

The young male offspring of dairy cows are usually killed at birth as they are obviously unable to produce milk. In the UK, these 'Bobby' calves were sometimes 'rescued', traditionally by dairy farmers' children, and raised on grass before being slaughtered for family use. This Bobby veal had more of the characteristics of mature beef but was still young, tender and succulent. Today, there is no market at all for crated veal in most countries, but rescued male dairy calves that are finished on grass are successful in the UK, where they are marketed as 'rose veal'.

---

[27] Some industry voices in the UK are now suggesting to reduce this to 12 months, to maximize profit and reduce emissions.

Quality of Life and Death

'All flesh is grass.'

— Isaiah 40:6-8

Breeding brings out and enhances desirable genetic characteristics, but that isn't enough to produce great meat. How the animal is treated – how it lives and dies – is of higher significance. Though it might not be possible to get a world-class steak out of some animals, no matter how well they're treated, a prize specimen can be ruined by poor treatment.

The factors that affect meat most after genetics will be feeding and the manner of slaughter.

Feeding and Finishing

Grass has a growth curve. When young and increasing in bulk, it's full of protein and then, as it matures, it contains more carbohydrate and sugars. Cows will eat grass throughout its growth cycle, but high-protein spring grass produces an unappetizing flavour in meat. Mature summer grass gives great flavour. Grass also contains chlorophyll, which breaks down to form terpenes. These are the volatile compounds that create vegetal, herby flavours.

This means that an animal ranging wild, grazing naturally, will produce different flavours of meat throughout its life. Obviously, that's not ideal for the farmer aiming for a consistent and reliable product.

The most cost-effective way to raise an animal, therefore, has historically been to let it eat naturally while it's growing, to create bulk, and then to control its diet in the months before slaughter to bring the meat to a peak of flavour and fatness. This process is known as finishing.

There are two main methods of finishing, which produce two very different types of beef: grass finishing and grain finishing.

Grass finishing

Grass finishing involves feeding cattle natural grass (if it's the correct time of its growth season), hay (which is grass that's been dried at its nutritional peak) or silage (which is grass preserved by a process of fermentation to produce even higher levels of sugar and carbohydrate).

Grass finishing means that the animal is consuming chlorophyll throughout the end of its life, creating the terpenes that produce a stronger vegetal or herbal flavour. Cattle can also be finished on grain, which is nutritionally consistent throughout the year and contains large quantities of carbohydrates and sugar, but which is much lower in chlorophyll. Grain produces excellent fat fast, but the lack of chlorophyll means fewer terpenes and a gentler flavour.

Both forms of finishing produce excellent meat, but generally, grass-fed meat has a stronger, meatier flavour while grain-finished meat focuses more on tenderness and unctuous texture. Both are desirable, but it is a continuum from which cooks can select. Grass flavour and grain texture are both great and both can be enhanced by different treatments in cooking. It's really down to individual preference, and I have no end of fun trying to match dishes to different steaks.

Grain finishing

In South and Central America, the Spanish colonizers raised their cattle wild, on grass, and the first Western settlers and ranchers in the US did the same. Some Eastern settlers, however, particularly around Appalachia, found success feeding their cattle whole maize plants. This technique of grain finishing was properly developed just after the Second World War by American scientists aiming to improve the beef industry. Ralph Durham, working at Texas Tech, developed a carefully calculated 'bovine ration' based on corn.[28]

---

[28] He also developed a method of injecting fat to create marbling which is, fortunately, forgotten.

Corn feeding fitted in with the growing and industrializing beef industry frighteningly well. Driven cattle had always been held in pens at the railheads before being freighted to cities as live transportation was essential in the years before refrigerated railcars. Now they could be 'finished' in pens with totally controlled diets, their movement restricted so they didn't exercise off any of their valuable fat. When refrigeration arrived, it became more sensible and economical to slaughter and process the animals before shipping. By the application of scientific methods, more and higher-quality beef could be shifted to an ever-growing number of customers at ever-more affordable prices. It seemed like an all-round winning argument.

This method did have downsides for the welfare of the animals, however. The faster and more efficient the fattening process became, the more it was balanced by symptoms like acidosis or liver abscesses. So, as soon as they became widely available, antibiotics were administered routinely and prophylactically.

Farmers had known for millennia that castrating young bulls made them put on fat faster than muscle, though they would not have recognized this as hormone control. But once scientists had isolated effective growth hormones in the lab, it became grimly inevitable that these would also be used on animals. Natural and synthetic hormones including oestrogen and testosterone gave even more control, creating leaner and more muscular cattle faster and on less feed.

Today, a typical American intensively reared calf will be implanted with a growth hormone while still suckling. It will be removed from its mother at 7–8 months, either for further grazing or grain feeding, and at this stage it will receive more growth hormones. After 12 months, it will be moved to a finishing lot, where it will receive antibiotics, further growth hormones and a corn-only diet until slaughter. Before the Second World War, 5 per cent of US steaks might have come from a grain-fed cow. Today it's almost 100 per cent.

Slaughter

An enormous amount of research and effort has been poured into making slaughter as low-stress as possible and, in most countries, there is a lot of regulation around the process.

After death, at least for a while, the body of an animal continues to process glycogen (the stored form of glucose) in the muscles in the same way it did during exercise. Increased acidity helps to reduce microbial action, so it's a preservative. It also helps to tenderize the meat. Stress burns glycogen, meaning that there will be less lactic acid in the carcass, leading to tough meat that will decay faster. Slaughter should be managed to minimize stress to the animal, both for the animal's sake and for the sake of the end product.

Animals should be transported in as calm a manner as possible and be kept at the abattoir for a period in a holding pen called a lairage, sometimes overnight, to calm them after the move.

Ideally, the cattle will be gently led to a path that restricts them to single-file movement in one direction. The animals should see only the animal in front of them in the chute, with no sensory distraction on either side. This encourages them to move forward in a controlled manner. At the end of the chute, there are a variety of arrangements, but the most common is a kind of curtain through which the animal pushes its head, or a tighter space that enables the slaughterman to access the animal's head from behind and above. Here, a pair of electrodes are used across the head to instantly stun the animal, or a captive bolt device is applied to the forehead, firing a retractable metal rod into the front of the brain. Both methods 'massively disrupt' the brain, instantly rendering the creature unconscious.

As much blood as possible must be removed quickly to avoid spoilage, so stunning is intended to stop the animal feeling any pain while the heart remains beating to keep the blood under pressure. As quickly as possible, the animal is hung up by its hind legs and its throat, including the key veins and arteries on either side of the neck, is cut.

Within minutes, the blood will pump out of the severed vessels or drain through gravity and the heart will stop. The animal will have died, we believe without pain and with minimum distress, of exsanguination – loss of blood.

Before rigor mortis commences, the carcass will be eviscerated and the skin removed, and the head and the lower ends of the limbs removed, too. It is then moved into a refrigerated area where it will be inspected by a vet.

Over the next couple of hours, the muscles run out of glycogen and surviving nerve activity makes the muscles contract and lock into position. Before rigor completely sets in, the carcass must be arranged so that the muscles will be extended by its weight before locking up.

After a day in this position, the muscles will begin to relax and the carcass can be split vertically, with a saw, producing two 'sides'.[29]

---

[29] Having experienced slaughter close up and many times, this point still feels immensely significant. The moment of stunning is hard to watch, but the final act of splitting the carcass, leaving two identifiable 'sides of beef' swinging on hooks is the moment to cease thinking of an animal and to begin regarding it as meat.

Butc

hery

The side of beef hangs in a refrigerator. It's been split into two
sections, the forequarter and the hindquarter at a line between
the 10th and 11th rib - between the rib and the wing-rib sections.
We're working with quite a neat little carcass but a quarter is
about the maximum one man can sling over his shoulder.

Hindquarter

The carcass hangs in the ageing fridge by its hind leg. Here you can see where the spine joins the pelvis – the 'aitch-bone', which has been cut through with a bandsaw.

We begin with the hindquarter, separating the leg at the hip joint.
Above the joint is the rump (see page 94). Working from inside the
pelvis we also recover the spider steak (see page 88), a delicate web
of tender muscle that holds the ball and socket of the hip together.

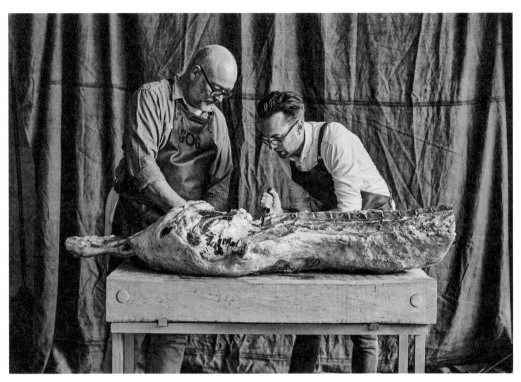

Separating the hind leg.

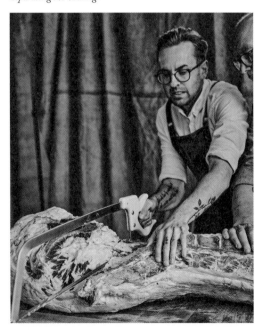
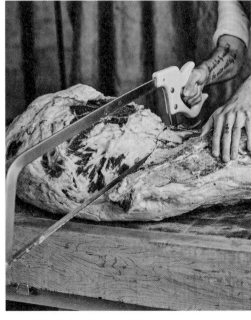

Sawing through at the hip joint. The aim here is to go through the very tip of the hip, preserving the maximum amount of loin.

Teasing out the spider at the hip joint.

Spider steak (see page 88).

Working around the ball of the hip joint.

We now separate the lower part of the hindquarter - the flank.
There are sheets and sections of abdominal muscle, low on the
animal's abdomen. In cross section not unlike streaky bacon,
but with care, sheets and strip-shaped steaks with longitudinal,
coarse-fibred muscle can be dissected out as steaks; one of these
is the flank steak (see page 90).

Close to the navel is the toro steak (see page 92), nothing to
do with the Spanish word for 'bull' but instead, named after the
prized fatty belly meat of Japanese sashimi tuna.

In the following photographs you will see the full length of the
sirloin still attached to the spine and the wide vertebrae of
the lower back. The fat end of the fillet, the chateaubriand, is
rooted inside the pelvis - overleaf you will see that it protrudes
to the right.

Flank (see page 90).

Flank – where we hope to find the toro steak.

Chasing the toro...

Trimming the toro.

Toro steak (see page 92).

Toro steak.

We remove the whole fillet (see page 102) as a single piece which is then trimmed and later sliced into separate steaks.

Sirloin section with the fillet in place. Notice how the fillet tapers off to the left. The chateaubriand has been left intact and is hanging out to the right.

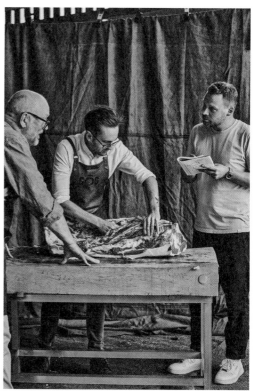

Removing the fillet whole.

Luke, our Art Director, takes notes as we cut.

Removing the fillet.

Untrimmed fillet.

Trimming the fillet.

Trimming the fillet.

Separating the rump (see page 94) from the loin, we are able to take our thick 'London Broil' steak (see page 194) from the rump side.

Separating the hind leg.

Pointing out the tri-tip[30] cut through when separating the sirloin from the rump.

Dan is counting the ribs, showing me where to separate the rump from the loin.

Separating rump from loin.

[30] The tri-tip (also known as the Santa Maria or Newport steak) is rather a newcomer in butchery. Several butchers in the LA area claim to have invented it after rescuing it from the mince bucket, some suggest for sale to US military caterers. It's a triangular portion of muscle called the tensor fasciae latae that's usually trimmed off the bottom of a US sirloin to square it up. It is a single muscle piece with a good layer of subcutaneous fat on one side.

Obviously, it wasn't really invented in LA, because French butchers call it the *aiguillette baronne*, in Argentine *asado* it is known as *colita de cuadril*, in Brazil it is known as *maminha*, it's called *Bürgermeisterstück* in Austria and parts of Germany and *rabillo de cadera* in Spain.

Whatever you call it, though, it's amazing when heavily marinated and seared on a charcoal grill.

Cutting our giant London Broil (see page 194) from the rump.

It's possible to take out the whole sirloin as a single piece (in the US this is called the strip, in the UK it's a larder cut) but for our purposes we're going to cut between the sirloin and the wing ribs (the last three ribs - see Cow Maps A and B on pages 76-79).

Chining a wing rib.

Sirloin to the left, wing ribs to the right.

Removing whole sirloin.

Removing whole sirloin.

Removing the sirloin from the spine/vertebrae.

Removing the sirloin from the spine/vertebrae.

End-view of whole sirloin.

The whole sirloin taken off as one piece (see pages 98–101). Restaurants love these as you can slice off clean, boneless, low-fat steaks as needed. This is why it's called a 'larder cut' in the UK.

If you remove the sirloin and the fillet as full pieces, it prevents you from cutting T-bone steaks. So, at this point, we also use a second hindquarter with the rump and flank removed, to slice into an assortment of steaks. Starting at the very back (thus including sirloin and chateaubriand) we cut a 'three fingers thick' Fiorentina - of which there is only really one; the last T-bone before the rump - then a series of T-bone steaks (see page 97).

Sirloin on the bone as a rack.

Cutting a sirloin steak on the bone. Notice the broad horizontal protuberances on the vertebrae.

Whole loin section on the bone.

Measuring a 'three fingers thick' Fiorentina steak.

Cutting off a Fiorentina steak.

Fiorentina steak (see page 97).

The Fiorentina steak 'stood up' on the bone.

Now we turn our attention to the forequarter, removing first
the neck and the shank (the lower end of leg), then the brisket.
See Cow Map B on page 78.

The huge barrel shape of the ribcage on the whole forequarter.

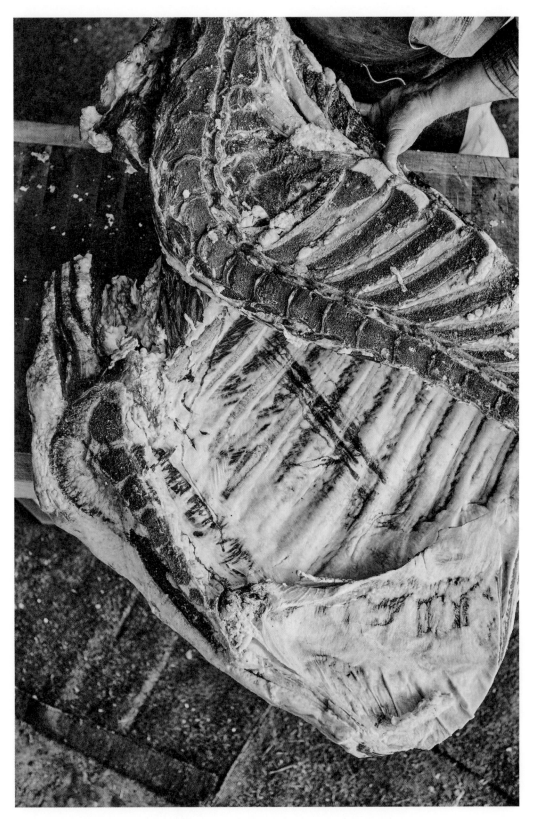

The forequarter. That's the neck toward the left — you can see the vast musculature that holds up the heavy head.

Whole forequarter before removing brisket.

Cutting away the brisket.

Removing brisket from rib eye section. The bottom layer of meat to the left-hand side is the spinalis (see page 110).

Cutting between ribs five and six we can separate the rib and chuck sections. The chuck contains muscles in the base of the neck and the complex structure of the shoulder blade (see page 112). Between the shoulder blade, and attached to the ribs and spine, is a further flat 'plate' of muscle which can be trimmed as a Denver steak (see page 114). The shoulder blade is removed, leaving the Denver lying against the ribs. At the bottom of the forequarter, attached to the ribs, are the skirt and goose skirt steaks (see page 116), which are carefully excised.

Taking off a wing rib.

A wing-rib on the bone. It comes from closer to the front of the animal so there's no fillet by this point.

Forerib to the left, chuck to the right.

Chuck section toward the neck end where the tall cervical vertebrae are. A lot of that complex musculature ties into the shoulder and the top of the leg. Again, the spinalis is visible at the bottom.

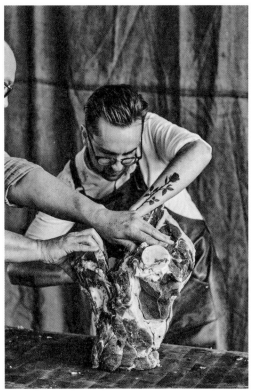

Removing shoulder blade from ribs.

Denver steak (see page 114).

Removing the skirt.

The skirt (see page 116). We tend to trim all the fat off this to make it look more appealing on the slab but in most of Central and South America, the fat is left on and the meat is better for it.

Finally, we're looking at the rib section. Here, all the musculature is outside the ribcage. The lower part of the ribs is removed, and the skirt and goose skirt are removed. The remaining 'rack' of spine and rib can be sawn into pieces to create rib eyes on the bone (see page 106) or txuletons. Leaving the ribs long and scraping them clean creates tomahawk steaks (see page 106).

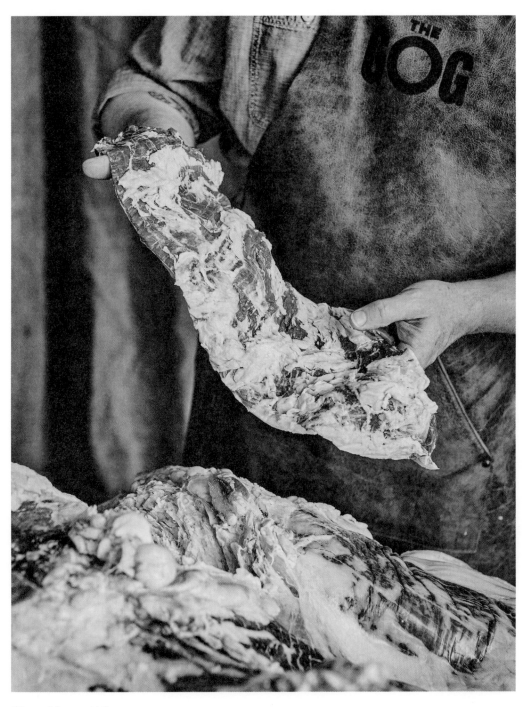

Skirt steak (see page 116).

Stripping the rib on a tomahawk.

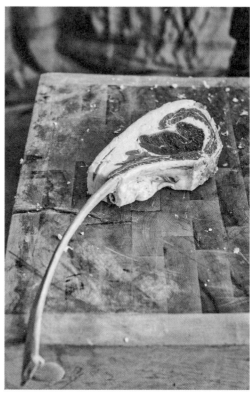

Tomahawk steak (see page 106).

Tomahawk to the left, chuck to the right.

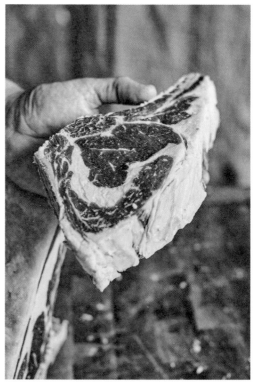

Rib eye steak (see page 106).

Alternatively, as we have done with our second forequarter. The whole 'rib roll' can be lifted off as one piece and then sliced into half a dozen or so boneless rib eye steaks, a set of which we've selected for the five-steak programme later (see page 132).

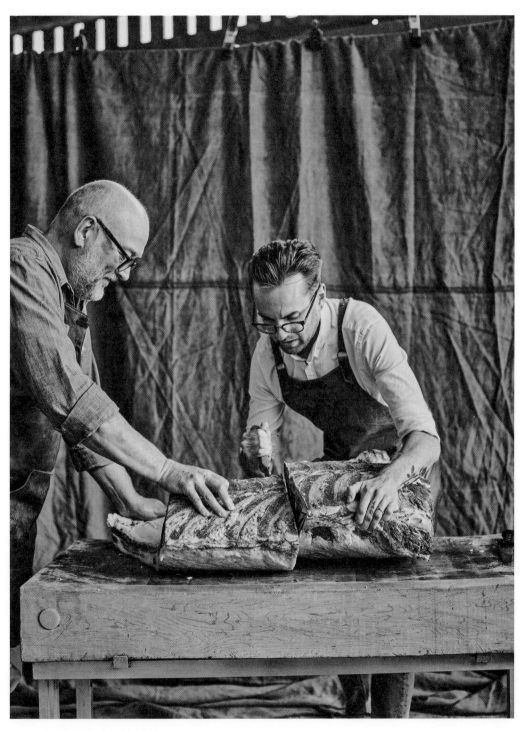

Here, we're taking off a 'set' of five rib eyes.

Mapping the Beast

I realize this is going to sound odd, but to understand how beef butchery works, I'd like you to start by finding a good friend and asking them to take their top off. I know, I'm sorry. Unfortunately, this is only going to get weirder. It's probably easiest if you pretend that you're offering them a massage, but what you'll really be doing is locating skeletal and muscular structures on a live subject – and, unless you have a live and reasonably compliant cow available, this is going to be the best way to do it.[31]

Take a look at the length of their back. You should be able to see the spine running down the middle, the shoulder blades on the left and right at the top and the pelvis at the bottom. By running your fingers down either side of the spine, you'll feel two sets of muscles just under the skin. There are two more of these long sets of muscles inside the torso, behind the spine and the ribs. On your live subject, you should be able to see or feel how the spine is basically a loose stack of roughly X-shaped bricks, held erect by the constant, gentle use of these four long groups of muscles. They are constantly pulling, balancing and adjusting to keep us upright and able to move around. Pilates teachers go crazy about this stuff.

If you move your fingers from the top to the bottom of your friend's back, you'll also find that there are ribs fixed on either side of the spinal vertebrae on the upper half of the torso. Then, at around the midpoint, we get to the abdomen, where the spine is doing all the work itself. This is the lumbar section of the spine – our waist – where we can swivel, bend and flex.[32] In this way, we are very different from cows.

OK. Clothes back on. Now we're going to do some yoga.

The yoga posture called 'cow pose' (*bitilasana*) can help us understand steak even better. Here's how it works. First, get on your hands and knees, with your hands directly under your shoulders, your fingers facing forwards and your knees directly under your hips. Keep your neck level with your spine. Now exhale, drawing your stomach towards your spine and gently rounding your back upwards, allowing your head to point down towards the floor. This is 'cat pose' (*bidalasana* or *marjaryasana*). Next, bring your spine back into the straight neutral position and, as you inhale, allow your belly to drop so your spine arches downwards, raising your head comfortably until you are facing just a little upwards.

---

[31] This is perhaps not as weird as it sounds. Throughout history, artists and sculptors have studied anatomy and even undertaken dissections in order to better understand the bodies they were trying to paint or carve.

[32] And, unfortunately, most often suffer back pain or injury.

Repeat this a couple of times – firstly because it's a good stretch for the muscles around the spine and so great for your lower back, but also because, as your instructor will no doubt tell you, yoga can teach you many things beyond just stretching. In this case, as your spine flexes from cat to cow and back again, it demonstrates how the muscle groups inside and outside the spine operate. As a standing human, your spinal musculature has a particular function, but once you put yourself into the position of a quadruped, you can quickly appreciate which muscle groups need to do more work and therefore will be better developed.

Humans are bipedal. We walk on two legs, so everything about our locomotion is about passing weight and stress down through the spine, hips, legs and feet. The muscles we need for this are quite small and refined. Now think about a cow. A reasonable-sized specimen at slaughter age can be anything up to two-thirds of a tonne. That's 650kg (1,433lb) of meat, fat and bone, supported at the corners, like a table. A cow doesn't need to bend in the middle like a human does – in fact, it needs a huge amount of muscle along the spine, in constant tension, to stop it sagging. This fact of animal physiology is what gives us steak.

Like most quadrupeds, most of a cow's strength is in the hindquarters, which supply motive power. The forelegs are usually more lightly built and practically 'hold up' the front of the animal. The area around the shoulders has a complex musculature with lots of strong tendons and connective tissue. It's noticeable that you rarely see 'beef shoulder' being sold in a butcher's shop like you would lamb or pork. Most of it leaves the slaughterhouse as mince (ground beef) or will be reduced, by the butcher, to cubed stewing meat or economical rolled slow-roasting joints. Don't reject this stuff, though, as the flavour is amazing – it just needs careful handling (see page 112). There are sheets of muscle around the bottom of the ribcage that can be tasty, too – this is where you're going to find things like brisket for long and low cooking.

It's once you get up top that things start to get most interesting, however. Take a look at **Map A** (see page 76). This cross-section of the carcass shows where those back muscles start to become significant. A nicely butchered chunk from here would give you a forerib roast, good for Sunday lunch and benefitting from long cooking. There are several distinct strands of muscle outside the ribcage, too. Some of these, like the *supraspinatus*,[33] help to articulate the shoulder joint, so naturally they peter out further down the spine. Around the outside of the rib eye is the *spinalis dorsi*, also known as the rib cap. A slice across here gives you a rib eye steak, either on or off the bone. It is not a single muscle, but rather a bunch of several with some fat and connective tissue included. In some styles of butchery, particularly in Korea or the US, muscles in this area are separated out to create small, single-muscle steaks.

Moving down the spine towards the rear on **Map B** (see page 78), we can see that the muscle bundle outside the spine resolves into a couple of large ones, the largest being the *longissimus dorsi*.

This big, simple muscle mass runs from here to the rump of the animal and is referred to as the sirloin (short loin in the US).

Behind the ribcage, there are wide projections on either side of the lumbar vertebrae, as demonstrated on **Map C** (see page 80). A slice across here gives us a T-bone steak, which is really a sirloin on one side of the bone and a slice of fillet on the other.

The fillet muscle group is small, tender, close-grained and free of fat or connective tissue. It's only there to balance the huge mass of the sirloin bundle outside the spine. It doesn't really have a lot of 'work' to do, so it's regarded by many as the best piece of meat on the carcass. In fact, the fillet is such an important and prestigious piece of meat that it's often removed and then separated into a variety of premium cuts (see page 102). Look at the longitudinal cross-section on **Map C**. You'll see that the fillet is roughly conical in shape, starting in a small point towards the back of the ribcage and then thickening gently before connecting into the complexities of the 'H bone' (the beginning of the hip). In short, the further you move towards the back of the carcass, the more the fillet enters the equation.

Because of the conical shape of the fillet, T-bones vary in their balance between sirloin and fillet. A steak cut at the front-end of this area will have a big sirloin side and a neat little nugget of fillet. The last couple of steaks, cut right at the back and close to the hip, will contain a big slice across the chateaubriand (the thickest part of the fillet), almost the same size as the sirloin. These are widely regarded as the best cuts on the animal, sometimes called porterhouse steaks.

The muscles in a piece of beef are made up of bundles of cells that form fibres. You can see them easily in most meat. These fibres tend to get thicker as the animal gets older and through exercise and movement. Usually, the more prestigious cuts have fine fibres and a close 'grain' structure, while coarser fibres give cheaper cuts a rougher texture that is initially harder to chew but which responds to long, slow cooking.

---

[33] Origin: the ventral surfaces of the transverse processes of the lumbar vertebrae and the last rib.
Insertion: trochanter of the femur.
Action: flexes the hip joint, rotates the limb laterally and flexes the vertebral column when the hip joint is fixed in position.

Under a microscope, the fibres are revealed as two separate types, referred to as 'white' and 'red' or fast-twitch and slow-twitch. Fast-twitch fibres are best for sudden, intense contraction. They are fast-growing but they're thick and tough. Slow-twitch fibres are best for sustained action. They usually come with plenty of intramuscular fat.

There are red and white fibres in every muscle, but as the animal grows, the proportions of red and white will alter depending on the use to which each individual muscle is put. Over the years, farmers have selectively bred beef cattle for rapid growth, so they've often favoured draft animals with a lot of fast-twitch muscle fibre. These animals tend to grow faster and larger, though the meat is consequently tougher, more fibrous and less juicy.

Breeds that spend more time standing around in fields and chewing develop more slow-twitch fibre in their muscles. They are consequently smaller, but the meat is often considered better.

What this means is that the texture, fat marbling and juiciness of a cut of meat can vary widely depending on the animal's breed, musculature, diet, age, rearing and the physical demands of its life.

The bundles of fibres are held together by a tougher outer wrapper of connective tissue, which also forms the tendons at the ends of the muscles where they join the bones.[34] Connective tissue is made mainly of collagen fibres which, though they are tough, can be rendered to softness through slow cooking. In butchery, the connective tissue is sometimes called 'silverskin' and can be taken off in trimming.

The role of fat in the flavour of beef is still a matter of some debate (see page 126) but, wherever you stand on it, fat – and its distribution through the animal – is important.

There are three important kinds of fat deposits in a cow's body, all of which have different culinary purposes. The thick layer of yellow fat on the outside, revealed when the carcass is flayed, is subcutaneous fat. This is the protective and insulating layer for the creature while it's alive and, when cooked, it softens to a pleasant, digestible consistency but doesn't fully 'melt'.

Around the organs are thick deposits of hard, white visceral fat that will actually 'snap off' the carcass. This melts easily and makes beef dripping, a fantastic frying medium for the world's best chips. The best stuff comes from around the kidneys and under the spine.

Finally, there's intramuscular fat, which forms thin layers between bundles of fibre in certain muscle groups, mostly the slow-twitch muscles that don't do a lot of work. Different breeds of cattle and different feeding regimes create more or less of this kind of fat, which is why a piece of 'A5', corn-fed Wagyu fillet can be almost white with the stuff while the same cut from a grass-fed ex-draft Chianina might be close-grained and lean.

Understanding what each muscle does and how they are constructed allows us to understand how the meat will behave. The large, simple muscles in the hindquarters of the animal have a high proportion of fast-twitch fibres to give impulsive force when galloping, fighting or pulling weight. The meat will be close-grained with less intramuscular fat and proportionately less connective tissue towards the rear. The complex bundles of smaller muscles around the shoulders are used for sustained 'propping up', so they'll have more slow-twitch fibres, more connective tissue and more intramuscular fat. Therefore, steaks are more 'complicated' and deliciously fatty towards the front and simpler and usually more 'juicy' towards the rear.

[34] This is called the 'insertion point'. Knowing where the insertion points for each muscle are on the body helps us to understand what each muscle does.

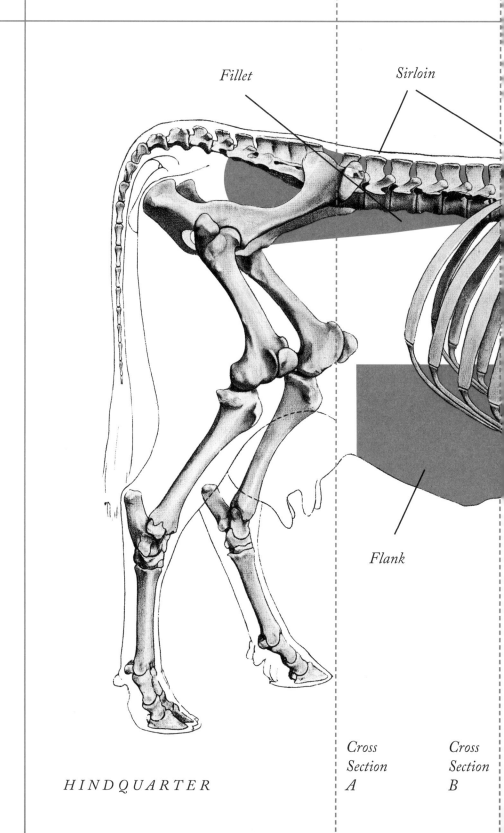

COW MAP A

Profile

Fillet

Sirloin

Flank

Cross Section A

Cross Section B

HINDQUARTER

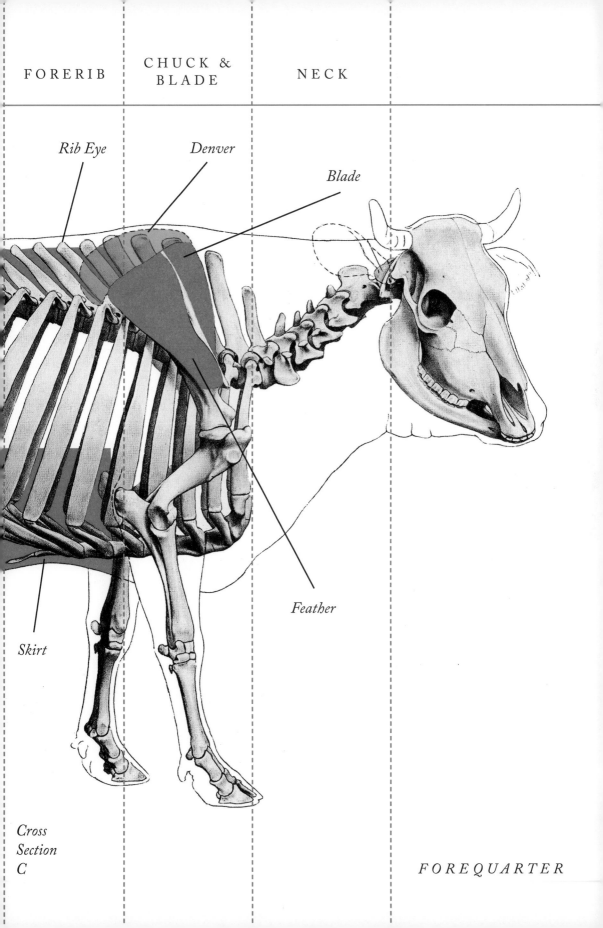

FORERIB

CHUCK &
BLADE

NECK

Rib Eye

Denver

Blade

Feather

Skirt

Cross
Section
C

FOREQUARTER

Above

COW MAP B

Because the sirloin is such a premium piece of meat, when removing it as a single piece the butcher will commonly stray further towards the front of the animal, into the wingrib – meaning more sirloin steaks.

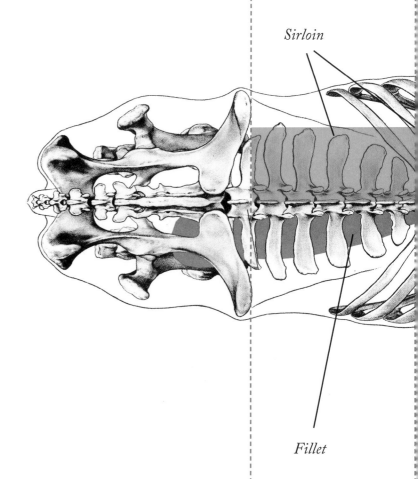

Sirloin

Fillet

*Cross
Section
A*

*Cross
Section
B*

HINDQUARTER

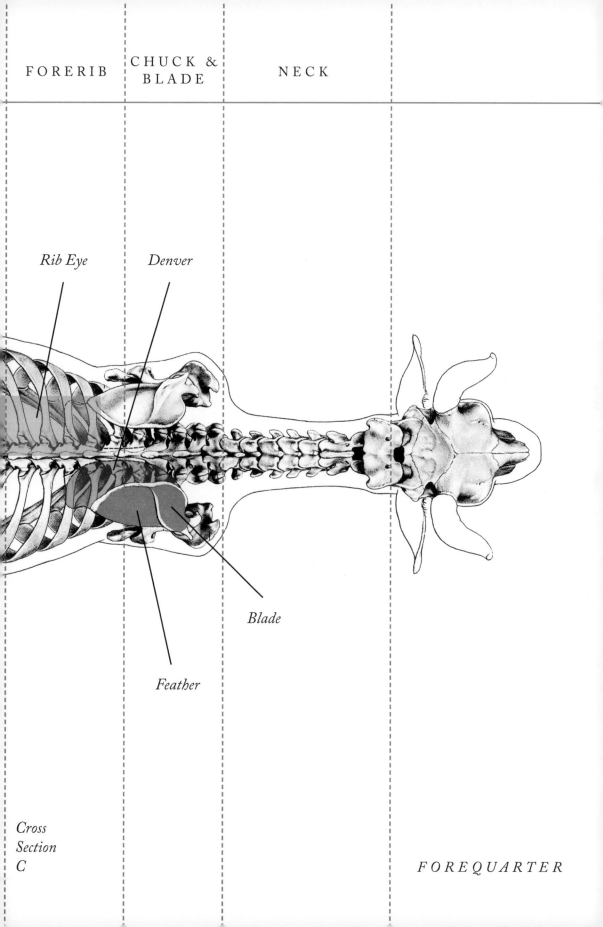

FORERIB CHUCK & BLADE NECK

Rib Eye

Denver

Blade

Feather

Cross
Section
C

FOREQUARTER

CHATEAUBRIAND

Tournedos can
be any size but is
tied into a drum shape

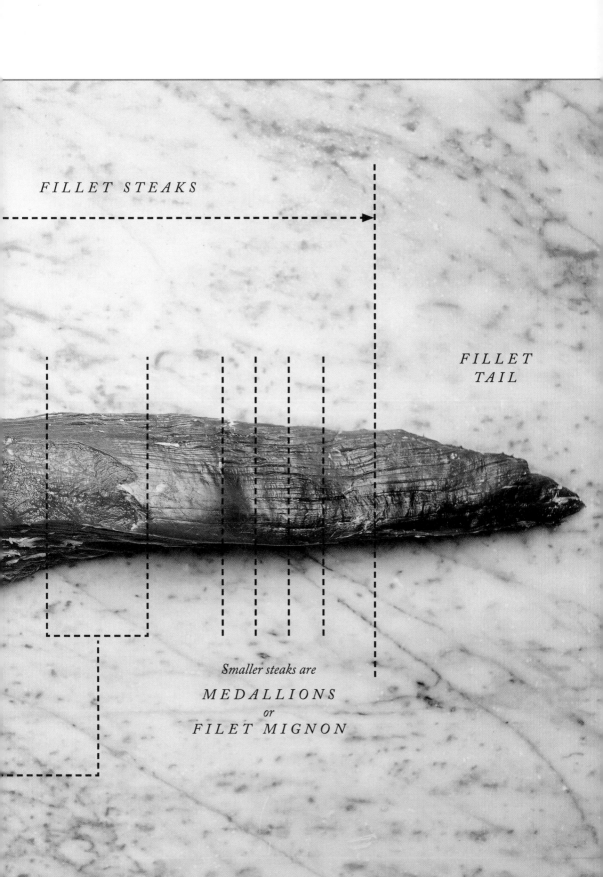

FILLET STEAKS

*FILLET
TAIL*

Smaller steaks are
MEDALLIONS
or
FILET MIGNON

Ageing and Storage

'Taking Down' the Carcass

Butchery is a complex process in which anatomy, power tools and business sense all come into play. There are different butchery traditions in different countries. In the UK, butchers often talk about 'joints' of meat – large sections that are often cut from the carcass with a handsaw or bandsaw. They include meat from several muscles, as well as bones, fat, connective tissue and often a literal joint. Other countries favour something closer to 'seam butchery', where individual muscles are removed from the carcass and then portioned.[35]

In a British butcher's shop, for example, you might be offered a standing rib roast – that's a lump of rib eye attached to several ribs and half of the longitudinally sawn spine. It's a great piece for roasting, as the bones add flavour and conduct heat well to help with the cooking. But offering a three-rib standing roast means there will be maybe five rib eye steaks that the butcher can't sell. Similarly, a steak cut like a porterhouse or a T-bone, which has a piece of sirloin and a piece of fillet either side of a central rib, means that the butcher has given up the chance to sell a whole fillet or have a sirloin to roll or slice. Knowing their customers and planning their cutting accordingly is one of the most important skills a successful butcher needs. A second consideration for the butcher is the trimming of fat. An increasing number of customers are turned off by large amounts of visible fat, while others see it as something they will eventually discard, so they don't want to pay for it. The butcher must decide exactly how much fat to trim away to please their customers.

Some butchers will take in whole or half carcasses and do all the work themselves,[36] while others will buy in 'primals' – a subsection of a side of beef – and cut individual pieces from them.[37] Buying primals allows a butcher or commercial kitchen to have a large stock of premium cuts, while whole sides provide a wider range of cuts of different prices and qualities.

Many restaurants with a steak on the menu will buy a whole vacuum-packed sirloin or rolled rib to cut off steaks to order. A restaurant that buys in a whole side, however, might have eight or so slightly different sizes of rib eye, ten sirloins, various fillet pieces and their own stewing steak, mince (ground beef) and beef stock.

Storing, Dry-ageing and Wet-ageing

Before meat is ever cut, the butcher is responsible for its storage, keeping it in peak condition through refrigeration or improving its flavour and texture through the ageing process known as 'hanging'.[38]

Stored in a clean environment, at a controlled temperature and humidity level and with a good

---

[35] Korean butchery has 120 cuts of beef (but only fifty are in regular use), while the French and English have thirty-five and the US has twenty-two.

[36] Like you've seen me and my butcher Dan doing on pages 50–71.

[37] A primal is different from a 'prime' cut, which is a US quality marker.

flow of fresh air, the composition and flavour of meat (particularly grass-fed meat) will change. Over time, water will evaporate from the surface of the meat, creating a more hostile environment for bacteria and concentrating the flavour compounds. The meat will become stronger flavoured and longer lasting. Many fans of ageing assert that the process particularly concentrates the grassy flavours of the terpenes (see page 45).

During ageing, the lactic acid remaining in the muscles of the animal following the slaughter process also continues to gently break down the meat, making it more tender and developing a characteristic slightly acidic taste.

Additionally, while dry-ageing is going on, some surface mould cultures may take hold, including the white bloom of *Lactobacillus acidophilus*, which can contribute to a faint smell that some associate with blue cheese.

This process of dry-ageing is expensive to the butcher, however. A properly hung piece of beef will lose 10–15 per cent of its moisture by weight. That means that 10kg (22lb) meat purchased from the abattoir will only yield 8.5kg (18¾lb) for retail. Worse still, a certain amount of the surface of the meat may be over-dried, mouldy or otherwise unattractive on the counter so will have to be trimmed away and discarded. This means that even a good butcher who is careful with dry-ageing and cutting can expect to lose a quarter of the weight of meat he bought in once everything is trimmed and tidied for sale.

In recent years, some butchers have begun to hang their meat in chambers lined with rock salt. I have to confess that the science of this eludes me. The salt doesn't seem to degrade over time, it isn't chemically capable of evaporating or in any way moving through the air and the drying effect is much less than that of a regular fridge. I've not been able to detect any flavour difference between 'salt-aged' steak and regular dry-aged steak… it certainly doesn't taste more salty.[39]

Ageing can continue to improve the quality and texture of meat for a month or more after slaughter, but the enemy is rancidity – the tendency of beef fat to oxidize, causing an unpleasant sour taste. Rancidity can be controlled reasonably easily in large cuts of grass-fed beef but for smaller cuts (with a correspondingly higher surface area) or highly marbled grain-finished carcasses, dry-ageing becomes increasingly difficult to do well.

The other option for hanging beef is wet-ageing, which involves sealing a cut of meat into a plastic pouch soon after slaughter. Because there's no oxygen, there can be no rancidity or mould and because none of the meat is exposed to the air, fats can't go rancid and there can be no evaporation and resulting weight loss. Lactic acid and other enzymes in the meat will continue to do their work, tenderizing and developing some flavours. Principally, though, the meat just sits in its own blood and juices, which can impart a kind of iron-rich, meaty kick to the flavour.

Freezing

Butchers may store meat by freezing it, so it's worth understanding the pros and cons of this process.

When water freezes, it forms ice crystals. If it freezes very quickly, the crystals remain small, but if it freezes slowly they become much bigger and the volume of the ice expands. This can rupture the cells in meat, allowing the juices to leak out. A poorly frozen steak will release a load of juice

---

[38] Hanging is the general term for keeping meat while it matures but, particularly in the case of game birds, it can also mean allowing partial decomposition in order to add a 'high' or 'gamey' flavour. This is rarely, if ever, the objective in hanging beef, so many butchers prefer to use the term 'dry-ageing'. Personally, I'm very fond of the Italian term *frolatura*.

[39] There is a chance that salt walls in a drying chamber can stop certain spoilage bacteria from proliferating, possibly increasing the time the meat can be aged, but this still doesn't seem to add anything that wouldn't be present in meat carefully dry-aged in a standard stainless-steel fridge with properly cleaned walls.

and blood as it defrosts and even more when it hits a hot pan and the damaged cells contract with the heat.

Abattoirs and meat-processing facilities use 'blast chillers' to freeze meat. These are very powerful freezers that drop the temperature to much lower than a domestic freezer in a matter of minutes. Usually, if meat has been blast-chilled at its peak and delivered via a secure 'cold chain' it will remain in the best condition.[41]

Though it's less common in the UK, some countries quick-freeze whole sides, then use power saws to cut steaks and joints from the solid, frozen piece.

If you must freeze steaks at home, remember to hit the 'boost' button on your freezer if you have one, wrap the steaks individually to prevent 'freezer burn' and place them in the freezer in such a way that there's plenty of space around them for cold air to circulate.[40] Once they're solid, you can bag them or stack them up any way you like, but separation gives them the best chance of freezing fast.

When it comes to defrosting a steak, do so gently, in its packaging. Room temperature is fine or, if you're in a hurry and the wrapping is waterproof, you can immerse it in a sink of cold water (hot water will cause much more juice leakage).

If you have time to defrost the steak overnight, this can be combined with dry brining. Unwrap the steak, sprinkle it liberally with salt and leave it uncovered in the fridge.

Tenderizing

When we say a steak is tough, we mean it's difficult to bite through and chew. Tenderizing means making that easier – breaking the meat down, interrupting strong fibres and also giving the teeth the head start.

Meat can be naturally tenderized through ageing, thanks to the presence of calpains. These are enzymes that, in the living animal, slowly break down muscle fibres so new ones can grow, allowing the animal to increase its size and strength. After death, there's no regrowth, but the calpains continue to function. This is a slow process and difficult to control, so various other methods can be used. These split into two categories; the physical, where careful cutting or vigorous bashing make the meat easier to get your teeth through; or chemical solutions, which actually alter or partially break down the structure of the meat.

Cutting Direction
Perhaps the most obvious solution to making meat easier to chew is in the way the meat is actually cut. In a muscle, the fibres run longitudinally, meaning that if you were to take a bite, the teeth would have to sever the fibres. Most steaks, however, are sliced from the muscle across the grain, so the longest fibre length at any time will be the thickness of the steak. Biting into it this just means parting the fibres or grinding them – far less effort. It sounds obvious, but the reason any steak is tender at all is because it's sliced 'across'.

Cutting thin
It is also unarguably logical that a thin slice of meat will be easier to cut through than a thick slice. High-quality steaks that are already tender can be served thick, while cheaper steaks are cut thinner to give them a better chance.

For some steaks, like bistro or minute steaks, the name describes the utility of the steak rather than the location on the carcass. These steaks can be cut from all sorts of nooks and crannies, but because they're sliced thinly, they cook through

---

[40] The cold chain is the logistical process by which frozen goods are transported to sale in a secure and guaranteed temperature window. If you were to buy a frozen steak, you would want to be sure that it had originally been quick-frozen to a certain temperature (say -20°C/-4°F) and had stayed within a particular temperature range (below -15°C/-5°F) until you take it out of the chiller cabinet to take home. Even a steak that's been well frozen can be destroyed if allowed to partially defrost and then refreeze.
[41] Using a vacuum sealer is a very good way to pack steaks for freezing.

'in a minute' forming a lot of delicious crust on their surface and at least have a better chance of being chewable.

Beating Thin

Another way to achieve thinness is by beating a steak between a couple of slices of butcher's paper with the bottom of a heavy pan or with a flat meat mallet or tenderizer. This forces the fibres apart, weakening the structure of the steak. Some tenderizing mallets also have a pattern of raised pyramidal teeth on their surface which takes this further. They don't just flatten the fibres and squish them apart, they actually penetrate the surface and force themselves between the fibres. Overdo it with one of these and you're in danger of beating a steak until it looks like a lace handkerchief, though at least you can then chew it without bothering with teeth.

Blade Tenderization

Taking physical abuse to its logical conclusion is blade tenderization. This can be done at home with a mallet tipped with small blades that actually sever the fibres across the grain. In commercial tenderization, blade tenderization takes place between huge toothed rollers or even giant frames of shaped needles that can treat a whole side at once. I recently found a small domestic version of this in a junk shop. By my reckoning it dates from around the 1950s and it looks like a tiny mangle that can handle a single steak at a time. It's a wonderful bit of kit with which any piece of meat, no matter how awful, can be made usable. I believe it would even make a shoe tender. Brutal but effective.

Electroshock

In some meat-processing facilities, whole carcasses are pre-tenderized before any cutting takes place through the use of massive electric currents. These cause the muscles to tense and release in pulses that are so intense that the fibres are separated or partially damaged.

Chemical Tenderizing

There are some naturally occurring enzymes that can perform the same function as calpains. For example, pineapple contains bromelain, which is so effective it can turn a steak into a kind of pulpy sponge if left to marinate too long. Papain, found in papayas, is also effective, and there are similar enzymes (though with a much weaker action) in raw onion (see page 206).

Acidic ingredients can also help, which is why you'll often see wine, vinegar or citrus fruits included in overnight marinades. Milk, buttermilk and yoghurt work, too, because they contain lactic acid.

In Chinese cuisine, bicarbonate of soda (baking soda) is also used effectively. This alkaline ingredient can be added to a dry rub or combined with salt for dry brining in the fridge, but don't try to combine this with any of the acidic tenderizers as they just neutralize each other.[42]

---

[42] Only a small amount of bicarbonate of soda is necessary. I'd use ¼ teaspoon to maybe 1 tablespoon salt to dry brine a single steak. Limit your marinating time, too. More than 30 minutes or so and the steak will become mushy.

The Cuts

As a general rule, cheaper, coarser meat comes from towards the front-end of the animal and the premium stuff comes from the top and towards the rear.

As you're doubtless already aware, there's not a lot of consistency in the naming of meat cuts. It makes sense that cultures that butcher in different ways have their own words for their own cuts in their own languages. We can also live, I guess, with the idea that though we share a language and an approximate pattern of cutting, British, American and Antipodean butchers vary in their naming of steaks. But it gets more complicated even than that. I have seen cutting guides for butchers with different beef maps for each large urban meat market in the UK (with Bristol-cut chops and Manchester-style sirloins) and, if I'm brutally honest, I can't even get the three brilliant butchers in my own small town to agree on the names for some of the obscure shoulder steaks.

Butchery is a craft skill that, until comparatively recently, would have been taught orally and through an apprentice structure. There was a certain amount of protectionism around trade knowledge and evolved local quirks.[43]

I've tried, as far as possible, to simplify things by using the most common British term, a North American name if different to that and whatever else seems appropriate when another culture is involved. Your butcher may well disagree with some of this (in fact, I hope your butcher will disagree), but ideally, using a combination of the diagrams, photographs and descriptions, you'll be able to find your way around a cow together.

---

[43] Why on earth does Barnsley get a chop and Bath get a chap, for example?

The Steaks

The following pages explain the shape and location of the steaks you'll most commonly encounter and most want to eat. The selection is personal… there are a few other names or cuts of steak that are not covered here, but this is the way I keep track of things in my own head and how I discuss steak cuts with my butcher.

In navigational terms it's worth remembering these things:

- The butcher will take a 'side of meat' that, for convenience of handling, will be split into forequarter and hindquarter.

- Working from the rear of the animal there are five sections: rump, sirloin, wing rib, forerib and chuck and blade.

- Some of the nomenclature is complicated. When we cheerfully bandy around the word 'sirloin' we might equally be referring to the whole front section of the hindquarter, the large single piece removed from above the ribcage (sometimes, confusingly, extending into the forerib section) and, of course, it can refer to the 14oz steak on your plate. Nobody said this was going to be easy. It's probably going to do your nut in.

- Most of the big-name 'prestige' steaks you might get in a restaurant come from around the animal's spine. These are the best known and most prized cuts on the animal. The kind a restaurant will namecheck on the menu, knowing they're recognizable to customers and justify a high price. They mostly deserve their reputation, but there is no guarantee of quality just from the cut. It's quite possible to have a leathery, tasteless filet mignon if the animal was poorly reared and/or the meat badly kept.

- Cheaper steaks, traditionally known as 'butchers' cuts', usually come from the lower parts of the carcass. The lower part of the forequarter is called the brisket and the lower part of the hindquarter is called the flank. These are the cuts without the instant recognition of the big stars but, nonetheless, loved by the cognoscenti. There's a whole tradition of butchery to create steaks out of other cuts and a whole toolbox of techniques and tricks through which cooks can turn 'tough but tasty' into something 'rich and rare'. In recent years, as we've become more aware of nose-to-tail eating, we've begun seeking out less obvious cuts, and this has resulted in a great revealing of butchers' secrets.

Butchers always knew there were places where you could cut out a usable piece of beef with great flavour at a much cheaper price point, but it was difficult stuff to sell. Firstly, they would have to explain to a sceptical customer where it came from. Then, since there are often few of the same cut like this on a carcass, if the customer developed a preference for it, they might not be able to sell them another one for quite a while. Worst of all, showing a customer something that was cheaper than a prime steak might mean a lost sale of the expensive stuff. Instead, the butchers wrapped up their deckles, spiders and onglets and quietly spirited them home to their doubtless delighted families.

- Butchers are great at marketing. 'Bavette' is the French word for a baby's 'bib' so you'd sort of expect it to mean 'brisket' but in fact it sounds so much sexier than 'flank or skirt' that it's used freely for any of them. Terms like 'bistro' or 'butler's' steak are similarly applied to the less prestigious steaks from the shoulder.

Spider[44]

The spider steak (or pope's eye or oyster steak) is the *gluteus medius*, a small muscle that holds the hip joint together inside the pelvis (see page 53). It's roughly semi-circular in shape, grainy, loose-textured and shot through with intramuscular fat rather than marbling. This steak can be the very devil for a butcher to dig out but it's worth the effort. The grain structure is coarse like flank (see page 90), but the fat is the most exciting part. It renders beautifully in a hot pan, effectively frying itself.

[44] Origin: the *aponeurosis* of the *longissimus* as far forward as the first lumbar vertebra.
Insertion: summit of the *trochanter major* of the femur.
Function: extends the hip joint and abducts the limb.

Flank[45]

This is the abdominal wall of the cow (see page 54). Unlike the abdomen of a bipedal human, which needs the core muscles to be strong in order to stay upright, the abs on a cow don't do much work. Structurally, this muscle just kind of hangs from its spine. It's a big, flat, grainy steak with plenty of intramuscular fat and longitudinal fibres. Due to its shape and flatness, it can't really be cut across to make steaks, so it's often grilled whole and then cut into strips, 'fajita'-style, to serve.

In the US, there are two types of flank, inner and outer, which are often run through a physical tenderizing process and are usually cooked after being heavily marinated. In the UK, flank is one of the favoured cuts for Cornish pasties.

[45] Origin: arises on the lateral border of the sternum as far forward as the third costal cartilage.
Insertion: the pubis, by means of the prepubic tendon.
Function: adapted to flex the lumbo-sacral joints and the lumbar and thoracic parts of the spine.

Toro

Toro might be the most recently discovered steak, or at least the one with the most contemporary name. To visualize where it comes from, imagine a piece of streaky bacon. This is cut as a cross-section of the belly of the pig. You can see in it long flat layers of muscle interleaved with layers of fat and connective tissue. The cow's abdomen has the same structure and some butchers will take the time to dissect out one whole piece of that muscle to make an absolutely superb steak (see pages 54–55).

The toro is located close to the umbilicus and is thin with pronounced longitudinal grain. It's spent its life in gentle tension, holding in the animal's substantial collection of stomach chambers but it's been encapsulated entirely by layers of fat. It cooks beautifuly, searing crisp, and all the effort of getting at it makes it feel somehow like the best and most secret of all steaks.

Rump

The rump is the last section along the animal's spine where a clean cut across will produce a good-looking steak, as once you go past the hip joint, you're into more complex musculature that controls the back legs (see pages 58–59). Rump steaks have good flavour and can be very large, without any connective tissue to interrupt a giant, *Flintstones*-style slab of solid meat with a clearly defined outer layer of fat.

These big steaks work well if you're showing off in a restaurant, but they can be quite challenging in texture. Some restaurants might sell rump as a prestige menu item, but it requires very special treatment if it's not going to be a tough chew. A rump will often be presented in such a way that it needs carving into thin slices for serving (see page 194), bringing into question the point at which a steak becomes a 'joint'.

T-bone/Porterhouse

Sirloin

Fillet

Cross Section A   *Cross Section A*

Counterintuitively, the T-bone is a lot easier to understand as a steak if you *don't* look at it with the bone forming a T. Once you lie it on its side so that you can see the 'crossbar' of bone as half of a vertebra, everything slots neatly into place (see pages 62–63). The big piece of meat at the top is the sirloin (see page 98) – remember the French, 'above the loin' – and the smaller piece is the fillet (see page 102). A good T-bone steak should, theoretically, give you the best of both steaks, but heat conduction through the bone alters the meat's behaviour while cooking and with fillet and sirloin requiring different cooking times to be at their best, one could argue that a T-bone is going to be a bugger to get right.

The closer the T-bone is cut to the rear of the animal, the more equal the sizes of the two pieces and it is at this point that it begins to classify as a porterhouse.

This is also the steak, usually taken from a large Chianina cow (see page 33) that is used for the classic *bistecca alla Fiorentina*, which is traditionally cut as thick as 'the length of a matchstick' or 'three fingers thick'.

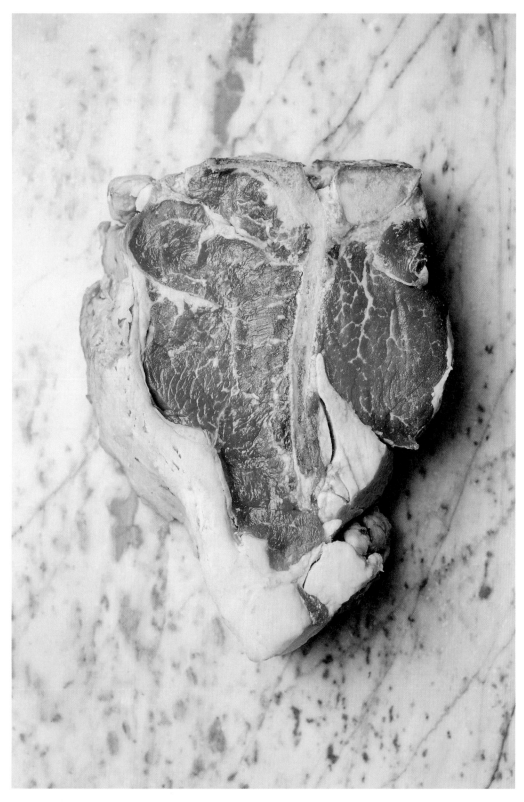

This is a Fiorentina. Sirloin on the left, fillet on the right.

Sirloin

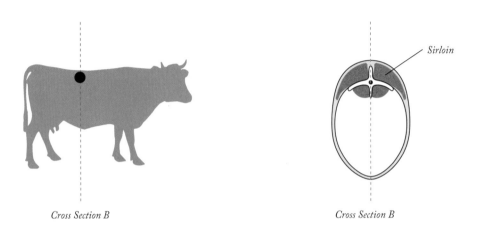

Cross Section B

Sirloin

Cross Section B

Let's get one thing out of the way straight off the bat. The name for this steak does not come from King Henry VIII knighting it 'Sir Loin'. I'm sure the guy was a keen beef eater and probably knew his steak, but he also spoke French fluently and would have been aware that they'd been calling it the *surlonge* ('above the loin') for ages. The more modern French term for the sirloin is, in fact, the *aloyau*.

Americans call this the strip steak or New York strip, which is a rather neat and apt description. It runs along the outside of the spine down towards the top of the hip bones (see pages 60–61) and can be removed as a single strip with a chunky, rectangular cross-section (see page 99). In most places, it comprises two pieces of muscle, but they are very closely unified – so much so that it's difficult to distinguish them in some carcasses. The result is an extremely neat steak. It is lean and without much marbling, with all the fat occurring

in a single easy strip along one side of the steak. This makes it a great steak if you're a 'cut-the-fat-off' kind of eater. It's also usually modestly priced and is easy to eat, so it's a great commercial crowd-pleaser.

It's generally accepted that the muscle does little work during the cow's life and is therefore tender, but it's actually fairer to say that the muscle is in constant, gentle tension keeping the animal standing and the spine straight.

A butcher can also tie the sirloin repeatedly along its length to create a round cross-section. This is usually done to create a roasting joint, but steaks cut like this, with the string still in place, look attractive on the plate.

Sirloin on the bone.

THE CUTS

Whole sirloin. This is such a popular and profitable piece of meat that it's often 'extended' by taking meat from the wing rib section, to the front or the rump to the rear.

Whole Fillet

See Cow Map C on page 80.

The fillet (or tenderloin in the US) is the shape of a long cone, pointy towards the front, chunkily tubular along the middle and with a big amorphous lump on the rear end (see pages 56–57).

A whole fillet, or one trimmed minimally at both ends, is sometimes served as an impressive centrepiece. It's usually tied – I suspect more to assist in carving than for any structural reason – and is roasted very quickly in a very hot oven. Each serving slice is, therefore, seared around the edge but medium-rare to bloody across the middle. It's a lovely thing but seems to me to run counter to much of our thinking about what constitutes a steak. If one's going to treat a fillet this way, one might as well wrap it in pastry and call it a Wellington…

Chateau/Tournedos/Tail

See Cow Map C on page 80.

If the fillet is taken off in a single piece (see pages 56–57) in can be sliced across into several of the most expensive, delicate and premium steaks on the carcass. The pieces sold as 'fillet steak' are usually cut from the middle, where you can get several slices of a pleasingly similar serving size – something that suits restaurant chefs perfectly. These pieces are also called 'medallions' or 'tournedos'. The smaller slices towards the point are often called filets mignon and the big lump towards the rear is the chateaubriand[46] (see page 191 for more on where this name comes from). Escoffier used this term for steaks cut from the

middle to the thick end of the fillet. At the legendary American restaurant Delmonico's, their signature steak was 'a 20oz centre-cut chateaubriand, flattened to an inch thickness' and called, naturally, a Delmonico (see page 23).

A chateaubriand or Delmonico steak on a butcher's counter or restaurant menu today will simply be a spectacularly chunky piece of fillet. It should be pan-seared or grilled and probably finished in the oven. Depending on the size of the original beast – and, therefore, the thickness of the fillet – it can be a thick, steak-like slice or a more cylindrical lump. If the latter, it may more commonly be oven-roasted at a high temperature.

In modern French cooking, the chateaubriand is still cut from the middle of the fillet and is 7.5cm (3in) thick, making it more of a cylinder than most classic steaks. Whether a seared piece of pure muscle, roasted in the oven and always served with a sauce, is actually 'a steak' is one of the knottiest questions in steak philosophy.

---

[46] Any steak cut from the fillet can be a fillet steak but the restaurant terms are a little more nuanced. 'Mignon' implies small, so the smaller steaks from the fillet 'tail' (which, confusingly, is at the front) are called filets mignon. At the fat end, the 'chateau', the cuts lose their neat cylindrical shape – this is often call a chateaubriand. Tournedos is a French restaurant term implying a cylindrical shape, the meat often tied and wrapped in bacon. But a restaurant might make tournedos out of something they could also sell as filet mignon. On an English menu, a nice tournedos would almost certainly be called 'fillet steak'. Confusing, huh?

Clockwise from bottom left: tail, filets mignon, centre-cut fillet tied as a piece, tournedos.

Rib Eye

Cross Section C

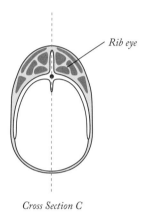

Rib eye

Cross Section C

Steaks are a little like children, in that you probably shouldn't have favourites, but I have to confess a quiet bias for the rib eye. It's the frontmost of the steaks, cut from an area where the musculature is still made complicated by the shoulder (see pages 70–71). Depending on the beast and the position of the cut, you'll be able to identify three or four distinct muscles with some pronounced lines of fat in between. In the middle sits the 'eye' of fat, which lubricates the steak as it cooks.

The rib eye can be a boneless steak or come attached to a neat little curve of rib.[47] This is useful as it imparts flavour and helps to hold the whole steak together in the pan or on the grill. If the piece is cut particularly thickly and contains one or two rib pieces, it's called a *côte de boeuf*, the classic date-night steak.

The bone can also be left long and scraped clean to make a tomahawk steak (see overleaf, left), good for grilling in the garden but useless for fitting in a pan.

The rib eye is also the cut that the Basques call the txuleton when it's taken from a well-aged, grass-fed animal, preferably the local Rubia Gallega. The txuleton is arguably the finest steak in the world.

---

[47] Butchers usually remove the spine from rib steaks. The forerib section is taken separately and the butcher will then saw through the tops of all the ribs, removing the spine in one piece. The resulting chunk means that the customer can choose how many ribs they'd like in a roasting joint and the butcher can slice straight through the meat without needing a cleaver or saw for the tough spine.

A trimmed rib eye. The spinalis or rib cap (see page 110) has been removed.

Rib left long and scraped to create a 'Tomahawk' steak.

THE CUTS

Another ribeye, cut further back on the carcass with the fat layer left untrimmed and showing how the spinalis has tailed off.

The French term *entrecôte* literally means 'between the ribs' and is a is a blanket word for any steak cut in the rib section. This steak is similar to rib eye but involves a different cutting technique that is now largely out of fashion – in fact, even in Escoffier's day this particular cutting style was already on the way out. The whole rib section would be bought from the butcher, already removed from the ribcage as a long cylinder of muscle. An entrecôte was then simply sliced off the end to the customer's specification.

Both Escoffier and Ranhofer[48] specify steaks in their menus by weight (a 560g/20oz entrecôte, a 450g/16oz rib eye), which is much easier to control if you're slicing from a continuous piece of boneless meat.

[48] Charles Ranhofer was the chef at Delmonico's Restaurant in New York between 1862 and 1896. In 1894 he wrote *The Epicurean* (1894) a work of similar scale to Escoffier's *Guide Culinaire*.

Spinalis/Deckle[49]

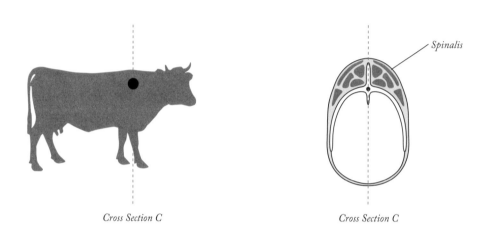

Cross Section C   *Cross Section C*

The *spinalis dorsi* muscle appears as a 'cap' on the upper perimeter of the rib eye (see pages 66–67). This gives a flat steak with longitudinal fibres like a flank, but which is texturally a little tighter. It's a very pleasant sandwich steak just as it is, but butchers collect them up and roll them two at a time into long cylinders that are tied and cut across into medallions. This makes a surprisingly good substitute for tournedos (see page 104) with a much better flavour and an almost equally yielding texture.

[49] Origin: first lumbar vertebrae.
Insertion: the spines of the last four cervical vertebrae.
Function: flexes the back.

The spinalis rolled and as a whole piece.

STEAK

Chuck and Blade

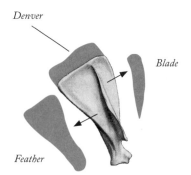

Denver

Blade

Feather

At the front end of the carcass, behind the neck and in front of the ribs, lies the chuck (see page 67). Counting back from the head, we pass the neck, then there are five vertebrae worth of chuck and five vertebrae worth of rib eye. It is effectively the area of the animal's spine that supports the shoulders and comprises a couple of interesting areas. The 'chuck roll' is a big bunch of muscles that support the animal's huge head as it constantly rises and falls while grazing. It's obviously very similar in structure to the rib eye, which sits behind it, so butchers will often cut serviceable steaks from this area. They should probably be called 'chuck steaks' but that term is so irredeemably associated with stewing and pies that you can be pretty sure the best of them will be passed as rib eyes.

Also included in the chuck is the musculature around the animal's shoulder blade. For many years this would have been regarded as meat for stewing or mincing, but modern butchery means that a variety of interesting cuts can be teased out and modern husbandry ensures the meat is good enough that they can easily qualify as steaks.

The shoulder blade itself is an isosceles triangle pointing downwards with the prominent ridge along the outside surface. The muscle lying along the front of the ridge is called the blade and the the muscle behind the ridge is the feather.

Along the top of the triangle, down behind it and attaching it to the vertebrae is the Denver steak (see overleaf).

To create additional confusion both the feather and the blade are similar with a length of tough connective tissue down the middle which may be cut out. Butchers often refer to both the feather and the blade as 'featherblade' steak.

Denver

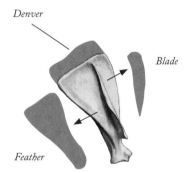

Denver

Blade

Feather

Denver steaks (sometimes also called the flatiron) come from the *serratus ventralis* muscle, which is mainly used to stabilize the shoulder and move the neck (see page 68). If you ever see a weightlifter working out, this is the great fan of muscle that pulls the shoulder blades in toward the spine, just below the neck.

It is quite a quite substantial slab of meat and the grain is longitudinal, so it is often cut across the grain into smaller steaks for cooking, making it more tender still.

Skirt

In the US at least, skirt steak is the dome of the cow's diaphragm (see pages 68–69). It is hugely popular in Mexico, where it is known as *arrachera*. It was originally imported there as offal, to avoid expensive import duties on steak.

Perhaps due to the association with offal, butchers in the UK and the US can be extremely coy about skirt, so it's often referred to as flank or bavette. Some US sources call both the skirt and the onglet hanger steak. This is confusing to everyone, so it's always worth asking your butcher to be absolutely clear where your 'skirt' steak is coming from.

Skirt responds well to marinating and needs to be sliced across to serve. Many Mexican recipes suggest slicing it across the grain into strips about 8cm (3in) wide, which, once the muscle has contracted from the heat of the grill, produces thin, finger-like strips with plenty of surface area to char and caramelize.

Onglet[50]

The onglet or hanger steak consists of a pair of muscles from the abdomen that support the diaphragm (basically, the muscles from which the diaphragm hangs). They are involved in the process of breathing, so are in constant, gentle use every moment the animal is alive. Historically, the onglet would be removed from the carcass during evisceration and would not be attached to a side of beef. This meant that the onglet was usually regarded as offal and rarely left the abattoir.

The line of tough connective tissue where the two muscles lie alongside each other needs to be cut out altogether, leaving two chunky ropes of loose-textured, well-flavoured meat that don't really look anything like a classic steak. It's a tough sell on the butcher's slab but, if seared quickly and sliced across the grain, it offers chunks of incredibly juicy meat with a lot of delicious char on the outer surface due to its long, thin shape providing plenty of surface area for maximum Maillard reaction (see page 127). Though a cheap cut, the onglet definitely needs no tenderizing.

[50] Origin: ventrally at the last rib, dorsally at the sternum.
Insertion: central diaphragmatic tendon.
Function: supports the diaphragm.

You can see the tough gristly line running down the middle of the whole onglet in the centre. The final trimmed pieces lie on either side.

ASADOR HORMA ONDO, BILBAO, SPAIN

It's interesting to speculate quite why there's such a wealth of interesting restaurants up in the hills around Bilbao. I've always reckoned it derives from the mercantile nature of the city. Like many big, industrial ports, there's a vague feeling everywhere of powerful people and business interests at work soaked into the fabric of the place. Manchester feels like that for me. Even the run-down and disused buildings feel like fortresses and cathedrals of commerce. So it's probably no surprise that expensive, discreet places with private dining rooms and immense cellars have grown amongst the golf courses and country clubs. It's all a bit thrillingly 'Corleone', so it feels appropriate that this is where you come to eat some of the best steak in the world.

Many of these places are asadors. The word has several meanings. An asado is a cook-out or barbecue, so an asador can refer to a) the place you go to do this, b) to the piece of equipment you do it with or c) the person who does the cooking. Uniquely, with Horma Ondo, c) does not apply. The person grilling the best steak in the world is an Asadora, a chef in the delightfully unexpected form of Jane Hardcastle, born in Blackpool but Spanish through and through. She and her husband built this place up from an old barn and now run one of the best-kept secrets in the area. I say that meaning that it's been consistently overlooked by Michelin while simultaneously being solidly booked by locals. My cab driver pretended to never have heard of the place until I convinced him that my intentions were pure.

For the completists amongst you, I'll briefly cover the other courses from my notes.

> Jamon croqueta. Looks unprepossessing. Large, slightly sagged ... what looks like grill bar marks and scorching? Then superlative ... best ever! Soft, hammy. Slight smokiness? Balance with rich bechamel ... full milk brought daily from local cows.

> Asparagus. Grill marks. Reduced almond milk sauce ... quotes ajo blanco but more delicate.

> Prawns a la plancha. Small, identical size, in ranks, jeweled with salt crystals. Only just off-raw.

Then they brought the txuleton.

It was big, charred dark on the outside and glistening with fresh salt. Sat, brooding on a wire rack, over a smoking tray of charcoals.

'Here it is ... it is rare. Would you prefer it well done?'

I'd obviously sooner be waterboarded, but I appreciated the gesture. There's something ingenious about presenting the thing at the point of perfection and then asking, 'would you like us to fuck it up?' More things in life should come in that order. They hustled it away to a side table for cutting. It only took seconds, but I have to admit I suffered separation anxiety.

It came back on the same rack but detached from the small section of rib and cut straight across in half-inch thick slices. What was most impressive was the way the inside was cooked ... but not. Like a big chunk of garnet-coloured glass. Large distinct fibres running unbroken across the slice and no leaking juice. Not a single ruby drop.

This is not, despite everything, a refined piece of meat to chew. Remember, this is an asado ... an informal, rustic cookout. The outside is charred in places. Nobody has got in there and butchered out the layer of silverskin just in from the outside edge ... that's your job. Some of the fat is sublime, some of it has caught in the heat and has a bitterness. You know these things, and you work to get the pure stuff out like a miner.

The fibres of meat will tease apart if you're into blunt dissection, but they also yield to the tooth in a way you're not prepared for. The nuggets you win are beyond value. It feels counterintuitive but, it's this stuff, at the core actually untouched by salt or flame, that is the most juicy, pure steakiness.

It is so pure that – like Wagyu, at the opposite end of the spectrum – you don't need much. This one is smaller than the great Fiorentina, yet it serves three happily, with bone and fat discarded. Three or four slices, draped over the tongue and contemplatively chewed, are absolutely sufficient for the whole incredible experience. Much like the craziest Wagyu, it feels like 'diminishing returns' to eat more.

That said, when the waiter asks if we'd like the bone stripped we happily agree and when after a few minutes she returns saying 'these are the best bits,' she's absolutely right. The little nuggets close to the bones are indeed sweeter. They win no prizes for beauty, but at least you're unlikely to waste time Instagramming them when you should be eating.

In the kitchen, Jane presides over a five-metre, five-bay set of charcoal grills. They're of a standard design with a broad, shallow tray for the charcoal and a stainless steel grating over the top that can be cranked up and down with a big wheel on the front. There's a framework up and over the top of each grill where most chefs keep a shelf for slow cooking or warming things. Jane has removed these and locks off the adjustable gratings at the lowest setting. 'We never use them,' she says. 'We have them set as low as we can over the coals and just take everything slowly and carefully.'

The five grills are set to different temperatures, by experience rather than anything as modern as a laser thermometer, and any heat modulation is achieved by moving horizontally between the bays.

She points me to the rig on the far end of the line where a slice of Basque cheesecake and a couple of croquetas are slow-grilling in metal baskets. That explains the grill lines but, god, Jane's confidence in her heat control is absolutely bloody awe-inspiring.

There are also screws to adjust the degree to which the grills slope towards drip channels along the front edge of the rig, but they're disused and caked with smokey tar.

'Tilting lets the fats and juices run off,' she pauses.

'Why would we want that?'

Jane explains her husband selects each piece of meat personally. These are 'bueys' – the nearest translation is 'ox' and it describes a male, bred for strength and castrated for tractability. They are draft animals and have a long working life in which they earn their feed through physical work. Where regular beef animals become uneconomic when they cease to grow at sexual maturity, an ox has value on the farm like a tractor and it's financially sensible to keep fuelling it. There are fewer and fewer draft animals these days, the best carcasses are difficult to track down and Jane's standards are high. My steak was from a ten-year-old beast, though they can be good up to fifteen years. The search is made more difficult by insisting on 'nine-rib sides' – in most animals there are only seven really good ribs in the primal area, forward of the short ribs and behind the chuck. Only the longer-framed, most powerful animals will have nine. Jane's husband has, on occasions, driven as far as Holland, chasing a single side.

They cure the meat in their own ageing room, the only place I wasn't allowed, using a variety of times and traditional techniques that vary with each piece of meat. 'Not too long, though,' says Jane. 'Too much spoils it.'

Note-taking as fast as I can, I ask about the charcoal, expecting some highly aromatic curated fruitwood, but apparently not. All the charcoal is 'encinada' which turns out to be the local holm-oak, but so carefully roasted that it imparts absolutely no flavour.[51]

'We just want the heat,' she says and then waves her hand at the other flavourings on the line; a big 'Gastro' pan of sea salt and a five-litre jug of green olive oil.

'Is that it?' I ask. She looks at me a little pityingly, as you would at a confused child.

'What else would you need?'

---

[51] The kitchen, notably, though only standard ventilation was installed, didn't smell of smoke at all.

Coo

king

Heat

The fundamental rule of cooking meat is that taking it up to a temperature of 64°C (147°F) will kill any bacteria in large single pieces and taking it to 71°C (160°F) will kill any bacteria in minced (ground) meat. Those are the important numbers that give you security and from which you can stray once you completely understand them.

Cooking steak is a special case, relying on the simple understanding that bacteria exist only on the surface of the meat where there is air supply. Inside the muscle there won't be any bacteria.

Once we move beyond this pure survival knowledge we can concentrate on the sensory and the way in which heat affects appearance, flavour and texture.

Connective Tissue

Many cooks believe that connective tissue gives flavour and texture to meat, and they are right… except when it comes to steak. The majority of connective tissue is made from collagen, which breaks down into gelatine in the presence of heat and water.[52] It only does this, however, when subjected to temperatures well above 71°C (160°F) over a prolonged period, so while a complex shoulder roast or chewy and gristle-veined piece of stewing beef might be made unctuous by long, slow cooking, a strip of connective tissue running through a steak is going to remain the texture of an elastic band after its brief flash in the pan. You'll still be picking it out of your teeth long after the meat has been destroyed by overcooking.

Fats

Heat does, though, melt the fat in a steak. Intramuscular 'marbling' fat will be entirely liquified at the temperatures and timings we're dealing with here. The fat doesn't add much flavour in itself, but it lubricates the meat and makes the experience of chewing much more pleasurable, while also acting as a vehicle for other flavours. Fat coats the tongue and naturally resists water, so flavours carried by fat tend to spread over the tongue and physically stick to it longer, resisting repeated attempts to wash them off with red wine.[53]

The outer layer of subcutaneous fat just below the animal's skin changes from an opaque solid to a translucent gel when cooked. On something like a sirloin steak, with a sufficiently thick fat band, you should be able to get the very outer surface of the fat dry and crisp and the interior very close to liquid.

Unfortunately, this miraculous substance seems to cause the human animal more conflict than almost any other food. The visible fat on a steak looks like… well, it looks like fat. There's no avoiding it. If you slice into it and eat it and you haven't carefully screened your fellow diners, you're going to get 'judged'. People just can't help it. In fact, even if you are a totally well-adjusted carnivore, it's still nigh-on impossible to tuck into a big lump of fat without a frisson of guilt. I refuse to be doctrinaire about this, though. The person with the fork has to make their own mind up, so I think it falls to the cook to simply leave the fat on and cook it to its best.

---

[52] There is more collagen in younger animals and it's lost with age. This is why, for example, veal bones make the richest stocks.

[53] Purer alcohol is capable of dissolving fat, which is why a martini can be such an excellent accompaniment to a high-fat, grain-fed steak.

Perhaps the very best fat on a steak is the 'eye' in the centre of a rib eye. Although it's in the middle of the steak, it's not *intra*-muscular marbling fat. It's actually a seam of soft fat that runs between the muscles in a bunch – *inter*-muscular fat. This eye of fat achieves its most perfect texture at exactly the temperature of a medium-rare steak, as if to prove that god loves meat. It is a uniquely delicious thing and should be honoured like the smallest spoonful of caviar, a transparent slice of a billion-yen tuna belly or the oysters on a roast chicken.

Colour, Texture and Flavour

The first and most noticeable change that cooking will make to a steak is surface browning. This requires a high temperature (well above the key temperatures mentioned) and involves causing heat damage to the muscle fibres. As these fibres heat up, they break down, scorch and release their juices and fats, leading to the Maillard reaction. This is a chemical reaction produced by heat that takes place between amino acids and the sugars released from the ruptured cells. It is what gives browned food its distinctive taste. This is followed by caramelization of the sugars, which darkens the exterior and produces a warm sweetness. Finally there is pyrolysis, where material is broken down by burning, which adds acrid, burnt flavours.

Any flavourings that have been added as part of a marinade or sprinkled onto the surface of the meat will also be altered by the pan heat. Volatile compounds will be driven off, combining the flavourings more closely with one another, with the crust and, to some degree, with the meat itself.

Throughout the meat, heat will also cause some proteins to break down into amino acids, some of which will be glutamates, producing an umami flavour.[54] This will combine with the terpenes in the meat, the juices and blood and countless other elements, all of which are, to a greater or lesser extent, affected by heat, either intensely at the surface or more subtly at the core.

---

[54] This might also include tryptophan, a biochemical precursor for serotonin. I'm not certain, but I think there's a tantalizing possibility that this might make steak an antidepressant.

As well as affecting the colour and flavour of the meat, heat changes its texture. Raw meat is roughly 25 per cent solid material and the rest is water. Cooking changes that ratio. Heat in the pan drives off some of the surplus moisture in the meat, tightening the texture of the fibres. This actually makes them easier to break through with the teeth, releasing the juices inside. Texturally, cooking makes the meat initially less 'wet' but more 'juicy' when chewed…

Juiciness

The word 'juicy' gets bandied about a lot when talking about steak. In fact, alongside 'tenderness', it's the way a huge majority of consumers would characterize their best steak experience. Juiciness is even a USDA certification criterion (see page 35). All this means it's worth breaking down exactly what it means in a physiological sense.

When you bite into a cooked steak, there are actually two separate kinds of juiciness at play. The first – let's call it 'primary juiciness' – is brought about through the liquid contained in the meat, which is released by the action of crushing and tearing the steak between the teeth and manipulation with the tongue. It's innate; a palpable component of the meat. Intrinsic juiciness.

'Secondary juiciness' is produced by the consumer. It comes from the saliva produced in the mouth, sometimes before a fork has been raised but certainly proceeding throughout chewing and swallowing. The saliva moves flavours around your taste receptors and enzymes in it begin to act on the meat, producing yet more flavours. This is extrinsic, acquired juiciness, provoked by all the senses, by knowledge of what makes a good steak, by the circumstances of eating and by the environment of the meal. It's as subjective as sexual response, as complicated and as numinous.

Just sit with that for a moment. One of the main ways you're going to judge whether a steak is good is *not completely dependent on the steak*. It's in the mechanics of your mouth and the wiring of your brain… it's all inside your head.

Technique

Temperature Curves

Meat will always tend towards equilibrium of temperature, both within itself and with its environment. In a hot oven, the surface of a steak will rise quickly to equilibrium with the surrounding air temperature and the core will rise at a much slower rate towards the same temperature.

Once the steak is removed from the oven, the surface of the steak will move towards equilibrium with the room temperature (i.e. it will cool) and the core will move towards equilibrium with the surface (i.e. it will continue to get warmer).

Cooking a thick piece of meat in a 200°C (400°F/ Gas 6) oven until its core reaches 50°C (122°F) will therefore result in a smooth gradient of temperature between the surface and the core.[55]

This means that our aim when cooking a steak is to ensure:

    1. Maximum heat on the surface.
    2. Consistent internal temperature at the desired level.

Once we understand how the temperature gradient works within the meat, it becomes obvious that the shape of the cut is important. A thin cut will cook quickly, with the core rising easily to equilibrium with the surface and making it difficult to

maintain a lower internal temperature. The higher ratio of surface to volume also means there will be more crust to meat. This is why quick-cook minute steaks can't really be served rare and instead rely on good marinades and a deliciously complex flavour in the outer crust.

For a big, thick steak, cooking will be a longer and much more controllable procedure, meaning we can sear the outside and gently bring the core to the *cuisson* (that's just French for 'degree of doneness') we want. The ideal shape for steak with a perfect medium-rare centre and a crisply crusted exterior might therefore be a squat cylinder, almost as tall as it was wide, with smooth sides that can be rolled around in the pan and a flat top and bottom. There's a much higher ratio of meat to crust here, so the steak should be high quality, tender and juicy. In fact, what I've just described is pretty much the definition of a filet mignon or tournedos.

Flipping

The shape of the meat also points us towards the way we should handle it in the pan. A thin steak will sear quickly on one side and, once flipped, will sear just as quickly on the other. While the underside heats up, the top will lose temperature but, by the time the second side is browned, the core will be either cooked or very close.

With a thicker steak, this simple flip won't work. If you sear a 3cm (1¼in) steak one side and then flip it, the top will start to cool and the bottom will brown, but the middle will remain well short of cooked.

---

[55] Frustratingly, this means that the bulk of the meat (arguably all of it except the point at the very tip of your probe thermometer) is actually above medium-rare.

Regularly flipping the steak in the pan from the very beginning of cooking slows down the browning of the exterior and ensures it is even and controllable while also giving the core more time to come up to temperature. This frequent flipping works the same way as a rotisserie, by constantly changing the direction of movement of the juices within the meat, either by gravitational pull downwards or by the heat from below driving them upwards.

On anything thicker than a minute steak, I flip consistently at around 30-second intervals which, even if no more complicated technique is used, reliably cooks a steak of all but the most absurd thickness.

Leidenfrost and Non-stick Pans

You'll have seen the Leidenfrost effect in action if you've ever put a drop of water into a hot pan or onto a hotplate and seen it skitter madly over the surface like an over-energetic hovercraft. And in fact, that's exactly what it is. When a water droplet, held in shape by surface tension, hits a hot enough surface, it produces a vapour layer underneath itself which both supports and insulates it. It hovers there, on a cushion of steam, not evaporating.

It's not a stable effect – sooner or later the little equilibrium breaks down and the droplet evaporates in an instant. There is a temperature below which the effect can't take place and another above which it breaks down. The lower temperature is dependent on many factors, including the cooking surface material, the air temperature, pressure and humidity. Figures range from 193°C (379°F) to 250°C (482°F) depending on your source, but that range is useable for our purposes.

Now, if you look carefully at the label on a non-stick pan, you'll see that it has an upper temperature limit. Usually, for Teflon (made from polytetrafluoroethylene, or PTFE), that's around 260°C (500°F).[56] Beyond that temperature, they say, your pan isn't guaranteed. We obviously want our steak searing surface to go well above that.

In reality, a steak is far too big to 'hover', but the water-drop test is a good indicator that a pan is hot enough to create steam very quickly. If you can heat a pan to above the Leidenfrost point and keep it there when a big raw steak is dropped into it, then you can be sure that there's going to be enough hot vapour under the steak that it won't have a chance to stick at the beginning. And, once it's been in the pan for a few seconds, the steak's own fats will begin to lubricate the surface, effectively making your cast-iron or stainless-steel pan non-stick at proper searing temperatures.

This is why cooking a steak usually requires preheating a pan to as hot as you can. Bear in mind that the cold steak is going to drop the pan temperature quickly on contact, so there needs to be enough heat energy pumped in there to bring everything back up to temperature almost instantly.

Back in the day, some diner cooks used the 'spitball test', in which they'd spit in the pan or onto the griddle and, when the ball danced, they knew it was time to drop in a steak. It's a deeply unpleasant thought to our modern sensibilities, even though the heat of the grill would kill anything unhygienic the grill monkey might transmit.

Still…

I think I'll stick to my laser thermometer.

All this means that for the purposes of the steak-cooking exercises and recipes that will follow, you should assume that, unless otherwise clearly specified, we're always cooking in a cast-iron or stainless-steel frying pan, rendered non-stick by the brilliance of Dr Johann Gottlob Leidenfrost and *A Tract About Some Qualities of Common Water*.

---

[56] The melting point of PTFE is actually 327°C (620°F), but Teflon recommend their pans don't go above 260°C and that you use adequate ventilation.

A Definition of Terms

Before moving on to the mechanics of cooking, let's try to define a few terms that differ between countries.

- Cooking in a hot pan or on a flat hotplate or plancha is referred to as 'frying' in the UK, even when no oil is used.[57]

- A plancha or hotplate in a commercial kitchen, though, is referred to as a grill… or sometimes a griddle.

- The British used to call the iron bar framework that is used for cooking over coals a gridiron, which was more helpful, but that's fallen out of use. Except in American football.

- Cooking on a metal grill over hot coals, gas or an electric element is now called grilling in the UK and in the US. Although both the Brits and the Australians will call it barbecuing if it's done outside.

- Cooking *under* a heat source such as a salamander (which is called a grill in UK domestic kitchens) is also, therefore, called grilling – though they call it broiling in the US.

- A good way to grill (or broil) a steak if you don't have a salamander is by cooking it in rapidly circulating hot air, for example in a fan oven or even an air fryer. This would usually be referred to as roasting in the UK, though it's technically baking if it's in an enclosed oven.[58]

- The Americans, though, will tell you that long, slow cooking in circulating air in an enclosed chamber is the only way to barbecue.

- Perhaps it's revenge but, in one final twist, the Americans favour cast-iron pans (aka skillets) with raised ridges to keep a searing steak above any steamy moisture while imparting desirable dark lines on the surface of the meat. They call these grill pans.

So, yes, it would be useful if we could define terms before moving on to the mechanics of cooking. But we obviously can't.

---

[57] The French have a separate word – *sauté* – for frying in a little oil. We don't. We do, however, cook bacon in a little oil and chips in great tanks of the stuff and call both of these *frying*.

[58] Real roasting takes place when a piece of meat is rotated horizontally or vertically close to an indirect heat source – so spit-roasting, hog-roasting, kitchen rotisseries, kebab rotisseries and authentic US BBQ are all examples. Spit-cooking directly over coals is therefore grilling, while doing it with the coals moved to one side to create an indirect source becomes roasting.

The Five-Steak Programme

The 'recipe' for cooking a steak is so simple, it's hardly worth writing.

Season. Sear. Rest. Serve.

Within that framework lies an inifinity of variation. Even a grill cook in a steak restaurant ordering hundreds of identically cut and weighed steaks every week will know that the meat will vary – from animal to animal, farm to farm, by age and by handling. If a butcher laid out fifty half-pound, 1-inch thick, top-quality grass-fed sirloin steaks in a line, the only thing you could be absolutely sure of is that no two of them would be the same.

Cooking steaks as well as a grill cook takes experience and an almost instinctive understanding of what's going on inside the steak as it's cooked. Everyone's approach is different, but for me there's a very clear picture in my head of what's going on at the core of the meat. Does it take years of cooking to develop this? Well, no. But it does take a bit of commitment, some effort and organization.

What follows is a brief course in steak cookery in which you'll cook five similar steaks in five different ways. All the steaks will taste good but some will taste better to you than the others. Read each section through first. Cook the steak according to the simplified instructions and then read the section again. This will help you develop your own mental model of what's going on. By the time you've cooked all five steaks, calmly and scientifically, you should have a much more developed grasp of what's going on. Combined with your knowledge of butchery, meat quality and provenance, this should enable you to cook pretty much any steak to your own degree of perfection.

You'll need six similar steaks before you begin. Have a proper talk with a decent butcher about what you're doing – if you're not already best mates with your butcher, this could be the most important step. Most butchers I know are enthusiasts for good meat, properly cooked, and once they know you're keen too, will start pointing you at interesting cuts, or letting you know when particularly promising carcasses are coming in.[59]

You'll also need a probe thermometer. A quick Google of restaurant supply houses should turn up cheap commercial models for under a tenner. These are so useful that I honestly believe no modern cook should be working without one. They're standard equipment in all commercial kitchens, and are even used routinely by the kid in a paper hat and a hairnet who slings the burgers at your drive-thru. This is a public health thing, not scary science.

On the other hand, if you want a probe as expensive and classy as your hand-forged kitchen knife, you can get a Thermapen for closer to £50. The real gamechangers though, are Bluetooth-enabled probes like the Meater (around £80). These offer the convenience of wireless connection when meat is inside a closed oven but, perhaps more importantly, they present a live, graph-style interface on your phone, which is incredibly helpful in forming the mental picture of what's happening in the core of the meat.

---

[59] I admit, I might be a meat nerd. There are lots of great independent butchers in my small town but my favourite three will text me with updates. On one occasion, one butcher sent me a message telling me that one of his competitors had taken delivery of an award-winning carcass.

You'll also need some 'Ziploc' plastic bags and an insulated 'Eski' or beer cooler, the largest you can borrow.

We only use five steaks in the programme, but the sixth is there for safety, so you can still complete the whole thing even if you have to repeat a section… but you almost certainly won't. You can do this with off-the-bone sirloins, if you wish. Your butcher will be able to easily manage half a dozen matched, 2cm (¾in) thick steaks from a single piece. I've done it with rib eyes, which I prefer for the extra fat content (and because I'm greedy). If your butcher is up for it, it's a good idea to get the steaks individually vac-packed.

This is a not inconsiderable financial investment so, though you can obviously do the whole programme in an afternoon, entirely alone, and eat a load of meat yourself, you might want to team up with a friend and do it together. You can also freeze the steaks and do the programme over a longer period… it just makes comparison a little more difficult.

Take it easy, take it slowly. Much like improving a golf swing or learning to drive, this is about rewiring your brain and muscle memory, but in this case you've got other senses in play too.

Steak Internal Temperature Chart

Rare:	**49°C (120.2°F)**
Medium-rare:	**56°C (133°F)**
Medium:	**60°C (140°F)**
Medium-well:	**65°C (149°F)**
Well done:	**75°C (167°F)**

Steak 1

Cooking by Time and Temperature

This first steak is cooked using the most traditional method. This is how professional chefs have cooked steaks for centuries and it's still respected for that reason. We will look at some simple principles here that will apply to every steak we cook. This method uses a cast-iron frying pan, but most of it will be equally applicable on a grill or plancha. Take this as the 'base steak' from which your understanding of cooking steak can develop.

1. Salting and drying

If you want to start a fight in a bar full of steak lovers, express an opinion about pre-salting and then go and hide under a table. Basically, the argument goes like this:

'You need to pre-salt your steak at least 12 hours before you intend to cook. The salt will penetrate the meat and enhance the flavours.'

'Are you entirely mad? If you salt the steak early, loads of juice is drawn out by osmosis. Look! It's sitting in a pool of pink juice!'

'Ha! That shows how much you know. That's water. Neutral water is being drawn out, concentrating the flavour elements in the meat. I always dry-brine overnight. This is a hill on which I'm prepared to die!'

'As God is my witness, salt will never touch my steak until it's rested and ready to serve!'

In fact, our protagonists are both wrong and right in equal measure. Salting bacon or ham involves burying the meat in crystalline salt or drowning it in a strong liquid brine for a matter of weeks. A light scrunching of salt on both sides of your steak is not going to 'penetrate' to any real degree in a matter of hours. It will draw out some pink liquid, which is indeed largely flavourless water. The purpose of hanging or ageing meat is in part to extract some of the moisture so that the flavours concentrate.

I favour salting early… but that's not the important thing. What's vital is that the steak is stored overnight in the fridge, uncovered and laid flat on a drying rack or grid. Why? Well, you know how vegetables stored in the fridge outside the 'crisper' drawer wilt in hours? That's because the circulating cold air absolutely sucks the moisture out of them. A fridge is actually a blindingly efficient drying cabinet.

We chill the steak overnight because when it hits the pan, it must be scrupulously dry. Imagine what's happening there, at the interface between the meat and the hot metal. Let's say the surface of the pan is 180°C (350°F) and you lay a big sheet of wet, fridge-cold meat on it. Most of the heat energy will immediately be drawn into evaporating the moisture. The pan temperature will drop quickly and the steak will sit on a layer of vapour, steaming. Steamed meat is grey, woolly, weird-tasting and ultimately unnecessary. If you haven't been able to dry your meat overnight in the fridge, dry it with paper towels as early as you can.

OK. Now we're ready to cook.

2. Temperature

The Maillard reaction (see page 127), which causes the browning and searing of the meat and builds the gorgeous crust you want, only starts to take place at around 150°C (300°F). We want the surface of the pan to reach at least 190°C (375°F), but if you can get above this then more the better. Many commercial kitchens use extra-hot charcoal grills like the justly famous Josper, which can create an air temperature around the meat as high as 350°C (660°F).

I use a laser thermometer to check the actual surface temperature of my pan, but if you don't have one, us the Leidenfrost/spitball test (see page 129).

Let the pan sit at this temperature for a good few minutes. We need stable heat across its surface and stored in the mass of the metal. Take your time getting everything else in order.

It is often suggested that you should take your steak out of the fridge before cooking so that it can come up to room temperature. The time needed for this is pretty hard to judge as the thickness of your steak and the temperature of your kitchen will vary. Either way, it's going to be a matter of hours before the core reaches room temperature, so just pulling it out of the fridge 10 minutes before starting will do nothing.

It is absolutely true that the core temperature of the steak at the start will significantly affect the time and temperature required to cook it to medium-rare, but the important thing is not actually the temperature but rather consistency. It may take a minute longer to cook right out of the fridge, but this time will be exactly the same if you follow the same method the next time you cook. Without wishing to sound like Yoda, fridge-cold or not, 'there is no try'. Just be consistent in everything.

Personally, I like the fact that a cold core slows down the cooking, meaning that the steak stays rare longer, and I like that the fridge is always at 4°C (39°F), while 'room temperature' can vary.

3. Timing

If you were going to cook steak this way for the rest of your life, like generations of professionals have, you would start from a fixed point and then refine everything – thickness, cut, pan type, temperature, etc. – over repeated attempts. If your diner served a one-pound rib eye, for example, your ingredient and equipment would be consistent and you'd refine your method by banging out forty steaks a day. It wouldn't take long to find a consistent technique for creating an excellent product. But we don't quite have the time for that. So, let's start with a simple recommendation of the sort you might find in a recipe for home-cooked steak.

We'll use the common estimate of 2 x 2 x 2 for medium-rare. That's a 2cm (¾in) thick steak, cooked for 2 minutes on each side. Results will vary depending on your setup, but you will learn as you go. Maybe get a couple of pieces of bread ready for when the steak is cooked – a steak sandwich never goes amiss.

Place the steak in the hot pan and time 2 minutes before flipping it over. Once flipped, watch the crisped upper surface of the meat carefully. With luck, at some point in the second minute, you'll start to see tiny 'jewels' of red juice forming on top. Meat contracts as it cooks, so – as the old grill jockeys knew – once the centre of the steak finally begins to just feel the effect of the heat, it starts to squeeze its juices up and out. The temperature at which the meat begins to tighten like this is around 56°C (133°F). Bear that in mind, because we're going to be seeing that number a lot.

After precisely 4 minutes, remove the steak from the pan and put it on a plate. Now season it again. It will need more salt, and any pepper you added earlier will have lost all its interest since the flavours in pepper are volatile and cook off at the slightest heat. Grind your pepper fresh and make it the last thing you add.

Take a picture of the finished steak, then slice it straight across the middle and take another picture of the cross-section.

1. PRE-SALT A 2CM (¾IN) THICK STEAK AND REFRIGERATE IT OVERNIGHT, UNCOVERED.

2. HEAT A FRYING PAN TO AROUND 190°C (375°F), USING A LASER OR THE LEIDENFROST TEST TO CHECK THE TEMPERATURE.

3. DROP THE STEAK INTO THE HOT PAN.

4. AFTER 2 MINUTES, FLIP THE STEAK.

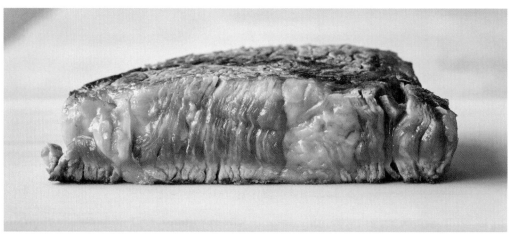

5. AFTER A FURTHER 2 MINUTES, REMOVE THE STEAK AND TRANSFER TO A PLATE.

6. SEASON AGAIN.

You should be looking at a pretty good steak. The outside will have browned, the Maillard reaction having turned the sugars to caramel and the salt and pepper doing their work. The centre should be pink and moist, not raw. You'll probably see juice flow out pretty freely, but mop that up with your bread before you assemble your sandwich.

OK. Now we can taste.

4. Tasting

I'm not going to suggest you take any kind of notes or, god forbid, create a spreadsheet. I mean, seriously, what kind of uncalibrated nerd would do something like that? Certainly not me…
And I certainly wouldn't be working out a fun, kind-of-informal system in which I marked the steak and my cooking on a scale between zero and five against criteria like…

- Crust quality
- Juiciness (primary)
- Juiciness (secondary)
- Beef flavour (immediate)
- Beef flavour (longer term)
- Salting
- Butteriness/fatty mouthfeel
- Acidity
- Textural elasticity ('poke with your thumb' test)

By the way, if you were hoping for some clever cheffy trick of counting your thumb along your fingertips and comparing the tenderness of the base of your thumb with that of the steak, forget it.[60] You have no idea how tender your steak is to begin with and I certainly have no idea how muscly your hands are.

---

[60] One cheffy trick you might want to try is the Skewer Test. Have a thin metal skewer standing by close to where you're cooking. Just before you remove the steak from the heat, stick the skewer into the meat so the tip is at the centre of its thickness. After a few seconds, pull the skewer out and touch it against your bottom lip. The principle is that the metal will heat quickly to the core temperature of the meat and your lower lip is one of the most sensitive parts of your skin. Is the test any use? That depends very much if you can distinguish heat by degrees or you can remember the exact sensation every time you cook. So, on balance, not really. But let's not write off core temperature reading quite yet…

Steak 2
Introducing Core Temperature and Resting

For the second steak in our programme, we're going to cook it exactly the same way as before but with two improvements. This time, we're going to get the core temperature exactly right, instead of guessing, and we're going to rest the cooked steak.

Once again, heat your pan to 190°C (375°F) and check that it's properly up to temperature with a laser thermometer or by using the Leidenfrost test (see page 129).

Drop your dry, seasoned steak into the pan, but don't bother starting a timer. This time, we're going to be much more accurate than a time estimate can be. Every twenty seconds or so, flip the steak using a spatula. (Using a two-pronged fork looks good, but you'll be piercing more holes in the crust than you need to.)

Flipping the steak regularly has a similar effect to cooking on a spit. Juices in the meat tend to gravitate downwards towards the hot surface of the pan where they might leach out and evaporate. Regular turning changes the direction of the flow constantly, meaning that more juices tend to stay inside.

After three or five flips, slide a probe thermometer into the centre of the meat at a 45-degree angle. Make sure you don't push through to the other side or prod too close to the pan surface and avoid landing the tip in fat or touching any bone.[61]

Now continue your flipping routine, probing for temperature every so often. I'm a bit obsessive and try to put the probe into the same hole every time, but that's probably a step too far. However you do it, though, try to form a graph in your mind of where the temperature inside the steak is going. This visualization technique may not work for everyone, but I have a very strong picture in my mind of what's going on inside the steak and the temperature probe feeds that.[62]

As soon as the core temperature reaches 56°C (133°F), pull the steak from the pan and transfer it to a plate to rest. We're going to rest this steak for 9 minutes.

Now the steak is out of the pan, there's no more heat energy entering the equation. The surface of the steak will cool a little, but the core temperature will stay pretty much the same. This means that the difference between the surface and core temperatures will reduce and the meat, which contracted quite violently with the initial heat, will relax, redistributing the internal juices.

---

[61] At this stage, we're probing well before we think the steak will be done. What we are doing is forming a picture of the speed at which the temperature is rising.

[62] There are some proprietary probe systems that link with software on a computer or smartphone to plot this graph for you. They're really better suited to roasts and larger pieces of meat, but if you have access to one, this is the time to use it. If you can see a graph on screen, you won't have to imagine it.

Resting means that a lot more of the juices will stay inside the meat and less of the good stuff will be lost when cutting it. Compared to the previous steak, this should entirely change your perception of 'juiciness', both on initial biting and as you continue to chew.

A steak gets better the longer you rest it, but many people seem to have a problem with steak going 'cold'. Some cooks, therefore, prefer to rest the steak in a warm oven – though do remember that if you do this, the oven mustn't be hotter than 56°C (133°F) or else you'll continue cooking the steak and will therefore undo all your good work. You can also rest the steak under an upturned plate or cover it with foil, both of which will slow the process down and keep things appetizingly warm. I tend to rest my steaks uncovered at room temperature. It certainly doesn't get cold anywhere near as fast as you might think and I find excessive heat impairs my ability to distinguish flavours.

Take a picture of the steak whole, then slice and take a picture of the cross-section. The *cuisson* should be perfect. Juices should be retained. Make any notes or scores you want to but, on the whole, this one will be worthy of serving on a plate and to friends. It should be an order of magnitude better than the last steak and your 'feeling' for what's happening inside the meat should be getting clearer.

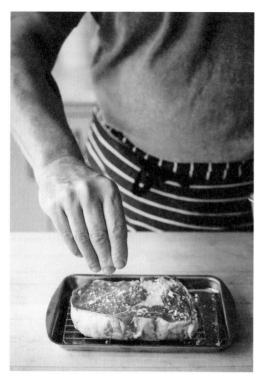

1. PRE-SALT A 2CM (¾IN) THICK STEAK AND REFRIGERATE OVERNIGHT, UNCOVERED.

2. HEAT A FRYING PAN TO AROUND 190°C (375°F), USING A LASER OR THE LEIDENFROST TEST TO CHECK THE TEMPERATURE, THEN DROP THE STEAK INTO THE HOT PAN.

3.FLIP EVERY 20 SECONDS.

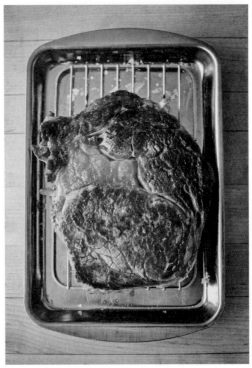

4. AFTER THE THIRD OR FIFTH FLIP, BEGIN TESTING THE CORE TEMPERATURE WITH A PROBE THERMOMETER.

5. WHEN THE CORE REACHES 56°C (133°F), REMOVE THE STEAK AND TRANSFER TO A PLATE.

6. REST AT ROOM TEMPERATURE FOR 9 MINUTES.   7. SEASON AGAIN.

Steak 3

Searing and Oven Finishing

By this point, we're aware of how we want the finished steak to be. We know what the internal temperature should be. We know we want the exterior to get as hot and charred as possible without compromising the core. We know that resting brings everything together before serving. We know how to store the steak before cooking and how best to season it afterwards. Now, we can try a slightly different route to the same result. In this method, we're going to separate the searing and the raising of the core temperature as much as we can, so that both are individually controllable.

Preheat the oven to 100°C (225°F/Gas ¼). Meanwhile, heat your pan absolutely as hot as you can get it. Please only do this with cookware that can take the heat, as this will completely destroy a non-stick pan or anything with a plastic handle.[63] If you have a laser thermometer, you should be looking at a surface temperature of 220–250°C (425–480°F). Hotter is even better.

Drop the dry, seasoned steak into the screaming hot pan. After 20 seconds or so, raise one edge with a palette knife and check that it's well browned. If not, continue to cook for a further 10 seconds, then flip the steak over. Sear the other side in the same way until you're happy with the char on the outside, then remove it from the pan and drop it onto a cold baking sheet.

Transfer the steak to the oven. Grab a beer and have a quick think.

The outer surface of the steak was seared at around 250°C (480°F). In a 100°C (225°F/Gas ¼) oven, and on an initally cold baking sheet, it won't sear more. During searing, the core of the steak didn't have time to come up to the desired temperature and, in a low oven, it will take quite some time to do so. So sit tight, finish your beer, then probe it. As before, after taking a few probe readings you should be able to visualize the speed at which the core rises in temperature.

Once the core of the steak reaches 56°C (133°F), remove it from the oven and transfer it to your favourite resting dish, leaving the probe inserted. For this steak, we won't rest by time, but far more accurately, by temperature.

We know that the core has reached 56°C (133°F) so the *cuisson* will be perfect. Now we're going to let it rest until it's at the ideal temperature to eat – potentially arbitrary, I admit, but we're told this is 50°C (122°F).

While the steak is resting, rub the surface with a little butter to give it a glaze and season it with some salt and pepper.

Once the internal temperature has dropped, take a picture of the steak. Cut it across and photograph the cross-section. Taste it and make any notes you like.

---

[63] You can also do this first stage on a barbecue.

This steak will be better than steak two. It will have rested longer, so it will have lost none of its juices and it will be enhanced by the melted butter. This is a definite keeper.

Most importantly, though, both the core temperature and the char on the exterior are now totally in your control. Too crispy? Drop the searing temp. Somebody wants their steak cooked medium-well? Leave it in the oven longer (take a look at the internal temperature chart on page 133).

Once again, the important visualization of internal temperature is improving with each steak.

This kind of sear and roast technique has one other important benefit that really good cooks can learn to use to their advantage. We know that some cuts – often the cheaper ones – are full of flavour but also contain more challenging stuff like fats and connective tissue. These benefit from 'low and slow' cooking.

Though the steaks we're working on in this five-step programme are all the same quality, you can see how, with a low enough oven temperature, you could effectively slow-cook a steak for hours without 'over' cooking it at all. Steak number four will take this logic to its extreme.

1. PRE-SALT A 2CM (¾IN) THICK STEAK AND REFRIGERATE OVERNIGHT, UNCOVERED.

2. PREHEAT THE OVEN TO 100°C (225°F/GAS ¼).
3. HEAT A FRYING PAN TO AS HOT AS YOUR SETUP WILL ALLOW THEN DROP THE STEAK INTO THE PAN.

4. AFTER 20 SECONDS, LIFT WITH A PALETTE KNIFE TO CHECK IF THE UNDERSIDE IS SEARED.

5. FLIP AND SEAR THE OTHER SIDE.
6. TRANSFER THE STEAK TO A COLD BAKING SHEET AND COOK IN THE OVEN.

7. WHEN THE CORE TEMPERATURE REACHES 56°C (133°F), REMOVE THE STEAK FROM THE OVEN AND TRANSFER TO A PLATE.

8. INSERT A PROBE THERMOMETER AND REST UNTIL CORE TEMPERATURE DROPS TO 50°C (122°F).

9.GLAZE WITH BUTTER AND SEASON.

Steak 4
Sous Vide

For our fourth steak, we're going to try one of the most scientific and controversial modern methods of cooking that has taken the world of professional cooking by storm over the past couple of decades – and which has also pushed traditionalists to the edge of raging madness. If you have a strong opinion on sous vide cooking (I know I have), I ask you to suspend it for the duration of this experiment. It is genuinely the penultimate step to enlightenment, and it involves a bit of science and a bit of bodging.

The basic principle of sous vide cooking is that food is sealed, along with seasoning, in a waterproof pouch from which all the air has been removed. This kind of vacuum-packing – aka vac-pack, or sometimes referred to by the tradename Cryovac – means that food can be stored longer, either under refrigeration or in deepfreeze, then cooked by immersing the bag in a water bath at a controlled temperature.

Originally, the idea was that meals could be prepared like this, then whipped from the freezer, cooked and then held at a perfect service temperature. It was intended to be a boon to the domestic cook but chefs, who knew what you now know about cooking steak, saw another advantage.

I'm hoping you're ahead of me here.

The first time I saw a sous vide 'steak line', I was reviewing a restaurant in which an internationally famous Michelin-starred chef was attempting to create a higher-volume, lower-cost operation. He proudly walked me to the steak section in his newly built kitchen. There was a charcoal oven running at, he said, over 400°C (750°F) and five clear plastic water baths. Each contained a bubbling heat element – a 'recirculator' – and on the five LED screens I could read the magic numbers: 49°C (120.2°F), 56°C (133°F), 60°C (140°F), 65°C (149°F), 75°C (167°F).

I couldn't help but smile at the absolute simplicity of it. The steaks floated in their plastic pouches with salt, pepper and a little oil. There was a colour code on the tops of the bags – fillets were red, rib eyes were yellow, sirloins were blue. 'We just load 'em up in the afternoon and let them sit,' the chef told me. And, of course, that was the absolute perfection of it. The steaks just held, never overcooking, and when an order was called in, they just sliced open the bag and slid the steak into the big oven. There was so much heat that any surface moisture vaporized immediately and they had a superb crust on both sides in 20 seconds. No need to rest, of course, because the temperature inside was already perfectly equalized and the juices distributed.

Neither the chef nor I was what you'd call 'happy' about it, but as he said, 'It deskills the process, but no one has to accept a badly cooked steak ever again.'

We're going to cook our sous vide steak following the same principles, only with a slightly cheaper home science kit. You'll need a beer cooler – the bigger, the better – a kettle, a probe thermometer and a couple of Ziploc freezer bags.

Season your dry steak and drop it into one of the Ziploc bags.[64] Fill the sink with cold water and seal the top of the bag almost all the way. Now, submerge the bag in the sink, keeping the open corner above the surface. This will drive out all the air, whereupon you can seal the bag. Place the first bag in the second and repeat the process. Your steak should now be double-sealed, water-proof and have no air surrounding it.

Half-fill the beer cooler using water from the tap and from the kettle, stirring it with a wooden spoon to mix. Keep checking the temperature until it's 57°C (134°F).

The reason we're using the largest possible cooler to do a single steak is that the increased amount of water will hold heat longer and, because there's plenty of space for circulation, convection currents will do some of the work of a recirculator.

Drop the bagged steak into the water and close the lid. After 10 minutes, open it up, give the water a stir and check the temperature. As soon as it begins to drop to 55°C (131°F) degrees, add more boiling water from the kettle to bring it back up.

Check the water temperature every 10 minutes for at least 2 hours. At this point you can unseal the steak and probe it to ensure it is 56°C (133°F) at the core.

After this time, heat your pan absolutely as hot as you can get it (with cookware that can take the heat). If you have a laser thermometer, you should be looking at a surface temperature of 220–250°C (425–480°F). Hotter is even better.

Fish out the bag from the cooler, open it up and take out the steak. Dry the surface scrupulously with paper towels before dropping it into the hot pan. After 20 seconds, lift the edge with a palette knife to check for browning, then flip to do the other side for a further 10 seconds.

Serve, photograph, cut and taste straight away.

You should find this one interesting. Assuming the sous vide part of the operation went to plan, the whole of the inside of the steak should be consistently pink and medium-rare. The outer layer will be thin and dark (to what extent will depend on the heat you managed to get to in the pan).

---

[64] If you have a Bluetooth probe, you can insert it into the meat and seal it into the bag with it. This will give you graphs of the internal temperature and that of the surrounding water bath. The software is a bit rough and ready, so try it at your own risk, but seeing the graphs on screen is infinitely pleasing.

By now, this should be making sense in regard to your conceptualization of what's going on inside the steak. There is no longer a need to visualize a graph of internal temperature because that temperature can't rise above the limit you've set, and time is no longer an issue.

Cooking the steak sous vide means that the meat has been very slowly poached and seasoned. This will have altered the flavour a little and you will be able to see how this might be a new route by which other appropriate flavours could be added. A little grated garlic, some thyme or rosemary, perhaps even a scrap of lemon peel would go a long way. The main advantage, though, remains that the steak can be 'held' for an extremely long time and swiftly 'finished to order'. The way we've done it is, admittedly, a hell of a faff, but the equipment to do it properly is expensive, takes up a lot of space and is not really appropriate for domestic kitchens.

Today, most big steakhouses have moved on from the pouch and water tank method of sous vide to a technique sometimes (inaccurately) referred to as 'air sous vide'. This involves a special, purpose-built oven with five drawers, each with its own thermostat, heating element and circulation fans. This allows the meat to be held at the perfect temperature, just like the 'wet' method, but with less faffing about with plastic bags and tanks. Steaks can still be held throughout a long service and quickly finished to order, and they can be dropped into the drawers straight from the freezer.[65] This is a technique that's easy to replicate at home, as we'll find out with our final steak.

---

[65] With this technique, however, there's no opportunity to add flavour during a 'poaching' phase.

1. PRE-SALT A 2CM (¾IN) THICK STEAK
AND REFRIGERATE OVERNIGHT, UNCOVERED.

2. FILL A BEER COOLER WITH WATER AT 57ºC
(134ºF).

3. SEAL THE STEAK AND FLAVOURINGS INTO A
DOUBLE LAYER OF FREEZER BAGS, EXCLUDING ALL
THE AIR.

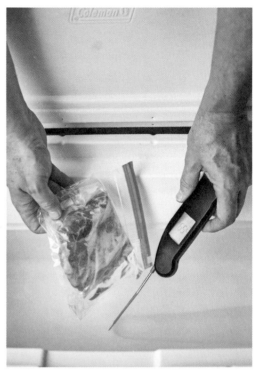

4. DROP THE BAGGED STEAK INTO THE BEER COOLER.

5. AFTER 10 MINUTES, OPEN THE COOLER, STIR AND CHECK THE WATER TEMPERATURE.

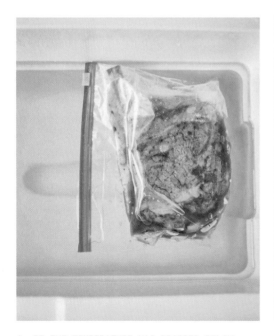

6. IF THE TEMPERATURE HAS DROPPED BELOW 55°C (131°F), ADD SOME JUST-BOILED WATER.

7. CONTINUE TO CHECK THE WATER TEMPERATURE AT 10-MINUTE INTERVALS FOR THE NEXT 2 HOURS, ADDING JUST-BOILED WATER AS NECESSARY.

8. HEAT A FRYING PAN TO AS HOT AS YOUR SETUP WILL ALLOW.

9. REMOVE THE STEAK FROM THE COOLER AND TIP OUT OF THE BAG, THEN DRY THOROUGHLY WITH PAPER TOWELS AND DROP INTO THE HOT PAN.

10. AFTER 20 SECONDS, LIFT WITH A PALLET KNIFE TO CHECK IF THE UNDERSIDE IS SEARED.

11. FLIP AND SEAR THE OTHER SIDE.

12. SERVE IMMEDIATELY - THERE IS NO NEED TO REST BEFORE SERVING.

Steak 5
Reverse Searing

Let's start this one off with a thought experiment.

If I put a 10cm (4in) diameter stone ball into an 80°C (176°F) oven and left it there for 15 minutes, what would the temperature of the surface of the ball be? That's correct, it would be 80°C.

What would the temperature at the core be? That's more difficult to tell without knowing a lot more about the conductive qualities of stone.

Now, If we leave the stone ball in the oven for 24 hours, the surface will still be 80°C. And we can be pretty certain that the core will be, too. The thermostatically controlled air temperature of the oven and the stone ball will be the same temperature because, though the temperatures may have been different at the beginning, they will move into equilibrium over a relatively short period of time and then stay there. Our grandmothers even had a name for this. They called it 'warming through'.

We can apply this logic to steak.

Theoretically, you could throw your steak into a 56°C (133°F) oven and keep it there for as long as you liked. The temperature of the steak would come to equilibrium with the oven and it would stay at that temperature. After a while, the fats and collagen would begin to soften and spread.

Sadly, most domestic ovens aren't accurate at such low temperatures. If you have access to a decent oven thermometer, you can try your own (particularly if you have a plate warming or proving drawer), and if you have an AGA, you can check the temperature of the slow oven. Some people have even managed to hold this temperature in a slow cooker.

Luckily for us, however, holding the temperature precisely at 56°C (133°F) isn't really necessary for this final method. All we're trying to do is lower the cooking temperature as much as possible (as long as it's over 56°C) and then monitor carefully as the core temperature rises, *as slowly as possible*. My fan oven, on its lowest 'warming' setting, sits between 55°C (131°F) and 66°C (150°F). Try setting your oven as low as it will go and starting from there.

For this method, the steak doesn't need a dry surface at all – it's going to have plenty of time to dry off in the oven – but you will want to season it so an overnight salting, uncovered in the fridge is still the best idea. I find that the slow-cooking part of this method is particularly helpful to black pepper, which usually has its volatile scents boiled off in the first seconds of searing. Similarly, grated garlic will sit on the warm surface of the meat, sharing its flavours rather than scorching to bitterness. Put your seasoned steak into the preheated oven.

Probe for a core temperature every 10 minutes, After a few probes, you should be able to visualize the way the temperature is rising and therefore be able to estimate when the core will be perfect.

A little before this happens, start heating your pan absolutely as hot as you can get it (with cookware that can take the heat). If you have a laser thermometer, you should be looking at a surface temperature of 220–250°C (425–480°F). Hotter is even better.

As soon as the core of the steak reaches 56°C (133°F), transfer it to the hot pan. Sear it on one side for 20 seconds, then flip it before adding a big dollop of butter. As the butter melts, spoon it over the steak, basting and glazing the top.

After a few seconds, flip the steak one last time and baste quickly before the butter begins to scorch, then transfer the steak to a warmed plate and pour over any melted butter and meat juices from the pan.

You should only need to rest it for a few seconds before cutting into it, but no harm will be done by waiting a little longer.

This reverse-seared steak should be as close to perfect as you can get. The exterior will be crisply seared and the butter basting will have added flavour. The interior will be quite uniformly medium-rare, though not as joylessly so as the sous vide steak. Take a picture, make your notes.

1. PRE-SALT A 2CM (¾IN) THICK STEAK AND REFRIGERATE OVERNIGHT, UNCOVERED.
2. PREHEAT THE OVEN TO ITS LOWEST AND MOST CONSISTENT TEMPERATURE (AS LONG AS IT'S ABOVE 56°C (133°F).

3. PUT THE STEAK ONTO A BAKING SHEET AND PLACE IN THE OVEN.
4. MEANWHILE, HEAT A FRYING PAN TO AS HOT AS YOUR SETUP WILL ALLOW.

5. WHEN THE CORE OF THE STEAK REACHES 56°C (133°F), REMOVE IT FROM THE OVEN AND DROP IT INTO THE HOT PAN.

6. AFTER 20 SECONDS, LIFT WITH A PALETTE KNIFE TO CHECK IF THE UNDERSIDE IS SEARED.

7. FLIP AND SEAR THE OTHER SIDE.

8. BASTE WITH MELTED BUTTER, FLIP AND REPEAT.

Programme Round-up

So, what have we learned? Initially, I imagine, that the simplest method of just throwing the steak onto a hot surface and turning it can produce a good result – but it will need either a lifetime at the grill or blind luck. We've learned that control of the core temperature is vital and what happens at the surface of the meat is secondary. This is a total inversion of the way most of us have learned to cook and it massively increases our control over the process.

Perhaps the most unexpected bonus of measuring internal temperatures – or even just of imagining them and cooking accordingly – is that it applies to all cooking. Understanding core temperature will revolutionize how you cook bread, fish, sponge cake, chips, carrots and custard.

One can, of course, take this too far. It's probably acceptable to reveal now that sous vide is not my favourite steak – I think it's because I find the total lack of temperature gradient across the core, or any variation, jarring. For me, once you begin to trust in the visualization of what's happening inside the piece of meat, the sous vide approach seems somehow artificial. People who eat a well-handled sous vide steak will enjoy it, no question, but are often slightly confused by the sensation. With a reverse sear, it's what you're used to, only infinitely better.

The key thing though, is that we now understand what the possibilities are, can control them and, whether you prefer reverse seared or sous vide, basted or charred, at whatever cuisson, you now have a better chance of producing it reliably and repeatably.

Tl
Rec

he
pes

Steak Tartare

Steak tartare got me started on this book and so it's fitting that it should be our first recipe. For me, it kind of sums up some of the key elements we've previously discussed. Sure, it's all about the superb flavour of well-reared beef, absolutely as rare as it will go. But, done right, it's also a tribute to all those waiters, in all those steakhouses, who've created so much of the lore and legend around steak, and maybe even a connection to our most primitive, innate and elemental attraction to good meat.

For a two-person tableside serving[66]

300g (10½oz) fillet steak
3 anchovy fillets (the canned oily type)
20g (¾oz) salted nonpareille capers
1 gherkin (dill pickle), finely chopped
2 large egg yolks
20g (¾oz) Dijon mustard
Olive oil, to taste
Lemon juice, to taste
30g (1oz) shallot, finely chopped
20g (¾oz) curly parsley, leaves picked and finely chopped
Tabasco, to taste
Worcestershire sauce, to taste
Salt and black pepper
Toast, to serve

Half an hour before you want to eat, put the meat into the freezer. Once thoroughly chilled and firm, you'll be able to slice and dice it much finer. Cut it into small dice, then go over the pile several times with the knife until the meat is effectively minced. Some modern presentations of steak tartare involve chunky diced meat, which is all very well but a long way from tradition.

Put the anchovies, capers and gherkin into a bowl and smush to a paste with the side of a knife, then whisk in the egg yolks and mustard. Slowly drizzle in the olive oil, whisking as you go, until the mixture is stiff, then add lemon juice, salt and pepper to taste.

Add the meat, shallot and parsley and combine thoroughly, tossing the ingredients like a salad. Add Tabasco and Worcestershire sauce to taste (in my case, a lot).

Modern brasserie practice is to serve tartare with chips but I'm a sucker for originality, so I stick with toast points.

---

[66] On the day, this served six in small starter portions. It would do four or three as larger starters or 2 mains (with fries).

Georgian Gridiron Steak over Coals

I wanted to honour the Sublime Society of Beef Steaks (see page 22), with a steak cooked like the ones they seared on their ceremonial gridiron. I'd made a good start by having it tattooed on my arm but, ultimately, it seemed important that I secure an actual gridiron. Fortunately a Victorian photograph of the original had survived in the club archives with which I approached several metal fabrication companies. They looked at it with some bewilderment, stroked their chins wisely and then talked about laser- or plasma-cutting and CNC machines. It just didn't seem right.

Then, while researching a book on knives, I met a (one-eyed) German blacksmith who specialized in authentic weapons for fantasy re-enactors. The bloke made halberds, heavy battle axes and swords with names. He had a beard and the sort of forge you'd expect to meet orcs in.

'It's not welded', he grunted, as he stared deep into the blurry photograph through his single piercing eye. 'See, there are rivets.' He was right. It was a rough bit of work, possibly even knocked up in the theatre, where they might have kept a small forge for mending metal parts. 'Yes,' he rumbled. 'I will make this.'

I lost track of him for about a year, but eventually, the gridiron arrived (see overleaf). Rough, heavy, functional and utterly beautiful. But what steak would be right to baptise it? I wondered whether Georgian thespians were into big, ugly T-bones or if they would prefer a more refined fillet. Then I came across the 'rump and dozen'.

There was a period in Georgian England when some of the aristocracy mixed freely with the lower and criminal classes around a shared enthusiasm for sport. They were called 'the Fancy' – a cult of unregulated, romantic, colourful 'racy'[67] types who gambled huge amounts on horse racing, dog fighting and bare-knuckle boxing. Particularly in the new London gentlemen's clubs, gambling became an obsession, with fortunes made and lost and duels regularly fought, not even on the turn of a card. There are accounts, kept in the club's 'wager books' of large bets being made on which way a cab would turn at the end of Pall Mall or, on days when such outdoor pursuits were unavailable, which raindrop would trickle to the bottom of the club window first.

---

[67] Yes. That's exactly where the term came from.

SIRLOIN

I know this is a rump, but it was a lovely plate...

Some of these wagers took a peculiar form. An issue of *The Sporting Magazine* from around the time jokes about 'The wager of a rump and a dozen[68] between Mr Giblet, the poulterer, and Mr Crimp, the fishmonger.' The term referred to a huge rump steak and 'a dozen [bottles] of claret'. The foundation, surely, of a decent meal for two sporting gentlemen and therefore, I reasoned, pretty good for a bunch of theatrical Whigs.

Contemporary records indicate that the steaks eaten by the Sublime Society were broiled 'over the fire in the painting room'. There wouldn't have been much use of wood as fuel in central London at this point. Gas was still half a century away and wood was heavy and expensive to transport and store. Coal was much more efficient, so there's a distinct possibility that the griddle was placed over a bed of glowing coals.

Coal burns with an interesting, bituminous smell. There's a touch of tar about it,[69] something resinous, but those are volatile compounds that are supposed to boil off when the coal begins to burn. It's a similar principle to 'self-lighting' charcoal – any residue is supposed to be all gone by the time the briquettes are glowing, but a tiny hint always remains. I thought it would make sense to do a similar thing with the coal. Glowing, hot and with only the faintest vanishing hint of proper London smog.

Coal is no longer easy to find in small quantities. In fact, I had to put out a plea on Twitter and somebody eventually got back to me, saying there was a small pile of it in the corner of their cellar that had been there since they bought the place. Judging by the state of the mummified rat on top of the pile, it might have been near contemporaneous with the Sublime Society. I'd been warned not to fill the barbecue entirely with coal as that would create a blast furnace, so I used half a dozen small pieces to 'seed' the top layer of my backyard grill and let everything burn down to a dull glow.

We know a fair bit more about steak today than they did back then. We know a rump can be quite tough, though full of juice and flavour. Fast, hot cooking, then, wouldn't be the best solution. I could maybe mark the steak on the bars, then finish it in a cast-iron frying pan to give it some time, but that didn't feel quite in the spirit of the thing. Instead, I used the barbecue controls to get the temperature of the coals down. My idea was to start cooking when the temperature of the coals would be dropping as the steak cooked.

The gridiron stood perfectly balanced on its stout little legs, right on top of the coals, and I gave it a few minutes to come up to temperature.[70] It wasn't a painting room and I hadn't removed a powdered wig to cook, but the smell of hot metal and coal was giving a certain 'early Industrial Revolution' vibe to

---

[68] Please don't Google 'rump and dozen' unless you wish to learn a lot more about the contemporaneous English predilection for flagellation.

[69] The smell of my Grandad. Wright's Coal Tar Soap.

[70] My very non-Georgian laser thermometer measured it at 180°C (350°F), with the metal ensuring that the temperature was reasonably consistent at all points.

the whole thing. The Sublime Society served their steak with potatoes roasted in their skins, so I wrapped a few in foil and propped them around the perimeter, buried in the coals.

I'd salted the steak the night before but left off any other ingredients. Marinating it felt… well, sort of un-British. The society was founded to celebrate the way that, while the French cut their meat into pieces and stewed it in garlic and sauces, the stout yeoman of England required nothing but the meat and the fire; the steak and the gridiron.

There was no point going for grill lines – this has always seemed to me like an American obsession and, let's face it, in 1776 we weren't getting on terribly well with America – so I flipped the steak constantly and obsessively. There's a trick in Argentinian barbecue of spraying the top side of the meat with a salty brine each time you flip. The brine salts the meat as it evaporates, but also cools it down so as you flip and spray, you're slowing down the cooking process, increasing the flavouring and giving everything more time to contemplate itself.

The society served their beefsteaks with 'port or porter' – thick, sweet, fortified wine or a dark, stout, treacly beer, reputedly first brewed for the huge and muscular porters at Smithfield meat market. As I cooked, I was drinking from a bottle of Guinness Export I'd obtained for the occasion. Guinness is an excellent porter, the same everywhere it's sold in the world except in Jamaica, where they've long kept alive a taste for a stronger, more bitter version that's reputed to replicate the taste of the original after it had suffered a long, hot trip on a sailing ship. I splashed a little on the top of the steak, let it sizzle off, flipped and repeated. It felt like the thing a bloke might do, staring at a steak in a fire, late at night, in an attic room in a theatre. I don't know… it was intuitive. I thought the bitter note would be rather nice with the smoky, tarry flavour from the coal. But then I suddenly panicked. What if it was too bitter? If only I had some dark, sweet, red booze.

For the last couple of flips, I sprinkled on some port,[71] which added a dark and glossy sheen to the meat, then I whipped it off[72] and put it to rest.

I think I'd characterize most of my friends as 'liberal' in that woolly, modern way, but I don't think any of them really embody the antagonistic, John Bull, anti-authoritarian, freedom-or-death bull-doggery of the original club members. They liked my steak and enjoyed the potatoes, but when one of them switched from porter to a full-bodied Rioja I felt I was rather losing my audience. The steak, however, was superb. A little tough – it wasn't going down without a fight – but the taste… meat, iron, blood, coal, tar, port and Guinness. If I knew any, I'd be singing patriotic songs…

---

[71] OK. I had a modest glass of that going too. It was research!
[72] C'mon… you know me better than that. There was no way I wasn't going to probe core temperature, no matter how out-of-character it might have been.

[73] Originally written for *The Grub-Street Opera* by Henry Fielding, which was first performed in 1731. The lyrics were added to over the following decades.

'The Roast Beef of Old England'[73]

When mighty Roast Beef was the Englishman's food,
It ennobled our veins and enriched our blood,
Our soldiers were brave and our courtiers were good.
Oh! The Roast Beef of old England,
And old English Roast Beef!

But since we have learnt from all-vapouring France,
To eat their ragouts as well as to dance,
We're fed up with nothing but vain complaisance.
Oh! The Roast Beef of old England,
And old English Roast Beef!

Our fathers of old were robust, stout, and strong,
And kept open house, with good cheer all day long,
Which made their plump tenants rejoice in this song.
Oh! The Roast Beef of old England,
And old English Roast Beef!

But now we are dwindled to, what shall I name?
A sneaking poor race, half-begotten and tame,
Who sully the honours that once shone in fame.
Oh! The Roast Beef of old England,
And old English Roast Beef!

When good Queen Elizabeth sat on the throne,
Ere coffee, or tea, or such slip-slops were known,
The world was in terror if e'er she did frown.
Oh! The Roast Beef of old England,
And old English Roast Beef!

In those days, if Fleets did presume on the Main,
They seldom, or never, return'd back again,
As witness, the Vaunting Armada of Spain.
Oh! The Roast Beef of old England,
And old English Roast Beef!

Oh then we had stomachs to eat and to fight,
And when wrongs were cooking to do ourselves right,
But now we're a... I could, but goodnight!
Oh! The Roast Beef of old England,
And old English Roast Beef!

Carpetbagger Steak

The 'carpet bag' or 'carpetbagger' steak has the kind of hotly contested culinary history that causes otherwise sensible food historians to start making stuff up.

Containing a quite logical combination of fresh oysters and good beefsteak, the dish was reasonably popular in steakhouses and restaurants wherever steaks were eaten at the turn of the nineteenth century. Both elements are prestige foods, with undercurrents of 'manliness', strength and virility. And both are standbys of the professional kitchen that also happened to be delicious together. It was then largely forgotten for years, but has since been noisily claimed by the Americans, Australians, New Zealanders and, unfathomably, the town of Mumbles in Wales.

For many years, the carpetbagger has been regarded by many as representing the lower end of the dubious 'surf 'n' turf' category, but I have a strong belief that it could be time for a reappraisal of this humble dish. There are several reasons. One is that our increased exposure to the food of different cultures has quickly made us realize that the supposed fish/meat barrier shouldn't hold us back. There are huge numbers of dishes combining prawns (shrimp) and pork in East Asian cuisines. Fish sauces that can be used in meat dishes such as nam pla, XO and garum have become hipster bait and the classic tuna and veal combination of Vitello Tonnato (see page 232) has seen a revival, too. Then, if we really think about it, we remember that we've been putting anchovies into our roast lamb for ages… and that Worcestershire sauce is packed with them.

In recent years, we've also seen an exciting trend for artisanal tinned fish, often from northern Spain or Portugal, which provides us with an abundant source of extraordinarily good, shelf-stable oysters, carefully precooked in their own juices.

Finally, many of the surviving recipes for this steak specify the use of fillet tail, an otherwise hard-to-shift cut with a superb texture, excellent flavour and usually a criminally low price tag. It's definitely time to reopen the carpetbag.

(Recipe overleaf…)

2 fillet tails (one per person)
1 x 113g (4oz) can of oysters
  (cooked in brine, not pickled
  or 'escabeche')
50g (1¾oz) butter, softened
¼ tsp cayenne pepper
4 slices of smoked streaky (regular)
  bacon
Olive oil, for frying
Sea salt and freshly ground black
  pepper
Roasted or sautéed potatoes,
  to serve

The night before you want to cook, season the meat all over with salt and place on a wire rack set over a tray. Place the tails on their cut ends so they stand up like cones. Transfer to the fridge to rest overnight, uncovered.

The next day, preheat the oven to its highest setting.

Using a long, thin and extremely sharp knife, push downwards through the tip of one of the fillets, then slide the tip a little to one side without cutting through to the outside. Withdraw the blade and turn it around, then insert it again and carefully cut outwards in the other direction. The aim is to create a triangular pocket in the steak, with the neatest possible opening at the top.

Open the oysters and drain off the brine, but reserve this in a separate container. Stir the oysters into the softened butter and season with salt, pepper and the cayenne pepper, then pack them into the tails one at a time. Buttery oysters are slippery, so this might be the only time you will ever hear me suggesting the use of cheffy tweezers.

Place the slices of bacon on your cutting board and, using the back of a knife, stretch them out along their length. They'll get about 50 per cent longer but will contract again when cooked – a quality we'll use to our advantage.

Wrap one piece of bacon around the bottom of each cone and secure with a small skewer or cocktail stick, then secure the top of the cone in the same way.

Heat a skillet over a high heat, then pour in a little olive oil. Roll the cones in the pan until they brown a little, then stand them on end and transfer the pan to the hot oven. Let the oven come back up to temperature, then reduce the heat to 150°C (300°F/Gas 2).

Check the meat regularly, probing through the tops of the cones, until the core temperature reaches 56°C (133°F). By not probing through the side of the meat, we keep all the juices inside. Remember that the oysters are already cooked and we don't want the core of the steak to reach more than 56°C (133°F). If you feel you can probe the meat reliably, avoiding the oyster pocket, do so, aiming for 56°C (133°F).

Once the fillets have reached the desired core temperature, remove them from the oven and set aside to rest for 5 minutes. Serve with roasted or sautéed potatoes.

If you'd like to pursue the recipe to a very traditional conclusion, you can combine the reserved oyster brine with any pan juices and a little Demi-glace (see page 271) to create a 'brown oyster sauce'. This will be strong flavoured and salty, so serve separately.

Bistecca alla Fiorentina

A *bistecca alla Fiorentina* is so good that it needs almost no intervention. Under the right circumstances, you can just cook it and sprinkle it with salt. Those circumstances, though, would be a wood-fired oven, a griddle and a small trattoria in Florence that's been in the family for three generations. For complete authenticity, it would also require the best porterhouse steak cut from a fully grown Chianina ox, measuring three or four fingers thick. Not easy to replicate.

The Fiorentina is ideal for cooking on a big barbecue or grill, as long as the temperature is controllable – you need to be able to drop it fast and accurately – and the top can be closed. If you do this, sear the steak directly on the grill first, then finish it in a pan placed on the grill. A small amount of oak or other aromatic wood would not be inappropriate.

For a small dinner party or a special family meal, a Fiorentina is little short of magical. Visually, it makes a stunning centrepiece. It's an absolute breeze to carve and then, on the plate, there are big, equal-size chunks of chewy, strong flavoured sirloin and lean, subtle fillet, all perfectly finished. There's plenty of excellent fat for those who like it and an incredible blend of meat juice and garlicky, herby oil to lubricate everything.

It's not a cheap cut but of all the grandest steaks, this is the one that will convince your guests that when meat is this good, you don't need so much.

Serves 2–4

1 large, extra-thick porterhouse
  steak
1 bunch of rosemary
1 bunch of sage
150ml (5fl oz) olive oil
4 garlic cloves, roughly chopped
Sea salt and freshly ground black
  pepper
Rocket (arugula) and Parmesan
  salad, to serve

The night before you want to cook, season the meat all over with salt and pepper and place on a wire rack set over a tray. Pack some of the herbs around the meat, then transfer to the fridge to rest overnight, uncovered.

Pour the oil into a saucepan and add the garlic. Roughly chop some more of the herbs (a couple of handfuls), reserving some for tomorrow, and add to the oil. Warm the oil over a low heat for about 30 minutes – don't allow it to boil or simmer. You want to infuse the flavours into the oil rather than cook them out. Strain the oil into a container and set aside.

The next day, preheat the oven to its highest setting. Put a cast-iron frying pan into the oven to get hot.

Tie the remaining herbs into a bundle to use as a brush.

(Continued overleaf…)

Brush the marinade herbs and garlic[74] off the steak and pat it dry with paper towels if necessary. Transfer the hot pan to the hob and sear the steak on both sides over a high heat.

Stand the steak up on the bone and brush the outside of the steak with the infused oil using your herb 'brush'. Fling a couple of pinches of salt at the sides so that some sticks to the oil. If you have a wireless probe thermometer, insert it now. Place the pan (with the steak still standing on its side) into the hot oven.

Allow the oven to come back up to temperature, then reduce the heat to 150°C (300°F/Gas 2).

After 10 minutes, open the door and baste the steak, using more of the infused oil and anything you can mop up from the pan. Check the core temperature.

Continue basting and checking until the core temperature reaches 56°C (133°F), then remove the steak from the oven and set it aside to rest. Italians traditionally prefer to eat their food at lower temperatures, so a really long rest is not a bad idea, plus you can continue basting throughout.

Serve with extra salt and an extremely simple salad, perhaps rocket dressed with olive oil, salt and lemon and, if you feel outrageously extravagant, some shavings of good-quality Parmesan.

---

[74] They have done their work overnight but they'll burn and become bitter in the heat of the grill. Cook the steak 'clean' and re-dress it with fresh herbs at the end if you wish.

TRATTORIA SOSTANZA, FLORENCE, ITALY

Whenever I go to Florence, there are four places to which I have to make pilgrimage. I join the queue at Nerbone in the Mercato Centrale for a lampredotto – boiled tripe with hot sauce, in a bap. Then the Riccardi-Medici Palace for Gozzoli's frescos. And then the Uffizi to see Jacopo Chimenti's 'Dispensa'.[75] OK, the last one's a bit niche.

Jacopo Chimenti, known as 'Empoli' after the town of his birth, did rather lovely still life paintings. Not a popular genre in Quattrocento Florence where everyone else was doing grand religious pieces and an unnerving number of plump nudes. But Jacopo had, to my mind, a far more compelling kink and painted, amongst other things, this sumptuously detailed interior of a Tuscan pantry.[76] The guy obviously knew and loved the cooking of his native Tuscany. There are chickens, a goose, some ducks in feather, a rather splendid-looking ham, and an earthenware crock that you just know has some kind of pâté or fat-preserved sausage packed into it. Scamorza cheese, truffles, a flask of red wine, vegetables, a side of pancetta, a 'capocollo', a really spectacular raised pie, and two hanging pieces of beef.

This is where things get really nerdy, because one is a long rib chop. You can distinguish, perfectly, the loin at the top and the intercostal muscle running along the rib. The end is left untrimmed, keeping on some interesting brisketty bits. A modern butcher might clean this up and scrape it into a Tomahawk, but sixteenth-century Tuscans were smarter than that. Looking at it again in my notes, I notice that the meat is pale and fine-grained and the length is quite modest. It might be 'vitello', the local veal. On the next hook, though, hangs a chunky joint. You can distinguish where the spine has been sawn through. The kidney has been left in place – not modern butchery practice, but it locates the cut along the spine. You can clearly pick out the very back of the ribcage. The butcher in me says we are in the rear of the loin

section here, but my inner art historian appreciates the way Chimenti has arranged, lit and painted it. He's showing off the cut end. Right there, you can see the T-shaped bone, the sirloin and a big, round, chunk of fillet. What is most tantalising is what's not here. This is the cut end of a side from which the precious Fiorentina has been removed. Is Chimenti telling us we are not worthy? He reaches across the centuries from 1624 and taunts us! Perhaps he has eaten it.

Once I've recovered my composure in front of 'The Pantry', it's time for the final station of my pilgrimage – Il Troia.

The Florentines, as well as having their own unique cuisine and their own artistic movement, have their own dialect and, in it, Troia has several meanings. It's derived from 'troiaio', a slang term for a 'piggery'. By extension, it is used as a nickname for a grubby, messy person and applied to women in the same way English used 'slattern'. This was the nickname of Guido Campolmi, who ran a restaurant out between the malodorous Arno river and the magnificent Santa Maria Novella railway station. It wasn't to do with his morals. He cooked good food without caring too much where his fingers went and, like many intuitive cooks, he looked a bit of a mess, but his Bisteccas[77] were regarded as the best in Florence.

Of course, you can't really call a restaurant, no matter how bohemian 'The Slattern' so across the front, in gloriously artless old Perspex lettering, is its name, Trattoria Sostanza. But everyone still calls it 'Il Troia'.

It was founded in 1869 by the Campolmi family. It was a tiny operation making soup for cab drivers, before Guido and his uncle Pasquale turned it into a modest trattoria in 1900. In 1933, they moved up the road and took over a small butcher's shop to convert into a restaurant. Since then, the only

[75] It means 'The Pantry'.
[76] See it yourself at:
www.uffizi.it/en/artworks/empoli-still-life.

[77] The Italian for beef is 'manzo' so there's likely to be truth in the story that the Italians borrowed beefsteak/bistecca from the English milords who visited cities like Florence on their Grand Tours. At the time, Italian food didn't enjoy the massive global appreciation that it does today, while English 'roast beef' was renowned internationally.

thing that changed is the floor. In 1966, the Arno rose and flooded the place out, so they replaced whatever had been there with a gloriously ugly terrazzo in brown, beige and black, like old men's teeth set in cement. Everything else is the same. White butcher shop tiles, lazy spinning electric ceiling fans, photos on the walls of the bohemians and celebrities who slowly patronized the joint: John Steinbeck, Eddy Merckx, Dario Fo, Ezra Pound. Marc Chagall's autograph is up there too between the various members of the Campolmi clan and their employees. Guido died in 1944 and in 1977 the staff bought the place from the family.

Il Troia is quirky, rough, romantic, soulful and authentic and might be my favourite restaurant in the world.

You're not allowed to cook over charcoal in Florence. The air pollution is a direct cause of the acid rain that eats away at the architecture and it's justly banned – except at Il Troia. It says something about the Florentine attitude to their culinary patrimony that they've weighed the cost of scrubbing down Renaissance buildings against the importance of a fine Bistecca and come to such a wise compromise.

I could see them cooking my steak. The bathroom is kind of behind the kitchen, so you can't really avoid it. There's a pile of glowing coals spread on a flat stone grate under a pre-war extractor hood. There's what looks like a wrought iron grill, on little stubby legs and my steak is lying on it.

One end of the grill is propped up higher. I'm not sure if that's so the fat runs to one side and doesn't flare up, or so the bone is a little further from the heat. If it's the latter, that's an astonishingly refined bit of physics – the bone conducts the heat to the middle of the meat, cooking it from the inside out, so a rare control could theoretically be applied by angle and placement. They're not doing a great deal of frenetic flipping, so they're probably aiming for grill lines.

I have no Italian, so I wasn't going to discuss the vagaries of *cuisson* but preliminary research suggested that such interventions weren't welcome.

These guys don't really need your opinion on how to cook. I wasn't sure whether that meant my steak was going to come raw or carbonized, but, to be honest, by this stage in the proceedings, I felt I was in the best of hands. I continued, hovering by the bathroom door and surreptitiously grabbing pictures.

The initial seasoning had been surprisingly simple. No obvious dripping marinades, no herbs, no garlic. Just a thick drift of salt and a grind or two of black pepper. And now the cook flipped it, settling it back on the bars and tweaking the angle.

There are a few well-worn stories about the Fiorentina. One is that it should be the same thickness as the length of a match. They also say that if it's less than 4cm (1 ½in) thick, it isn't a Bistecca Fiorentina, but carpaccio, which probably should have alerted me to what *cuisson* to expect, too. The Florentines themselves seem to agree on 'three or four fingers thick' which, having just waved my fingers over a ruler, is a bloody thick piece of meat.

Finally, the chef lifted the steak off the bars and transferred it to a beaten old metal tray. I'd like to have stayed to find out if it was just resting or whether he would keep it near the fire to cook through further, but I'd overstayed my time at the bathroom door. People were looking at me suspiciously and a small queue had formed. I slipped back to my table to find it partially occupied by Belgians.

I don't know. Maybe they were Eddie Merckx fans, but you should know Il Troia is proud of its bohemian and socialist roots and so you may have to share one of the six tables, in a spirit of International Brotherhood.

I had a small bowl of tortellini in brodo while waiting for the main event, which was finally borne to the table, with a flourish, by a waiter who wouldn't have looked out of place in a fresco. God, it was a beautiful thing.

I'd ordered one of the smaller ones on offer, around a kilo uncooked. It was a chunky little thing, the two 'sides' nearly equal in size, flanking a bone cut short. They took the meat off, sliced it into tranches about a centimetre thick and fanned them back on either side of the rib. The exterior was dark and crusted – actually carbonized where it had been in contact with the bars – and the centre deep carmine and evenly translucent like clouded red glass or Turkish Delight. No juices leaked … at least not until I bit into it.

Englishmen get emotional in Florence. All the beauty, the culture, the sheer weight of religious opulence and artistic excess disorientates as it delights. We're inclined to swoon or write poems. I took a good minute and a half, enjoying the first slice. Revelling in the way it played over my tongue. Chewing slowly, interspersing judiciously with red wine. The dawning realization that the simplicity and austerity of the presentation, the rigour, if you will, just made it the steakiest expression of steak that a human mind could encompass.

I let out a muted and involuntary moan and realized that my eyes had closed. The Belgians applauded.

They'd ordered the chicken, and I'd definitely got the better-looking plate.

I was so overwhelmed with joy and International Brotherhood; I gave them a slice.

Tournedos

First, let's get this straight. The name 'tournedos' is nothing to do with violently rotating columns of air emanating from thunderstorms. It's also not plural. You can't have a single 'tournedo'. The word first appeared in the 1800s and is derived from the French *tourne dos*, meaning to turn one's back. This might have been a reference to the stalls in the back alleys of the Les Halles meat market, though the *Larousse Gastronomique* prefers a more apocryphal tale: supposedly, when the composer Gioachino Rossini first ordered filet mignon topped with foie gras, served on a croûton and drenched with Madeira sauce, the staff were obliged to deliver the thing 'behind the backs' of other customers.

Naaah. I don't buy it either. Though it does make me think how amazing Rossini's supposed invention would be in a toasted brioche bap…

Tournedos Rossini is one of those dishes that almost everyone has heard of. It's an icon of old-school fine dining, bringing to mind imperious maîtres d', faffing with the napery, too much silverware and fuss. Few people get the chance to eat it any more and even fewer understand quite how big of a deal it used to be.

It was, without doubt, the poshest and most high-status cut. A small, neat piece with no chance of bone or connective tissue, it is easy to cook beautifully in lots of ways and easy to eat. It is also the perfect serving size and, if we're completely honest, is tender enough to eat with bad teeth and reticent enough in flavour to take whatever sauce a French chef wanted to throw at it.

To give you some idea, Auguste Escoffier's masterwork, *Le Guide Culinaire* (1903), contained ninety-five recipes for tournedos and only fourteen in total for entrecôte and sirloin.

My personal favourite tournedos recipe is the rather more elegant variation that Ian Fleming describes James Bond eating in the restaurant of the Hotel Splendide in *Casino Royale* (1953). A single, small tournedos, resting on a trimmed, poached artichoke heart and napped with béarnaise sauce (left). Now that I can really get my head around, and I don't even need the bap.

Tournedos No-ssini

Tournedos Rossini hasn't really stood the test of time, possibly because foie gras has fallen out of favour – and because it was always extremely challenging to flash-fry such an expensive ingredient. It's a shame, though, because the combination of the liver-iness of the foie and the incredible richness of the sauce do go a long way towards enlivening a tournedos. Perhaps, then, it's time for a more modern take on the Rossini... something that takes all that dirty sauce and meat-on-toast action and makes something less operatic and a bit more contemporary.

In the first step towards this, we'll use a crumpet rather than a neat little brioche croûton. The intention here is to mimic the effect of something like devilled kidneys or mince on toast... it's all about the gravy soaking in. We could potentially smear the toast with a layer of good duck liver parfait, in the style of a Vietnamese *bánh mì* sandwich, but I reckon it's a much better idea to go back to basics with a couple of lobes of chicken liver, crisply browned in a pan and left rare at the centre. I suspect Escoffier would have removed the bacon wrapping from his tournedos after cooking to make things easier to cut delicately at table, but we won't have any of that nonsense... Rossini apparently enjoyed his tournedos with shavings of truffle as a final garnish.[78] I reckon that's inordinately pretentious – though I did, just once, add some leftover morel mushrooms that I'd stewed in butter the night before. I did not regret putting them on top.

Serves 4

4 slices of smoked streaky (regular) bacon
4 small, 3cm (1¼in) thick filets mignon
4 chicken livers
Plain (all-purpose) flour, for dusting
4 crumpets (see opposite for homemade)
100g (3½oz) cold unsalted butter, cubed, plus extra for basting
100ml (3½fl oz) Madeira
100ml (3½fl oz) Demi-glace (see page 271)
Sea salt and freshly ground black pepper

Combine all the crumpet ingredients in a bowl and whisk together to create a smooth, thick batter. Rest at room temperature for 30 minutes until it's very bubbly and risen. Oil two metal rings and place them into a frying pan over a medium heat. Pour some of the batter into each ring and cover the pan with a lid. Cook for 10 minutes, then check the crumpets. The bottoms should be cooked and just starting to tan. Continue cooking until the tops of the crumpets are dry, then flip to briefly seal the top. Transfer to a wire rack to cool.

Place the slices of bacon on your cutting board and, using the back of a knife, stretch them out along their length. Wrap the bacon around the edges of the steaks and pin in place with a small skewer or cocktail stick. Season both sides with salt and black pepper.

Trim the livers carefully. I usually separate each one into three lobes, discarding any tubing or other odd bits. Season a little flour with salt and pepper, then toss the livers lightly in the seasoned flour.

---

[78] I am, as is probably self-evident by now, obsessed with the origin myths of food. When we try to seek out where a dish came from, though, it's worth remembering that we're not dealing with a 'folkway' or an evolving human behaviour, we're talking about a product. A dish, if it has a name, was usually created to be sold and, subsequently, its origin story is part of its marketing. I'd love to believe in Rossini's personal involvement but, if I do, I'd have to extend the same suspension of disbelief towards Captain Morgan, Tony the Tiger and Ronald McDonald.

For the crumpets

235g (8¼oz) plain (all-purpose)
   flour
7g (¼oz) fast-action dried yeast
1 tsp sea salt
1 tsp sugar
½ tsp baking powder
240ml (8fl oz) semi-skimmed (2%)
   milk
15g (½oz) butter, softened

Heat a dry frying pan over a high heat and sear the steaks on both sides. Toast both sides of the crumpets in the pan at the same time, to reheat them and to absorb any juices. Remove the crumpets, then add a generous dollop of butter to the pan and roll the tournedos on their edges to cook the bacon. At the same time, drop the chicken livers into the pan. They will seal and brown very quickly, so watch them carefully. I remove the livers when my probe thermometer reads 45°C (113°F). They will continue to cook once out of the pan and I love them rare.

Continue to cook the steaks until core temperature reaches 56°C (133°F), then place them on top of the crumpets to rest and top with the livers. Deglaze the pan with the Madeira. Allow it to bubble, then add the demi-glace and reduce further. Whisk in the cubed butter so that it thickens and becomes glossy. Pour the sauce over the tournedos in abundance, making sure that the crumpets are in a good position to soak it up.

Tournedos BP

Once you try tournedos, you realize that it's no wonder Escoffier loved these little beefy nuggets. Steak, plus something else, on a bread product, with a sauce to soak into it is a highly flexible and pretty much unbeatable combination.

I rather enjoyed creating a tournedos McMuffin, with a toasted English muffin, two rashers of smoked bacon and a topping of appalling yellow burger cheese and a fried egg. Transgressive but delicious. That was the gateway tournedos for me. Since I run a restaurant that's got a great reputation for brunch, I was led on to combine a tournedos with the off-menu 'special' that the chefs knock up for me – eggs Benedict with the bacon swapped out for a slab of top-quality black (blood) pudding, known as 'eggs BP'. In honour, then, of Damien and the chefs at Fitzbillies, I offer you the tournedos BP.

Serves 4

4 small, 3cm (1¼in) thick filets
   mignon
4 slices of smoked streaky (regular)
   bacon
4 slices of black (blood) pudding
4 English muffins or crumpets (see
   above for homemade crumpets)
Béarnaise Sauce (see page 282),
   to serve
Sea salt

The night before you want to cook, season the meat all over with salt and place on a wire rack set over a tray. Transfer to the fridge to rest overnight, uncovered.

Place the slices of bacon on your cutting board and, using the back of a knife, stretch them out along their length. Wrap the bacon around the edges of the steaks and pin in place with a small skewer or cocktail stick. Season both sides with salt and black pepper.

Heat a dry frying pan over a high heat and sear the steaks and black pudding on both sides. The black pudding may take slightly longer, but you can use the extra time to rest the steaks. Meanwhile, lightly toast the muffins or crumpets.

Stack the steaks onto the muffin halves, then balance the black pudding on top and pour over the béarnaise sauce.

Tournedos No-ssini

Tournedos BP

Steak Diane

Steak Diane is still one of the most popular dishes to cook tableside on a guéridon cart. You probably won't need to do this at home, but you will need to work at the same blinding speed as a hassled waiter, so this recipe is simple and sure-fire, as long as your mise-en-place is completely squared away.

Arrange your chopped shallots and garlic in little piles on a plate alongside your sliced mushrooms, so everything is close to hand. (For pure retro authenticity, I sometimes use tinned button mushrooms – thank you, Len Deighton – but it's also sensational with reconstituted dried porcini.) Put the butter onto the plate in a big ugly lump and have the mustard ready on a teaspoon, too. Measure the brandy into a shot glass and have the cream ready to pour, either in its original container or a jug. Open the Worcestershire sauce. Then you're ready to go.

Serves 1

1 sirloin steak
50g (1¾oz) butter
3 shallots, very finely chopped
150g (5½oz) small button
  mushrooms, thinly sliced
2 garlic cloves, very finely chopped
50ml (1¾fl oz) brandy
1 tsp Worcestershire sauce
2 tsp Dijon mustard
250ml (8fl oz) whipping cream

Heat a dry cast-iron skillet over a high heat until it's as hot as you can get it, then sear the steak on both sides. Use a probe thermometer to check the internal temperature and remove the steak when it reaches 56°C (133°F). Set aside on a plate to rest.

Reduce the heat a little and add the butter. While it's still foaming, add the shallots, allowing them to soften and become transluscent.

Add the mushrooms and keep stirring until they start to brown a little at the edges, then add the garlic.

Pour in the brandy and the Worcestershire sauce, then add the mustard and allow everything to bubble until you can smell that the alcohol has boiled off. You can set fire to it if anyone is watching, but it doesn't add much beyond theatre. Now add the cream, stir it through and reduce to a simmer.

Pour in any juices from the rested steak, then pour the sauce over the steak and serve.

Monkey Gland Steak

The story behind 'monkey gland' steak is one of my favourites. Much like Café de Paris Butter (see page 267), the recipe is really an exercise in jazzing up a possibly quite undistinguished piece of meat by throwing the entire mise-en-place at it. But it also has one of the most bizarre and troubling origin tales, which taps directly into the odd inadequacies of 'men who love steak'.

Serge Abrahamovitch Voronoff was a French surgeon with odd ideas and an eye for publicity who, in the 1920s, began treating the upper classes of Europe with monkey testicles.

No, really. His 'monkey gland' treatment was supposed to reduce the signs of ageing and, of course, to increase sexual potency. The even more ick-inducing detail, however, is that he didn't feel it was sufficient to administer the treatment by blitzing the monkey nuts into a nourishing smoothie or serving them devilled on toast. No, he sliced them finely and then surgically implanted the pieces into the testicles of his patients. I'll just leave that thought hovering there as I uncross my legs and consider how widely this treatment seized the public imagination.

Voronoff became rich and his treatment became the subject of popular music, a beloved topic of comedians, the base of numerous quips in Hollywood movies and, of course, it became immortalized in the names of cocktails and dishes in fashionable nightclubs. I suppose our closest parallel today would be something like a huge tomahawk steak served with a coating of gold leaf for a performatively ridiculous price tag. Thank god we don't do that sort of thing any more…

Monkey gland steak passed from fashion not long after Dr Voronoff's methods were comprehensively discredited, but the sauce is still popular as a braai meat dressing in South Africa. It's a cooked preparation of onions and tomatoes that's flavoured with Worcestershire sauce, vinegar and a local hot chutney called – with wonderful appropriateness – Mrs Ball's. In many ways, it's like a North American BBQ sauce but a bit punchier.

I found an old hotel recipe for monkey gland steak lurking in the pages of one of my favourite old books, *The Restaurateurs Guide to Guéridon and Lamp Cookery* by John Fuller (1964). For many years, it was a set text at catering colleges, clubs and officers' mess halls. This is a much more manageable take on that recipe, with less bulk and sweetness in the sauce. It involves a useful trick with mustard and the sort of flambéing that would guarantee a healthy tip for a keen waiter. As for steak Diane (see page 185), make sure you have all your ingredients prepared and close to hand before cooking.

Serves 2

20g (¾oz) butter
1 shallot, very finely chopped
2 single-portion sized fillet steaks
20g (¾oz) Dijon mustard
1 tsp Worcestershire sauce
75ml (2½fl oz) cognac
30g (1oz) crème fraîche
½ bunch of curly parsley, leaves
  picked and chopped
Freshly ground black pepper

Melt the butter in a cast-iron frying pan over a medium heat, then add the shallot and cook until translucent. Scoop out with a slotted spoon and set aside, making sure no pieces remain in the butter (scorched shallot is bitter).

Press or beat the steaks to flatten them a little – this will speed up the cooking time. Smear both sides of the steaks with the mustard, then season with plenty of black pepper.

Increase the heat to high, then drop in the steaks and sear both sides. The oil content of the mustard becomes the frying medium and the keen initial heat of both mustard and black pepper is volatile, so that is quickly driven off while the more aromatic elements penetrate the meat. The mustard will form a dark crust both on the meat and in the pan. Flip the steaks regularly and check the core temperature with a probe thermometer.

As soon as the core temperature reaches 54°C (129°F), splash in the Worcestershire sauce and pour in the cognac. As soon as the cognac begins to boil, light it.

As the flames subside, lift out the steaks and set them aside to rest. Scrape any dark bits from the base of the pan and mix into the boiling liquid using a small metal whisk. Add the crème fraîche and allow it to simmer and reduce until a sauce-like consistency is achieved. You can add the shallots back into the sauce at this point if you wish.

Serve the steaks with the sauce spooned over. There is no culinary reason whatsoever to sprinkle it with fresh parsley, but it feels tremendously authentic to do so.

BRASSERIE GEORGES, LYON, FRANCE

You can't understand the steak at Brasserie Georges in Lyon unless you start with the building. No, not even that – its location. Lyon is France's second city, three hours south-west of Paris by rail, historically a powerhouse of food production and industry. Lyon is so important to Paris that it has its own train station in the capital, and, like any other second city, the relationship is complicated.

Brasserie Georges was built just outside the main railway station in 1836 by a local brewer, Georges Hoffherr. From the front it looks like a stolid, neo-classical engine shed and inside it is a vast,

single-span room kitted out in a muscular art deco style. It's an incredible thing to see as a kind of projection of regional pride. It was the first and last thing a visiting Parisian would see in Lyon and Georges was going to make damn sure he didn't let the city down. In fact, Georges is still there. A bronze bust sits on a plinth as you walk in, positioned so he stares you level in the eye. He has a fine set of side whiskers and the mien of a well-dressed rhino. His eyes communicate a low tolerance for fools or frippery and his brasserie is a brilliantly functional eating factory.

The nice thing about France is that places like this are still full every lunchtime. I can't really imagine an old place out near the station filling up every day in somewhere like Manchester or Hamburg, but here it's still buzzing with the contemporary equivalent of 'commercial' travellers, *hommes d'affaires*, bourgeoisie families and old geezers who take even less crap than Georges.

The waiters are lifers. Wiry men of all ages with thousand-yard stares and feet that probably ache like bastards by the end of a shift. These are the pros, the absolute Special Forces of front-of-house. Economical in movement, frighteningly effective.

The beef, the waiter tells me, with precisely the correct amount of nationalistic pride, is Charolais. This just makes me grin gleefully. Of *course* it's Charolais. The French national breed, raised specifically for beef, usually on grass. It's built like a leather-covered armoured car, with short, thick-kneed legs and hulking shoulders.

This animal will not have 'worked' like a draft animal, but it won't have been over-fattened with a high-calorie corn diet, either. It will be strong and muscular, just from moving its own huge weight around a field – like one of those rugby players who has no speed but who stays upright in a tackle through a combination of muscle and attitude.

There is no discussion of *cuisson* as the waiter has explained it should be served *saignant* (rare) and I don't feel equipped to argue. He plonks down a steak knife.

The meat arrives, cut thick by a local butcher and already coated with peppercorn sauce. This being France, it is of course on the menu as entrecôte. We would immediately recognise it as a boneless and beautifully trimmed rib eye. It's a cross-section of the three *longissimus* muscles that keep the spine straight and hold the animal up. It was probably slaughtered at three years and those muscles have been in use for that entire time. There is good fat around one side and in little reserves through the centre. There's also some connective tissue between the muscles.

It's not tough, but it's certainly not what the USDA would regard as tender. You need a serrated knife and you need to chew… but god, it's worth the effort. The juices, carefully husbanded by an excellent grill cook, flood over your tongue. Sharp, a little irony, but properly beefy. The peppercorn sauce, in this context, is a real complement, the extra beefiness of a highly reduced demi-glace perked up with little explosions from the briny, fragrant peppercorns. You can see why this sauce has survived for so long – it's so well judged that you can't really discern where the meat flavour stops and the sauce begins.

It's a no-nonsense steak, for people who understand quality, value for money and haven't been shy about demanding both for nearly two centuries.

It is, however, a proper chew, so if your teeth aren't up to it – as the waiter gleefully points out – the same meat also comes as a tartare, made table-side. It's the first time I've heard steak tartare being offered in this way, as an easier-to-chew alternative, but I'm reminded that the French once regarded it an excellent fortifying meal for invalids and ideal nutrition for sportspeople.

I decide to order the tartare as well. In this context, I really reconsider the dish. Pre-chopped, it's obviously easier to chew. You can definitely detect the same irony taste of blood as you do in the rare steak, but the melted, liquid fat of the hot meat is replaced by something else. The waiter starts the tartare by emulsifying olive oil with mustard, effectively creating a delicious, semi-liquid fat which he then works the meat into. The salt and the vigorous beating mean the meat juices flow into the dressing and combine and, after a thorough two-minute pummelling, the waiter forms the now smooth and sticky combination into a ball, then spoons and pats it onto the plate.

I look at it with new eyes. It's what a pretentious young chef would doubtless call 'steak, two ways' – one an honouring of it in its simplest form, the other an effective de- and re-construction. For me, now completely immersed in steak, it was a rare opportunity to experience French steak entirely raw alongside the same meat, lovingly and traditionally cooked.

Chateaubriand

The chateaubriand is going to cause us some trouble. Most of us know it from contemporary menus as the most expensive piece of meat on offer. But, historically, it's been the term for a particular cut of meat, a method of cooking and a sauce. So, let's start from the beginning.

I'd always imagined that the name 'chateaubriand' came from some Parisian bon viveur who'd had his favourite steak named after him, but it turns out that that's not entirely true. François-René de Chateaubriand was a bit of a Byronic character, who had failed to kill himself as a teenager and then gone on to be a writer, historian, diplomat and politician. Though his life was full and his achievements great – he considered himself the greatest lover of his age, though no corroborating testimony survives – there's little evidence that he was keen on his nosh save the one steak they named after him. This strange link is investigated in *Kettner's Book of the Table* (1877):

> 'A chateaubriand is cut from the best part of the fillet, and is nearly twice the ordinary thickness of steak: but is this all? The thickness of the steak involves a peculiar method of cooking it. It is so thick that by the ordinary method it might be burnt on the surface when quite raw inside; and there-fore – though the new method is neglected and is even forgotten very much – it was put upon the fire between two other slices of beef, which, if burnt upon the grill, could have been thrown away.'

What on earth was that all about? Is the fierce searing going to drive all the fantastic juices of the cheap steaks into a spectacularly tender piece of fillet? And what's this got to do with our guy Francois René? It goes on:

> 'It may still be asked, what has this to do with chateaubriand, that his name should be attached to a steak so prepared? Here we come into a region of culpable levity. Chateaubriand published his most famous work under the name of *Le Genie du Christianisme* (The Spirit of Christianity). The profane wits of the kitchen thought that a good steak sent to the fire between two malefactor steaks was a fair parody of the Genie du Christianisme. If I remember rightly, it was at Champeaux in the Place de la Bourse that this eccentric idea took form and burst upon Paris.'

These days, a thick, rounded 'cushion' of meat from the head of the fillet is usually marked on the slab as a chateaubriand.

(Continued overleaf…)

I've actually tried the sacrificial steaks trick, wrapping a thick fillet in two cheap rumps and grilling it at the sort of terrifying heat I could only really obtain in a Kamado-style charcoal grill, cranked to maximum. As soon as the core temperature reached 56°C (133°F), I whipped it off the heat and pulled off the steak wrappers, which had carbonized on the outside as expected, but which certainly hadn't imparted any goodness into the fillet. In fact, the main steak was a decent medium-rare throughout but just lacked any Maillard crust on the exterior. Kettner doesn't record whether the 'original' chateaubriand was finished with a quick pan-sear or another fast pass over the hot coals, but that's what I did, and the result was, indeed, fantastic.

What was most exciting, though, was the realization that the most legendary, decadent, high-status cooking method in the history of steak was actually a perfect reverse sear (see page 152).

Kettner does leave us with one other tantalizing hint. Not quite a whole recipe, but helpful, nonetheless:

> 'The peculiarity of the steak is in its thickness, and in the way of broiling it; but sometimes also it is served with a peculiar sauce, namely, Spanish sauce diluted with white wine, then considerably reduced and at the moment of serving enriched with a pat of maître d'hôtel butter.'

Hmmm. We've seen that somewhere before. 'Espagnole' mother sauce with added wine that is then considerably reduced is demi-glace… which we might just find in the freezer next to the maître d'hôtel butter.

Serves 2–4

1 chateaubriand steak, large
   enough to serve two people
375ml (12½fl oz) dry white wine
2 shallots, minced
10 black peppercorns
1 tarragon sprig (or thyme if you
   prefer it), leaves picked and finely
   chopped and stems reserved
200ml (7fl oz) Demi-glace (see
   page 271)
50g (1¾oz) butter
Sea salt and freshly ground black
   pepper

The night before you want to cook, season the meat all over with salt and place on a wire rack set over a tray. Transfer to the fridge to rest overnight, uncovered.

The next day, preheat the oven to 120°C (250°F/Gas ½). Transfer the steak to a roasting tin and roast in the oven until the core temperature reaches 56°C (133°F).

While the steak is cooking, put the wine, shallots, peppercorns and tarragon stems into a small saucepan and simmer until reduced to 50ml (1¾fl oz).

When the meat hits the target temperature, remove it from the oven. Pour any juices into the saucepan with the reduced wine and add the demi-glace. Allow to simmer gently.

Heat a dry cast-iron frying pan over a high heat until it's as hot as you can get it, then sear the steak aggressively on both sides. Go for as dark a crust as you can, but don't faff about. The meat shouldn't be in the pan for longer than about 4 minutes and it should be moving for most of that time. Pull it while it's still a little pale rather than overcook it.

A reverse seared steak doesn't really benefit from resting but I usually let it sit a couple of minutes while I finish the sauce.

Pass the sauce through a sieve, then whisk in the butter and stir through the finely chopped tarragon leaves. Serve the sauce separately in a sauceboat.

London Broil

You won't find a London broil anywhere in London, because it's actually a terrific piece of American menu-writing creativity. This is a way of cooking a big and showy (but actually rather cheap) piece of meat to its best advantage and then giving it a name redolent of gentlemen's clubs and aristocracy.

Originally, London broils were chunks of flank steak, but they can also be taken from the rump, the rump cap, the top round and even the sirloin – anywhere on the cheaper parts of the carcass that you can cut a big, rectangular piece that is 6cm (2½in) or more thick, with the grain of the muscle fibres running lengthways.

This kind of cut is going to be quite tough, but the flavour will be great. This is why it's worth employing all our best tricks to make the very best of it.

The idea is to marinate it, preferably overnight, in a liquid with enough acid content to tenderize the meat. Then, you need to cook the steak as fast and as hot as possible. We want a seared, maybe even a charred, exterior for maximum flavour. It should be served rare, carved into the thinnest possible slices across the grain. That way, the meat will have astonishing flavour and will be easier to chew because of the physical structure of the slice. Be sure to give it a long rest, too, so the fibres have the best chance to relax and all the juices are retained.

I always imagine London broil to be the kind of steak they would serve in a Scorsese movie. It's a multi-person dish that needs a bunch of wiseguys to finish it – guys who like big flavours and a huge piece of meat and who aren't afraid to use their teeth. If the cook messes up, they'll probably shoot him.

In a surprising twist, if you keep the flavourings of the marinade suitably Italian and serve it over dressed rocket (arugula), it becomes the fabulously sophisticated steak *tagliata*.

'Broil' is the American term for savage overhead heating of the kind supplied in restaurant kitchens by a salamander or at home by a grill. It is possible to broil on some barbecues – you just need to rig them in a way that the meat is protected from any direct heat underneath while a lot is deflected back down from the lid. Another great way to broil (and, therefore, get a good, dark charred crust) is in a pizza oven, particularly those fashionable little tabletop ones that seem to be popping up in everyone's gardens.

(Recipe overleaf...)

Serves 2–4

2 tsp balsamic glaze
25ml (1fl oz) soy sauce
1 tsp Worcestershire sauce
1 tbsp English mustard powder
1 large, thick steak with longitudinal grain
Buttery mashed or baked potatoes, to serve

The night before you want to cook, combine all the ingredients, except the steak, in a shallow dish and mix well to create a loose marinade paste. Add the steak and slather the marinade all over it, massaging well. Transfer to the fridge to marinate overnight. If you get a chance, flip the steak a few times during this time, spooning the marinade back over the top before returning to the fridge.

The next day, arrange one of your oven shelves towards the top of the oven. Preheat the oven to its highest setting, then, just before cooking, switch to the overhead grill on high.

Scrape the marinade off the steak and pat it dry with paper towels, then place the steak on a baking sheet and quickly slide it under the grill.

Cook, flipping the steak often and brushing the top with the marinade each time you do, until the core temperature reaches 56°C (133°F) on a probe thermometer.

Remove the steak from the oven and set aside to rest for absolutely ages, then slice very thinly across the grain before serving. The steakhouse favourite accompaniment would be mashed potatoes – highly enriched with cream and butter – or baked potatoes.

Steak in a Tin

I first spotted this method in a very small Italian restaurant.[79] Though the place was justly famous for its glorious Neapolitan-style pizzas, one of my guests insisted she needed a steak. I kept my eye on the kitchen, through the open hatch, because I was interested how they were going to handle the order with a wood-fired oven and no noticeable stove or grill. Sure enough, the old *pizzaiolo* ferreted around under the bench and pulled out a small tin. It was a knackered old thing, maybe 6cm (2½in) deep, with very slightly sloped sides and just a little bigger than the fat rib eye he pulled from the fridge where it seemed to have been stored, like in many really old-school joints, under oil.[80] The tin looked very much like the sort of simple, cheap steel container you might use under an old car to collect oil drips.

In retrospect, however, the tin was critical. It was the kind of pan an Italian baker would use for a focaccia. Like all bread tins, it transmits oven heat immediately – in a focaccia, that's what causes the oily dough to 'fry' and crisp against the sides.

He seasoned the steak generously and then slid it into the pizza oven where the bottom of the pan instantly heated up against the stone while the top of the steak was seared by the flames in the dome above. After about a minute, he pulled the tin from the oven and flipped the steak with a fork before tucking fresh thyme and roughly crushed, unpeeled garlic cloves around the meat. Then he added a glug of olive oil and a huge lump of butter.

After another minute or so, he flipped the steak again, then after another minute he forked it out onto a hot serving plate and slid it into the mouth of the oven to rest.

The bottom of the tin must have been a mess of garlic, herbs, oils and meat juices – I couldn't see from where I was lurking – but, in no particular hurry, he used his fork to scrape up and abuse everything left. He then slid it back, next to the resting steak, and got on with everyone else's pizza.

(Continued overleaf…)

---

[79] I tried to find out what they called it, but my Italian is hopeless and the cook's English was even worse. On the top of my notebook page it just says 'steak in a tin', so that's going to have to do.

[80] In the very first diner I ever worked at, the old Swiss chef stored his carefully trimmed and portioned rib eye pieces in olive oil. In many ways, it makes sense. When refrigeration isn't necessarily up to the most modern standards, it keeps the meat absolutely out of contact with the air. There can be no oxidation or drying out, the lactic fermentation of ageing (which is actually anaerobic) can continue and when the meat is eventually pulled out to cook, the extra oil will cause brief 'frying' of the exterior when it hits the hotplate, kickstarting the Maillard reaction.

In the last second before calling for service, he slid the steak back into the pan, rolled both sides in the oil, put it back on the plate and gently spooned some of the oil over the top.

It was an absolute masterclass in everything you need to know about steak cooking, but also the brilliance of any evolved cooking procedure. This worked and looked effortless because this old guy had been buying the same cut of meat, from the same butcher, for probably forty years. He'd used the same oven, the same procedure and, crucially, the same damn tin every single time. Like evolution itself, there was no point at which he, himself, was aware of change, but over all that time, every single action had become pared back to a perfect functionality.

Could you or I cook a steak like that? Probably not the first time. Probably not the first fifty times (and that's a lot of steak for a civilian). But as I stood at the hatch, like an idiot, diligently making notes and timing things on my phone, I learned that the most important thing, sometimes, is just to keep doing something good and let it get better.

I've got my own tin now. I repurposed one I inherited from my nan that no one else wanted for baking. It does a pretty good job in a very hot oven, where the fan-driven hot air can get to the base and I can turn on the overhead grilling elements. It works even better in my ceramic outdoor grill, with a pizza stone installed and a good, long preheating time.

I can't tell you how to do it – which is why this is more of a parable than a recipe – but I can tell you for sure that the sooner you start, the younger you'll be when it gets good.

Steak on a Plank

Search online for 'steak on a plank' today and you'll find many references to *plankstek*, which is undergoing a revival in Sweden following its restaurant heyday in the 1970s. Cooking steak on wood is an interesting method that was supposedly imported from the United States, where steak on a plank has been popular since at least the 1950s.

I found an old live recording of Cab Calloway singing 'Everybody Eats When They Come to My House', recorded some time between 1950 and 1957, judging by the band line-up. The lyrics go like this:

> Steak on a plank for Frankie
> Corn on the cob for Bobby
> Chilli con carne for Barney
> Everybody eats when they come to my house

This version doesn't crop up in any of the online lyric archives, so it must have been an ad lib, making reference to something that would have been relevant to his audience in the room. (And it's tantalizing to think that 'Frankie' might be Sinatra.)

Steak on a plank must have been quite the thing and it would have been a really impressive presentation in the grand dining rooms of the American post-war boom. It was fashionable – but it was already a revival of an older trend.

The February 1917 edition of *Good Housekeeping* ran a piece called 'The Plank versus the Platter' by Katherine Campion. In it, Campion writes:

> 'Until very recently, a Beefsteak Chateaubriand was always cooked and served on an oaken plank. But now the custom of broiling the steak and serving it from a silver platter has replaced the plank.'

So why serve a steak on a building material? There are two reasons.

Firstly, it's a time-tested way of cooking meat well. There is a long history of grilling protein on wood in many cultures, since a flat piece of wood can hold food close to a fire in the absence of a metal pan. Hardwood, particularly when it's soaked in water before use, is a strong insulator against heat (unlike a pan, which transmits heat efficiently), so the side of the steak that's against the plank doesn't get much heat. Cooking a steak on a piece of damp oak or cedar therefore means it cooks more slowly, with the aromas of the wood being transferred to the meat. As the wood dries and begins to char, there's also the gentle addition of a smoky flavour.

This is probably the original reason that steak was 'planked' but, though the wood could be reused a couple of times, it was essentially a trick for outdoor cooking. When the method reached North American steakhouses, however, things changed. The plank became a superbly clever way of both cooking and serving.

A steak is cooked under the grill until one side is done, then it's placed on a board and a border of duchess potatoes is piped around the outside. The standard Swedish accompaniments of a stuffed tomato and either green beans or asparagus wrapped in bacon were also chosen to heat at the same time. The whole thing is then finished off in the oven.

It's a little miracle of practical catering design and it's no wonder that the presentation became an instant classic. By the time the second side of the steak is browned and the meat is medium-rare, the potatoes have browned perfectly, the stuffed tomato is hot and scorched and the green vegetables are on point.

Like most restaurant recipes, this one requires some advance prep, but it's good to know that all the work is done and that finishing will be extraordinarily stress-free.

Serves 4

4 single-serving steaks
1 large bunch of asparagus
4 slices of smoked bacon or
   smoked, air-dried ham
1 quantity Duchess Potatoes
   (see page 204)
2 tomatoes, halved
Olive oil, for cooking the vegetables
Sea salt and freshly ground black
   pepper

To serve

Your favourite steak butter
   (see pages 267–270), sliced
   into discs
Your favourite steak sauce
   (see pages 271–277)
Parsley sprigs (optional)

You'll need four 18–22mm (¾–1in) planks of oak, applewood or cedar. You should be able to pick these up wherever you buy your barbecue supplies, or you might also find them as cheap cutting boards. Don't use coniferous softwoods – the regular building timber – as the taste is a bit mentholated and medical. Also avoid anything that's been treated. No creosoted fencing or, god forbid, decking planks, which are routinely pressure-treated with cyanide. Avoid anything that's been varnished or polished unless you like your sirloin smoked with Mr Sheen. The boards need to be big enough to fit a steak, surrounded by trimmings, yet small enough that two will fit on one oven shelf.

The night before you want to cook, season the meat all over with salt and place on a wire rack set over a tray. Transfer to the fridge to rest overnight, uncovered.

The next day, soak the boards in cold water for at least 30 minutes.

Meanwhile, divide the asparagus into four bunches and wrap each one with a slice of the bacon, then tie with kitchen string.

Bring a large saucepan of water to a simmer, then drop in the asparagus bundles and cook for 2 minutes. Remove and plunge into iced water to stop the cooking. Drain, cover and refrigerate.

Preheat the oven to its highest setting and arrange two shelves inside. If you have the option to turn on overhead heat, use it.

Pipe the mash around the edges of the boards.

Season the steaks again, then place them on a baking sheet and place them under the grill. Grill for 2 minutes.

Meanwhile, rub the asparagus bunches with a little oil.

Place the steaks onto the planks, browned-side down. Place a tomato half next to each steak and find a space to tuck in the asparagus. Place a slice of your chosen steak butter onto each steak.

Place the planked steaks into the oven. After a minute, swap the two shelves and then continue to cook for another minute or so. You can check with a probe thermometer to gauge doneness, but you should find that the steak reaches perfection just as the potato browns and the vegetables approach al-dente perfection.

The steaks won't need much resting, so you can just pour over your favourite sauce (béarnaise works brilliantly with asparagus but I have a soft spot for peppercorn, too). A sprig of parsley would be ridiculous, though thoroughly retro and quite amusing.

Duchess Potatoes

Duchess potatoes are a type of mashed potato that's designed to be 'held', so that they can be piped cold and reheated under a grill. The potatoes are mixed with butter and eggs so that the mixture browns nicely, and piping (particularly through a star nozzle) means there's plenty of surface area to colour.

Makes enough for the recipe on page 203

1kg (2lb 4oz) potatoes (Maris Piper or Yukon Gold)
100g (3½oz) butter
Handful of cheese (optional, but Gruyère or Parmesan work well), grated
100ml (3½fl oz) double (heavy) cream
4 egg yolks
Freshly grated nutmeg, to taste
Sea salt and freshly ground black pepper

Proceed by whatever means you prefer to make mash. You can peel the potatoes and steam or boil them, or you could bake them and then split them before scooping out the flesh. The latter method produces a drier mash, which can absorb more fat, and also provides 'shells' into which any excess duchess mix can be piped.

Pass the potato flesh through a ricer (or a sieve if you're old school and have forearms like hams, or servants). The mash needs to be smooth but don't be tempted to use any kind of mechanical blender or food processor as this breaks up the cells of the potato and makes the mixture unbearably gluey. Transfer the hot, smooth potatoes to a large bowl.

Use a large silicone spoon, spatula or, best of all, a spoonula to beat in the butter. There is no scientific basis for my assertion, but I think these things have a tremendous effect on mash. They make it possible to beat in unbelievable amounts of butter. I've listed 100g (3½oz) of butter for this recipe, but if you want to you can manage much, much more. If you appreciate the taste, you can also beat in the cheese at this point.

Stir in the cream to lower the temperature a little, then quickly beat in the egg yolks.

Adjust the seasoning with pepper, salt and a scrape of nutmeg, then spoon the mixture into a piping bag fitted with a large star nozzle. Store in the fridge until needed.

Tip: Use plastic piping nozzles. If the mash doesn't behave when it's time to pipe it out, you can microwave the whole thing for a few seconds.

Chaliapin Steak

Feodor Chaliapin was a Russian opera singer with, we are told, a gorgeous bass voice and a naturalistic acting style. He was also fond of a steak and in 1936 he walked into the Imperial Hotel, Tokyo, and requested an extra-tender one.

Why are there so many stories like this? What is it with opera? Why on earth are these people so unreasonably demanding? I've been told I've got an agreeable light baritone but I'm pretty sure it's never going to give me the cojones to walk into a grand hotel and demand they devise an entirely novel 'steak Hayward'.

What's interesting about this particular recipe, though, is that it was a Japanese master chef who was asked to make the steak tender – and he utilized an entirely different culinary tradition to solve the problem.

The Chaliapin uses the technique of cross-hatching with a knife, which was usually used to tenderize squid. In essence, this is actually a much more refined version of the blade tenderizing that is used to create the cheap US 'cube steak' (see page 225). It also employs long marination in finely chopped onion. The liquid that leaches out of onion when it's cut contains a lot of oxalic acid – that's the stuff that makes you cry – and proteolytic enzymes, which as well as adding flavour, break down the meat a little.

The tenderized steak is grilled in the usual way and, in the original version, was served with a classic red wine-based French sauce. Personally, I can't see the onions go to waste and it seems proper to honour the dish's origins by adding more umami with soy sauce. Fiendishly brilliant.

Serves 1

1 x 2cm (¾in) thick sirloin steak
2 large onions, very finely chopped
   (reserve any juices)
2 tbsp dark soy sauce
2 tbsp clarified butter or ghee, plus
   extra as needed
50ml (1¾oz) red wine
Sea salt and freshly ground black
   pepper
Steamed Japanese rice, to serve
Chopped spring onions (scallions),
   to serve

Place the steak on a board and use a sharp knife to make shallow cuts across the face of it about 2mm deep and 2mm apart. Turn the steak 90 degrees and repeat to create a crosshatch pattern. Flip the steak over and do the same to the other side.

Put the onions into a bowl, add half the soy sauce and stir thoroughly. The salt in the soy sauce will season the steak and encourage more juice out of the onions.

Add the steak to the bowl and coat it with the onion sludge, then transfer to the fridge to marinate overnight.

The next day, scrape off and save the onions and pat the steak dry with paper towels.

Heat a dry cast-iron frying pan over a high heat until it's as hot as you can get it, then sear the steak on both sides. Add the butter, then flip and baste until the internal temperature reaches 56°C (133°F) on a probe thermometer. Remove and set aside on a plate to rest.

Pour the red wine into the pan and use it to scrape up anything adhering to the base. Allow it to bubble until you can smell that the alcohol has cooked off, then pour in the onion marinade. Reduce the heat a little to avoid scorching the onions, add a little more butter and continue to cook down until you have a chunky, textured sauce. Adjust the seasoning with the remaining soy sauce.

Slice the steak thinly and drape it elegantly over the rice. Pour the onions on top and sprinkle with the chopped spring onions.

(Pictured overleaf…)

Steak Tataki

It is said that tataki was invented by Sakamoto Ryōma, 'a nineteenth-century rebel samurai, who picked up the European technique of grilling meat from European visitors to Nagasaki', which is a lovely idea, and sounds like exactly the kind of thing you'd print on a menu. In fact, the method was applied to fish in Japan long before it became popular as a meat treatment in the West.

Most steak tataki recipes concentrate on incredibly intense searing so the outside is sterilized and the inside remains raw, which conveniently complies with health and safety requirements. I prefer to focus on the marinating, using a wrapping technique used to keep fish in constant contact with liquid flavourings. Don't worry about getting an intensely seared crust. That was never what tataki was all about.

Serves 2

400ml (14fl oz) dark soy sauce,
  plus extra to serve
120ml (4fl oz) rice wine vinegar,
  plus extra to serve
150ml (5¼fl oz) mirin
50ml (2fl oz) sake
50ml (2fl oz) sesame oil, plus extra
  to serve
Honey, to taste (optional)
75g (2½oz) fresh ginger
2 garlic cloves
1 beef fillet, fat chateaubriand end
  and the pointy 'tail' removed.

Prepare a marinade by combining the soy sauce, rice wine vinegar, mirin, sake and sesame oil. I'm not keen on sweet marinades, but if you are, consider whisking in a little honey to taste. Bring to a simmer in a saucepan, grate in the ginger and garlic, then remove from the heat and allow to cool. When cool, place the marinade in the freezer until very cold, but not actually frozen.

Look down the centre of the fillet and find the faint line between two muscles. Separate the muscles with a sharp knife.

Carefully trim away any extraneous fat or silverskin, then sear the meat in a hot, dry pan. Work as fast as you can. Keep the meat moving constantly. Don't allow any part to be in contact with the pan for over 45 seconds.

Transfer the meat to a piece of muslin and roll it tightly into a neat cylinder, tying the ends. Place the wrapped fillet in a container just large enough to fit it, then pour over the chilled marinade. Cover and refrigerate overnight.

Remove from the marinade and unwrap the muslin. While the meat is still very cold, slice very thinly with a deadly sharp knife. Arrange on a plate and allow to rise to room temperature before serving with a dipping sauce made of soy sauce, rice wine vinegar and a few drops of sesame oil.

The Schnitzel Family

Veal doesn't have a very strong meaty flavour and it doesn't really benefit from being cooked rare. In fact, the brief for a 'good' piece of veal has historically been 'bland, zero fat and easy to chew', so most recipes that use it depend on things other than the meat to do the heavy lifting, flavour-wise.

These next few recipes all work on the principle that a piece of veal, beaten out until thin so it cooks quickly and is highly tenderized, can be made infinitely more interesting by being breadcrumbed and fried.

There are, of course, arguments about exactly where this idea originated. The most creditable claimants are two ends of the Hapsburg dynasty: Italy and Austria. The Italians claim that Catherine de' Medici was somehow involved in exporting veal Milanese to the grateful Viennese and the Austrians, quite naturally, assume they thought of it first and told the people of Milan later.

We will probably never know which is true, but let's start in Vienna, because their take is the simplest and it's taxonomically useful to be able to classify all of these dishes under the name 'schnitzel'.

The Wiener schnitzel calls for a veal cutlet (the eye of a veal chop) to be trimmed of fat and bone, beaten out to less than 1cm (½in) thick, seasoned and then dipped in flour, egg and breadcrumbs. This is the absolute key to all the schnitzel family recipes: a thick breadcrumb coating that absorbs fats and flavours. In this case, principally an enormous quantity of butter. Good Wiener schnitzel can be one of the most glorious pieces of meat on earth, but it might as well be vegetarian, because 99 per cent of the flavour comes from the crisp, butter-fried breadcrumbs – and there's nothing wrong with that.

As a side note, since modern tastes no longer include the strangely pernickety preference for very pale and subtle meat, the following veal recipes would work as well, if not better, with any beefsteak that can be tenderized by beating out.

Wiener Schnitzel

To add to the international confusion surrounding breaded veal cutlets, if you serve your Wiener schnitzel with a runny fried egg on top, it becomes German – though 'schnitzel à la Holstein' is the name usually given to this preparation, which is, confusingly, French. And it's most popular in the US. No wonder Europe spent so much time at war with itself. *(Pictured on page 215.)*

Serves 1

1 boneless veal cutlet
100g (3½oz) plain (all-purpose) flour
1 egg, beaten
100g (3½oz) dried breadcrumbs
75g (2½oz) clarified butter or ghee, plus extra as needed
3 anchovy fillets (the canned oily type) (optional)
Juice of ½ lemon (optional)
15g (½oz) salted nonpareille capers (optional)
Squeeze of lemon juice (optional)
Sea salt and freshly ground black pepper
Mustardy lettuce salad, to serve

Place the cutlet between two pieces of greaseproof or butcher's paper and pound with a flat meat mallet or the bottom of a heavy pan until 0.5–1cm (¼–½in) thick. Look carefully at the beaten cutlet and, if it looks like there's any tightening around the outside edge where a membrane may be pulling inwards, just make a neat snip through the edge in a couple of places. This will stop the cutlet rolling up when it's cooked. Season generously with salt and pepper.

Spread the flour on a plate and dip both sides of the beaten cutlet into it. Flip several times, patting to achieve good coverage and adherence.

Pour the egg into a shallow dish and put the breadcrumbs onto a plate.

Dip the floured cutlet in the egg so both sides are fully coated, then lay it on the plate of breadcrumbs. Flip to coat both sides but don't push the breadcrumbs into the meat to make more stick. Compressing the breadcrumbs makes the crust denser.

Heat half the butter in a cast-iron frying pan over a medium-high heat and fry one side of the breaded cutlet until golden, then add the remaining butter. Flip the cutlet and continue to cook, flipping occasionally, until both sides are equally golden brown. Don't be afraid to add more butter at any point. A schnitzel is best when it's effectively shallow fried rather than slid around a modestly lubed pan.

You can top the cooked schnitzel with the anchovies or create a quick sauce by adding a little more butter to the pan, then rolling the capers around in it and squeezing in some lemon juice.

Serve with a very simple salad of roundhead lettuce with a mustardy vinaigrette.

SCHNITZEL, VIENNA, AUSTRIA

I flew to Vienna for the schnitzel. Yes, sure, I love Klimt and wanted to sit in cafés and pretend to be an important nineteenth-century philosopher, but mainly, it was the meat. All over the world, there's a consensus that the best way to treat a steak is to go for thickness and rareness, yet here, comparatively close to my home country, there's a culture that beats the damn things as thin as a postcard and fries them. I had to go into the belly of the beast and so booked myself into one of the grandest and most famous of old cafés. Local friends warned me

that the place was 'touristy', but I usually disregard that kind of advice. If you live in the city yourself, then a café full of foreigners paying over the odds for the most obvious local specialities is everything you'd want to avoid. But to the traveller … well, those places don't get famous by being crap, and if these guys were promising the most *echt* schnitzel in town … I booked a table.

The place was ecclesiastical. Columns and vaulted ceilings. Uniformed waiters, many of advanced age, glided between tables like king penguins on hover-boards and every table was packed with locals. This had been exactly the right decision. I kicked off with sausages and mustard as a palate cleanser and an excellent steak tartare. The cultural issue with rareness doesn't seem to be total, though personally, I'd have been happier if they'd stopped chopping before they'd achieved the texture of toothpaste.

I was with friends. The wine and conversation flowed. We were still there, carousing, when the penguins were stacking the chairs on the tables and sweeping around our feet, and it was a glorious evening in every respect. Except the schnitzel.

It should have been revelatory. I mean, the location couldn't have been more authentic, nor the circumstances more propitious but, honestly, the schnitzel was exactly as I had feared. About 3mm thick, grey in colour and entirely cooked through, beyond merely 'well done'. It certainly wasn't too hard to cut, and the crust was pleasant enough, but I was left … baffled. Is that all there is?

The following day, I was to fly home, but I'd planned to have lunch at a nearby restaurant to try another Viennese speciality. Plachutta is just behind the gorgeous Opera House and seemed to be serving only the most glossy of international business people on their beautiful terrace. They all seemed to be enjoying exactly what I'd come for: Tafelspitz. A truly terrifying prospect. Plachutta's best-selling Viennese speciality is top-quality beef cuts boiled in clear broth with vegetables. There's a marrowbone in there, too. They serve it with an array of mustards, bread – on which to smear the bone marrow – and salt to dress it. Everything comes in a polished copper saucepan.

When you order, they give you a kind of cow map and a list of cuts that reads like Wagner…

'Act 4: Kruspelspitz woos Beiried in the magical forest of Lungenbraten. They are surprised by the three Hüferscherzl – Fledermaus, Tafelstück and Zunge – who salute them with a traditional Hüferschwanzl.'

As you can see, I have no German at all, but the cuts are all brilliantly described in English on the menu, with forensically accurate delineation of fat content, texture, variations of fibrousness, degree of chew and delicacy of flavour. But after about a week in the poaching stock, they obviously all look utterly identical on the plate. It seemed important to understand this stuff, if only because it ran entirely counter to anything I knew about cooking beef, but I ploughed on.

Actually, Tafelspitz is amazing. Obviously, it's all about the broth, which is as clear as a mountain lake, every bit as deep and complex as a consommé or a top-grade ramen broth and, in the most pure sense, the absolute essence of beef. The clear broth of a Tafelspitz tastes like the juice you want to flow out of your steak as you bite into it … only they serve it in bucket-sized containers … and they give you a spoon.

Sure, I thought, they're eating the meat because this is a traditional dish, from a time when you could be tortured by cardinals for wasting food, but all of it – the veg, the potatoes, the meat – is just by-product. Leftovers from the kind of broth that's more delicate than a Rhinemaiden's tears and strong enough to bring a demigod back from the grave.

But then I bit into the hüferschwanzl; tender meat, they told me, from around the 'aitch-bone'. This was effectively a chateaubriand but looked like it had spent a month in a school stewpot. As my teeth went through the fibres of the meat and the broth bathed my palate, I realized that this was just astonishingly good. Sure, the colour was a touch Farrow & Ball, but the texture was that of extremely tender steak and the flavour was supreme. The fat had achieved a state of textural sublimity. It was almost as if all the best parts of steak had been deconstructed and then reassembled in my mouth. I closed my eyes – partly in bliss and partly because I didn't want to ruin the experience by gazing at that grey, boiled meat again.

And then they brought me a Wiener Schnitzel.

It was of a modest size. None of the crazy 'overhanging the plate nonsense' you might get in Italy. It was puffed up like a pitta and the egg and breadcrumb crust shattered at the touch of my knife. The steak within was veal, so of course, pale in colour and delicate in flavour, but it was reasonably thick and properly juicy when I cut into it. I squeezed over the lemon in its little white cotton shower cap and dived in. This time all the flavour was there. Subtle, evanescent beefiness but just enough to balance the insane, buttery richness of the crust. It was glorious.

A lot of this was down to some pretty spectacular ingredients and some top-quality cooking, none of which comes cheap. But there was also something else going on. It was almost as if one of those brilliant and troubled young Austrian philosophers had sat in a café and asked the un-askable question:

What if it isn't about rareness?

It's the only way I can imagine this coming about. A kind of culture-wide decision only to eat fully cooked meat and then a couple of hundred years of improving on the idea.

And for me, weirdly, it was a kind of breakthrough. Prime steaks are our most sought after, highest-status food, and they, uniquely, taste good when close to raw. But there are other dishes, other ways, that beef can be eaten where that pre-supposition isn't there.

A week after flying home, I picked up a particularly good Fiorentina from my favourite butcher. He assured me this was a special one – an older beast, strong flavour, might have a bit more chew than usual. So, rather than slinging it on the grill bars in the customary way, I decided to reverse sear it; I'd do 4 hours in the oven at 55˚C (131˚F) and then a red hot skillet to finish.

Dear reader, I screwed it. Comprehensively. When I carved, I nearly cried. I'd got my thermometer readings wrong and I'd cooked it to medium-well – no, I'll be honest – well done!

I brought it to the table, wracked with shame and everyone nobly dug in and, you know what, it was one of the great steaks of my career. The slow heat had done wondrous things to the texture. The flavour was clean, clear and well developed. The fat was crisped and rendered, yet appeared to have self-basted the whole piece, imbuing it with the flavour of a Tafelspitz broth and the richness of a buttery schnitzel crust.

My mind was, frankly, blown. Well-done steak. And it was good! My whole *Weltanschauung* twisted like a pretzel.

I don't even know who I am any more.

Veal Milanese

Cotoletta alla Milanese may have been the OG schnitzel or it could be a later schnitzoid. The claim for the former comes from the story of a banquet thrown in 1134 at the Basilica di Sant'Ambrogio in Milan. Records of the banquet state that it featured *lombolos cum panitio*, or breaded small veal bits. Personally I reckon veal Milanese is worth talking about because it went on to become an Italian-American steakhouse classic that brings a load of extra flavours to the table.

A Milanese is a cutlet that has been beaten out but left on the bone, creating a convenient handle. It's also worth mentioning that the idea that it should be absolutely bloody huge, hanging over the edges of a large plate, is a far more recent Italian restaurant tradition. Some – and I must stress here only some – Italian cooks add Parmesan or pecorino to the breadcrumbs.

Serves 1

1 veal cutlet on the bone/veal chop
100g (3½oz) plain (all-purpose) flour
1 egg, beaten
100g (3½oz) dried breadcrumbs
20g (¾oz) Parmesan or pecorino (optional), grated
75g (2½oz) clarified butter or ghee
Sea salt and freshly ground black pepper
Tomato and onion salad, to serve
Pasta in tomato sauce, to serve (optional)

Beat out the cutlet following the instructions for the Wiener schnitzel on page 214, but keep away from the bone as you clobber it.

Prepare and fry the cutlet following the instructions on page 214, adding the cheese to the breadcrumbs if you like.

Serve with slices of fresh tomato dressed in olive oil and balsamic vinegar and sprinkled with chopped onions. Some restaurants would serve this with a simple tomato sauce dolloped on top to 'cut through' the butter, but why on earth would I want to do that? You could compromise, perhaps, with a small serving of pasta tossed in a tomato sauce.

Veal Piccata

If you follow roughly the same procedure as the Milanese but leave out
the egg and breadcrumb stages you will make veal piccata, another fast,
crowd-pleasing Italian-American restaurant classic that looks elegant on
the plate. This is particularly good served with mashed potatoes, but I'd
recommend making it with olive oil rather than the usual butter and cream.
I yield to no man in my love of highly enriched mash, but served with a sauce
that's predominantly butter, it can be too much.

Serves 1

1 veal cutlet on the bone/veal chop
100g (3½oz) plain (all-purpose)
  flour
75g (2½oz) clarified butter or ghee,
  plus a knob extra
2 garlic cloves
75ml (2½fl oz) dry vermouth
150ml (5fl oz) chicken stock
25g (1oz) salted nonpareille capers
1 lemon
Sea salt and freshly ground black
  pepper
Olive oil mash and green salad, to
  serve

Place the cutlet between two pieces of greaseproof or butcher's
paper and pound with a flat meat mallet or the bottom of a heavy pan
until 0.5–1cm (¼–½in) thick, avoiding the bone.

Pour the flour onto a plate and season well with salt and pepper.
Dip the veal into the flour, coating both sides evenly.

Melt the butter in a cast-iron frying pan over a medium-high heat and,
once foaming, add the garlic and the cutlets. Fry for 2–3 minutes on
each side, flipping regularly, until evenly golden.

Lift out the cutlets and add a knob of butter to the pan, then remove
the garlic and pour in the vermouth. Allow it to bubble and reduce.

Add the stock and the capers and reduce further. Squeeze in the
juice of the lemon, then roughly chop any squeezed-out bits and
throw them into the pan, too. Continue to cook for a minute more,
letting the lemon scorch a little, then pour the sauce over the cutlets.

Serve with the olive oil mash and green salad.

Veal Parmigiana Sandwich

Veal Parmigiana, or Parmesan, is an Italian-American dish in which tomato sauce is poured over a breaded veal cutlet before a cap of mozzarella is melted over everything. It's the culinary equivalent of the thing they built over Chernobyl… it looks a bit like overkill but you're very glad it's there.

Given that veal parmigiana is a 'red sauce' restaurant special, you can be pretty sure the breadcrumbs will contain cheese and, almost certainly, some garlic powder and oregano. And, in a final departure from any historical accuracy or even human restraint, the parmigiana can be served as a large, sloppy, grilled 'hero' sandwich – and I am not the man to complain about it.

Serves 1

1 boneless veal cutlet
100g (3½oz) plain (all-purpose) flour
1 egg, beaten
100g (3½oz) dried breadcrumbs
20g (¾oz) Parmesan or pecorino (optional), grated
¾ tsp garlic powder
¾ tsp dried oregano, plus extra for sprinkling
¾ tsp cayenne pepper
75g (2½oz) clarified butter or ghee
1 ciabatta loaf
100ml (3½fl oz) Italian tomato sauce (whichever is your favourite recipe)
100g (3½oz) low-moisture mozzarella (the cheap block stuff), sliced
Sea salt and freshly ground black pepper

Place the cutlet between two pieces of greaseproof or butcher's paper and pound with a flat meat mallet or the bottom of a heavy pan until 0.5–1cm (¼–½in) thick.

Spread the flour on a plate and dip both sides of the beaten cutlet into it. Flip several times, patting to achieve good coverage and adherence.

Pour the egg into a shallow dish and put the breadcrumbs onto a plate. Add the grated cheese, garlic powder, oregano and cayenne to the breadcrumbs and stir in.

Dip the floured cutlet in the egg so both sides are fully coated, then lay it on the plate of breadcrumbs. Flip to coat both sides but don't push the breadcrumbs into the meat to make more stick.

Heat half the butter in a cast-iron frying pan over a medium-high heat and fry one side of the breaded cutlet until golden, then add the remaining butter. Flip the cutlet and continue to cook, flipping occasionally, until both sides are equally golden brown. Don't be afraid to add more butter at any point.

Split the ciabatta and place cut-side up on a baking sheet. Toast under a hot grill, then place the cutlet on the bottom piece of ciabatta. Pour over a thick coating of tomato sauce, then lay the slices of mozzarella on top.

Cook under the hot grill until the cheese is bubbling, then remove and sprinkle with a little more dried oregano. Apply the lid of the ciabatta, then enjoy.

Chicken-fried Steak

The final bastard child of the schnitzel family is the Southern diner favourite chicken-fried steak which, in many ways, takes the schnitzel to its logical intellectual conclusion. The breadcrumbing here is well flavoured and the steak need not be veal. In the places it's served, it's considered a clever way of using steaks that are full of good flavour but cheap and perhaps too tough for more refined uses. The steak for chicken-frying is often flank that has been ferociously beaten or 'cube steak', a usually unspecified piece of flat cow meat that's been put through a blade tenderizer. The rollers are coated in razor-sharp blades that make incisions in the meat, almost mincing it into tiny 'cubes' but leaving the pieces attached. It's a remarkable technique that turns something as tough as shoe leather (though delicious) into a kind of lacy meat-matrix that soaks up flavour and is as easy to chew as a burger.

Chicken-fried steak is served with a pan gravy that uses the leftover frying fats to make a roux that is then used to thicken milk. This is important. The gravy collects up every last available droplet of flavour in the pan and makes sure none of it goes to waste. The main additional flavouring is copious amounts of black pepper – and by that I mean quite a lot more than you think is wise. You want enough pepper that there's not just heat but a fantastic, almost fruity fragrance. A shot of coffee can also be added to fine effect.

Danny, a rather intense chef I once worked with in South Carolina, was a Marine Corps vet and, possibly as a consequence, had a deep, abiding respect for ingredients that came in cans and pouches. He used the tinned 'au jus' broth concentrate, which is a staple in US kitchens, and half a pouch of dried onion soup mix to make a gravy that had our quite sophisticated diners howling for more. I wouldn't recommend you do the same but, whenever I make French onion soup, I freeze a couple of portions that can double as gravy for future chicken-fried steaks.

In this recipe, I've swapped the regular flour for potato starch. That's the secret weapon the Japanese use for their fried chicken *karaage*, which has the puffiest and most spectacularly crunchy coating. The baking powder also helps with this.

(Continued overleaf…)

Serves 1

1 flank, bistro, minute, bavette
  or other 'cheap frying steak'
100g (3½oz) potato starch
1 egg, beaten
½ tbsp baking powder
½ tbsp garlic powder
½ tbsp House Creole Seasoning
  (see page 291) or similar spice
  mix
75g (2½oz) bacon grease, dripping
  or lard
2 tbsp plain (all-purpose) flour
60ml (2fl oz) cold black coffee
Splash of Worcestershire sauce
200ml (7fl oz) whole (full-fat) milk
50ml (1¾fl oz) double (heavy)
  cream
Sea salt and freshly ground black
  pepper
French fries or salad, to serve

Place the steak on a board and pound with a spiked meat mallet or heavy-based pan until roughly 1cm (½in) thick. If your knife skills are up to it and you enjoy a challenge, you can also crosshatch the steak lightly (see page 207). Season generously with salt and pepper.

Spread the potato starch on a plate and dip both sides of the beaten steak into it. Flip several times, patting to achieve good coverage and adherence.

Pour the egg into a shallow dish and dip the steak into it so both sides are fully coated.

Add the baking powder and spices to the remaining potato starch and re-coat the dipped steak. Flip to coat both sides. Double dipping like this will make sure the coating adheres and that it puffs up to the maximum.

Heat half the fat in a cast-iron frying pan over a medium-high heat and fry one side of the steak until golden, then add the remaining fat. Flip the steak and continue to cook, flipping occasionally, until both sides are equally golden brown. Don't be afraid to add more fat at any point. Keep it deep – remember, you're frying a steak like fried chicken.

Remove the steak from the pan and pour out all but a tablespoon or so of the fat. Lower the heat, pour in the flour and stir to form a smooth paste, then continue to cook until it begins to brown.

Use the coffee to deglaze the pan, scraping up any burnt bits and combining them with the roux to make a thick paste. Add the Worcestershire sauce and then the milk and cream. Bring everything up to a simmer, then reduce to a good pouring and coating consistency. Taste and adjust the seasoning.

Pour the gravy over the rested steak, then serve with French fries for total authenticity. You should also probably have ketchup and maybe bottomless black coffee served by a waitress called Blanche. A slug from the bottle of Bushmills in your bag is optional. Me? I reckon it works well with a crisp green salad or maybe an iceberg wedge with blue cheese dressing and bacon sprinkles.

Steak Salad

OK. I need to share something here, in the spirit of full disclosure and no little element of catharsis: I often cook too much steak. It's quite difficult to do this, because I've discovered from long and wearying experience that my family and friends will consume as much steak as I put on the table (so my secret plan is often thwarted), but the idea is this: I want to have enough left over for a cold steak sandwich or salad the following day.

That's right, a salad. Intentionally cold steak makes an utterly amazing salad. A proper salad, as god intended, with lots of meat in it.

What I'm not going to do here is give you a formal recipe for steak salad. It's far more interesting and versatile than that. Instead, here's a series of suggestions and notes that you might want to consider when designing your own.

Choose the right steak

Cold beef fat can be unpleasant.[81] Or, there is at least the possibility that someone you might want to share a salad with might find it hard to deal with.[82] The ideal steak, therefore, is going to be one with little intramuscular fat and with subcutaneous fat that's easy to trim away. We don't want it to be hard to chew, so rump might be a little too much and a rib eye would have far too much to make for elegant slices. A good, thick sirloin will be best.

You have time

Unlike with a hot steak, there's no counting the seconds as you rush from the kitchen to the table, watching perfection ebb away. You've got all the time in the world. You can, if you wish, marinate the steak before you cook – a particularly good idea considering that the crust on the steak is going to be such an important part of the finished salad. Cook the steak by whatever method you prefer but be sure that a very hot searing is part of the process and that you pull the steak from the pan a degree or two short of your target core temperature. This one's going to get a terminal rest.

(Continued overleaf…)

---

[81] Once you've read this sentence I'd like you to forget it. Well actually, I'd like you to remember it, but to forget it was me who said it.

[82] Let's be honest. People are going to have enough trouble with a meat salad. Let's not challenge them to cold fat too.

Cool

Don't rush the cooling process. We don't want to do anything that might frighten out any juices. In fact, we want the juices to rest extremely gently and then, only once they're thoroughly reabsorbed and redistributed through the meat, do we want to fix them in place with refrigeration. I let the steak cool for a couple of hours at room temperature, uncovered, and then wrap it loosely in greaseproof paper before refrigerating. Leaving it open to the air means any steam will dissipate and the crust will dry out beautifully before you wrap. The fridge will continue the drying process, concentrating the flavours.

Choose your greens

I find the iron-rich flavour of some darker greens harmonizes with the juices of the meat, but there's a sort of spectrum; a sliding scale from which you can pick the greens that suit you. Right up at the challenging end is raw kale, which makes salads that are immensely pleasing but frankly gaseous. In their shockingly brief season, you could also try finely shredded baby Brussels sprouts. Blanched and shocked cavolo nero takes us more into the realm of the acceptable, as does similarly treated purple sprouting broccoli. Finally, you can default straight to rocket (arugula) and watercress.

Add some enlivening bits

It's a great idea to include onions. Red onions, sliced micro-fine with a mandoline, are a fiery[83] little accent. Depending on the cultural slant you're taking, you could also consider shaved pickled onions (the pub-style ones) or even pickled walnuts.

Capers! There ought to be capers!

But the more controversial addition is likely to be anchovies. I love them and often drape them whole into the salad, but I realize I may be in the minority here.[84] You can chop them extremely finely or even include them in the dressing (overleaf). Or just use capers or thinly sliced gherkins.

(Continued overleaf…)

---

[83] If you're worried about breathing on anybody, you can soak them for 30 seconds in boiling water and then cover with rice vinegar for 30 minutes. The onions, not the person.
[84] There is a perfectly lovely Thai beef salad called 'weeping tiger' that utilzes lots of nam pla fish sauce so we're not operating entirely without precedent.

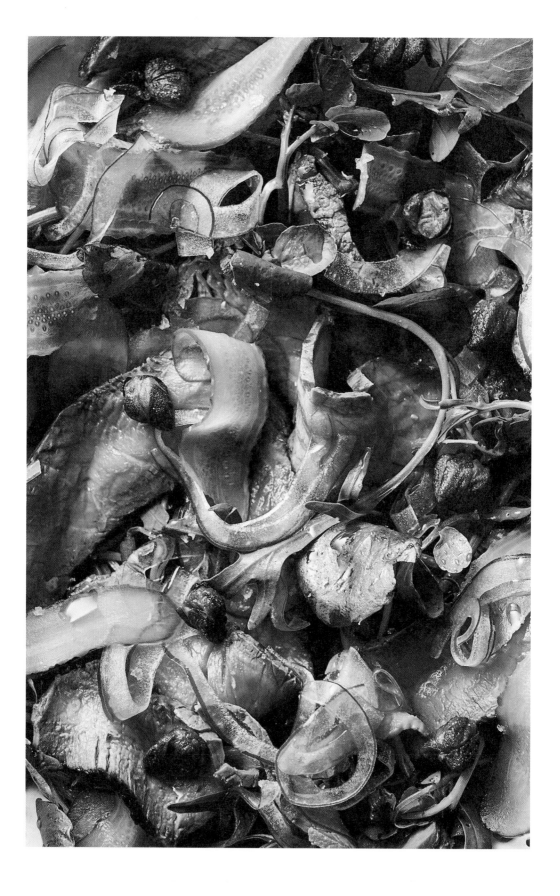

Get dressed

Choose your dressing depending on what you've already got in your mix. You can obviously go with a simple vinaigrette, but crank up the mustard because … well, because beef. That feels like a bit of a cop-out, though. The garlic/Parmesan/anchovy dressing you might put on a Caesar salad would work here, almost without tinkering[85] but, once we're heading down that route, we get to my absolute favourite, tonnato dressing (see page 232). For this usage I make it a little runnier with the addition of some sour cream and then top it with a sprinkling of deep-fried capers.

Finish

Slice the steak finely. I like it fridge-cold, but you may prefer at room temperature – it only takes a few minutes to warm up after slicing. You can assemble the whole salad and then drape the beef slices over the top, but I prefer to add it in, along with any remaining juices, and then toss the lot with the dressing.

Finally, have a taste and ask yourself whether it needs cheese. Some combinations might really benefit from a few shavings of Parmesan, others from a modest crumbling of blue cheese.

---

[85] Remember you can get just a hint of anchovy by using a splash of Worcestershire sauce if that fits your design.

Veal Chop[86] Tonnato

Vitello tonnato is a Venetian dish in which thinly sliced, cold, poached veal is served with a mayo-like sauce that is strongly flavoured with canned tuna and anchovies. It sounds entirely mad on paper, but in real life it is the most spectacular combination. I can't get enough of tonnato sauce and pour it on everything from cold boiled potatoes to steamed broccoli. Strangely, though, no one seems to be serving it with grilled veal, which seems to me a monumental oversight. It is remarkable with a veal chop.

Serves 1

1 x 145g (5¼oz) can of tuna in
   olive oil
1 x 50g (1¾) can of anchovies in
   olive oil
2 egg yolks
Zest and juice of 1 lemon
½ garlic clove, grated
25g (1oz) salted nonpareille capers
Olive oil (as needed)
Pinch of sugar (optional)
1 veal chop
Knob of butter
1 thyme sprig
1 rosemary sprig
1 garlic clove
Sea salt and freshly ground black
   pepper
Rocket (arugula) and pecorino
   salad, to serve

Drain the oil from the tuna and the anchovies, reserving it in a bowl.

Put in the egg yolks into a container that fits the end of a hand-held blender and add the tuna, anchovies, lemon zest and juice, garlic and half the capers and blitz to a smooth paste.

With the blender still going, start drizzling in the saved oil. It should quickly turn into a smooth emulsion, stiff at first and then getting runnier as you add more oil. If you run out, carry on with more plain olive oil until you have a pouring consistency. Adjust the seasoning with salt, pepper and more lemon juice if needed. (I find supermarket lemons in the UK are never as sweet as the ones you find in the Mediterranean, so often find myself adding a pinch of sugar to compensate.)

Heat a dry cast-iron frying pan over a high heat until it's as hot as you can get it, then sear the chop on both sides. Use a probe thermometer to check the internal temperature and, just before it reaches 56°C (133°F), add the butter, thyme, rosemary and garlic and baste the chop for a final minute.

Remove the chop and set it aside to rest. Pour the remaining capers into the butter and crisp them up a little.

Pour the tonnato sauce into a pool on the plate and top with the chop. Season with black pepper and sprinkle with the fried capers.

Serve with an absurdly Italian salad of rocket dressed with a little oil and topped with shavings of pecorino.

---

[86] A chop? In a steak book? Well actually, yes. Take a look at the picture. With our freshly acquired brilliance in bovine anatomy, we can look at this piece of meat, identify the bisected vertebra with its wide lateral protuberance, that fine textured cross section of uninterrupted muscle, and confidently announce in a loud, clear voice: 'Why, of course. It's a sirloin on the bone!'

Steak and Egg Breakfast

There really are very few occasions when it's acceptable to have steak for breakfast. A proper, full-on steak is far too big and is probably going to spoil the opportunity for a much more interesting lunch. But it's undeniable that the therapeutic and restorative qualities of steak can help with a colossal hangover.

I know American brunch joints would serve it with most of the trimmings of a fried breakfast alongside, but I find all that far too difficult to organize with blurred vision and a screaming headache. A modestly sized steak of medium thickness and without too much fat – maybe a neat little sirloin – will hit the spot and can be prepared, even when seriously impaired, with less skill and effort than a slice of toast. Fry it in a dry pan, then, once the steak has been lifted out and put on a plate to rest, turn the heat right down, add some butter and gently and contemplatively fry two eggs.

Unlike many people, I believe eggs benefit from quite slow 'frying', arguably more like poaching them in the oil or butter. That way, the yolk reaches 'just right' at precisely the moment that the whites have set. The time required, by an amazing coincidence, is precisely that needed to assemble a bloody Mary – assuming your tomato juice is chilled and you have pre-made your mix.[87]

Serve the steak topped with the eggs and flanked by the Bloody Mary and a strong coffee. Contemplate, before you eat, how many good things are spread before you in this sophisticated, brilliantly planned and entirely virtuous act of self-care.

---

[87] The mix isn't complicated, just Worcestershire sauce, Jalapeño hot sauce, a squeeze of lemon and a grind of black pepper. I make it up in quantity and store it in the fridge in a squeezy bottle labelled 'BVM' (after the Blessed Virgin Mary). I am a keen advocate of minimal breakfasts so I have a Virgin Mary every morning along with a couple of espressos. The immense cunning in this plan is that my family has grown so used to seeing me consuming part of my 5-a-day, a great bolt of vitamins and enough Lycopene to help me live forever, that they never notice the rare occasions I slip in a shot of frozen vodka as a hair-of-the-dog.

Breakfast Taco

I was introduced to the breakfast taco by my daughter, who has a fine feel for these things. There are times, when trimming a steak for dinner, when small pieces of meat are 'set aside'. I must confess that I often buy meat with this in mind. 'Shall I neaten it up for you? Trim off the rough bits? The fat? The cap?', the butcher asks? They are keen to help, but the answer is always no. Those bits can be trimmed off at home and tucked into a quiet corner of the fridge with a little dry marinade, leaving you to get on with dinner. The following morning, there's a surprise for breakfast.

You can use packaged corn tacos or make your own if you feel up to it. I'm not keen on the bread sold as 'wraps', which honestly seems to contain enough preservatives that they embalm my insides, but I'm not here to proscribe. I've even had these with flatbread leftover from dinner. I make mine with a lot of yoghurt[88] instead of water which means they stay soft for a couple of days and have a pleasant sour flavour.

Even up the steak trim so all the pieces are roughly the same size and shape. I like to make a very simple salsa of onion and tomato with maybe a little coriander leaf if I have it to hand or a shot of hot sauce if I don't. Then it's all a matter of order.

Heat a dry frying pan and sear the meat on all sides. As soon as you have a core temperature reading of 56°C (133°F) on your thinnest piece of meat, tip them onto a board to rest and use the hot pan to heat through or cook your taco or flatbread. One side will suck up any oil or meat juices, the other will then heat and brown a little in the hot, dry pan.

Remove the taco or flatbread to your serving plate, oily-side up. Turn off the heat under the pan, drop in a large knob of butter and crack in an egg.

The egg will take a while to cook to your taste and you can splash the melted butter over the top of it if you prefer the yolk sealed. While this is going on, arrange the meat on the taco or flatbread so any leaking juices won't be lost. Grate over a little cheese while things are still hot and, as it melts, spoon over the cold salsa. As soon as the egg is spot on, lift it carefully on to the top of the piled filling and then sit back and pour a coffee. It will take a few seconds for the cheese to melt and for everything else to settle nicely together.

Tear through the egg yolk with a fork, roll the taco or flatbread and eat as messily as possible.

---

[88] Combine 400g (14oz) flour, 300g (10½oz) liquid (half yoghurt, half water), ½ tablespoon yeast and 2 teaspoons salt. Knead for 10 minutes then split into small balls and allow to rise overnight in the fridge.

Steak Pie

One of the most popular items on the menu at the bakery chain Greggs is the 'steak bake'. It retails for less than a couple of quid and is basically a rather delightful square pasty or hand pie with a very rich meat and gravy filling. It's gorgeous, particularly with a hangover, but the key question for us is this: at that price... can it really be considered steak?

Of course, the answer is yes, because English butchers have long since sold cheaper or tougher cuts as 'stewing steak' or 'braising steak'. Usually pre-diced into 2cm (¾in) cubes, it's good stuff, carefully butchered from all those places on the carcass that might not constitute a 'proper' steak, but which are nonetheless full of flavour and respond well to long, slow cooking — particularly in gravy and especially when enclosed in a container... like maybe a pastry jacket.

What really enhances a Greggs steak bake, or indeed any meat pie bought hot from a bakery, is that it's probably been held for a while in a heating cabinet. These are the glass-fronted display units referred to by aficionados as 'the piequarium' where, by UK environmental health rules, steak bakes can be 'displayed for up to two hours at a temperature above 65°C'. Can you imagine what two hours at that temperature does to a pie filling? It's like the best possible braising of a world-class Michelin chef. It will render every fibre of the meat perfectly tender and combine meat, juices and gravy in ways I don't even have words for. Is it steak? Hell yeah!

A few years ago, Greggs released the recipe for their steak bake and, though it was tempting, I don't think I need to repeat it here. Seek it out online. Instead, here's a recipe for a very simple and classic beef pie. You can use stock, ale, stout or even wine for the braising liquid, you can add mushrooms, pickled walnuts or even, classically, kidneys, but what's most important here is that we're not going to cook the filling separately. Making the filling first is a good way to control the flavours, but it always somehow feels like you're just wrapping some pastry around a poncy French stew. If you're the kind of person who pre-makes a filling, I have a suspicion that you're also the kind of person who would make a pie with a top and no bottom (which is, of course, not a pie).

This recipe, like the immortal Cornish pasty, relies on strong pastry, careful seasoning and long, slow cooking so that the filling is perfectly braised. If you like your gravy thicker, you might consider adding a medium-sized potato, grated into the other filling ingredients. It will break down and thicken the juices.

Ask your butcher for stewing steak, but suggest that a bit of brisket wouldn't go amiss in the grand scheme of things. Brisket is full of gelatine and connective tissue, which will make the gravy even richer. Don't bother with a pie funnel — ask your butcher for a short length of marrowbone instead. And, remember to start this recipe many hours before you plan to serve it.

Serves 6

360g (12½oz) plain (all-purpose)
   flour, refrigerated to chill
200g (7oz) cold butter, plus extra
   for greasing
600g (1lb 5oz) stewing steak
   (diced chuck and possibly some
   brisket)
1 onion, finely chopped or grated
100ml (3½fl oz) water, stock, beer,
   wine or a combination thereof
½ tsp vinegar from a jar of pickled
   walnuts
1 marrow bone
1 egg, beaten with a little milk to
   make an egg wash
Sea salt and ground white pepper
English mustard and pickled
   onions, to serve

Pour the flour into a large bowl and grate in the butter, stopping occasionally to lightly stir so that the butter is well distributed into the flour. Once the butter is all mixed in, add a big pinch of salt, then place the bowl in the fridge.

Pour some very cold water into a jug and add some ice cubes.

Grease a 23cm (9in) loose-bottomed cake tin and, if you believe in a belt and braces approach, line the bottom with baking parchment. Put the tin in the fridge.

Remove the flour mixture from the fridge. Splash in a small amount of the iced water and then stir the crumbly dough with a silicone spatula until it just comes together. Use your hands to work the dough into a sausage, then cut off one-third. Wrap both pieces in cling film and return to the fridge.

Put a good, thick baking sheet or roasting tin onto the middle shelf of the oven, then preheat everything to 200°C (400°F/gas 6).

Roll out the larger piece of pastry between two sheets of baking parchment until it forms a circle about 30cm (12in) wide. Drape the pastry over the prepared tin and work it down into the bottom, allowing any excess to hang over the edge. Return to the fridge.

Put the meat into a bowl and season it heavily with salt and white pepper, then stir in the onion, water (or stock/beer/wine) and vinegar. Place the marrow bone on its end in the middle of the pie casing and add the meat mixture around it. Brush the rim with the egg wash.

Roll out the remaining pastry until it's just a little wider than the tin and cut a cross shape in the centre. Lower the lid over the pie, guiding the bone through the cross. Crimp the edges and trim any excess pastry. Brush the top with more egg wash, being sure to gloop plenty around the protruding marrowbone.

Bake the pie in the oven on the hot baking sheet for 25 minutes, then reduce the temperature to 180°C (350°F/gas 4) and continue to cook for a further 70 minutes. Check occasionally towards the end of the cooking time and if it's showing any signs of burning or scorching, give the whole pie a foil hat. Use a probe thermometer to check the temperature of the filling, which should be somewhere north of 85°C (185°F). Now, drop the temperature of the oven to that of a piequarium – i.e. as close as you can get to 65°C (149°F) – and leave to sit for 2 hours. This will not raise the temperature of the pie any further, it will just make the filling more unctuous, give it more chance to mingle with the crust and generally become a greater and greater boon to mankind. Serve with mustard and a pickled onion.

(Pictured overleaf...)

Steak Sandwich

So much in the world of steak is about display, luxury and status, and perhaps that's why nothing feels quite so decadent, quite so much like ultimate self-care than a quiet, solo steak sandwich. Sure, you can make one for someone you love very much, but as the eminent philosopher RuPaul clearly expressed it: 'If you don't love yourself, how in the hell you gonna love somebody else?'

I should begin by saying that almost any steak tastes great between a couple of slices of almost any bread, but there is a textural issue. Bread tears easily in the teeth, but steak has a strength and resilience that requires carnivorous tearing (on that note, how did the tyrannosauruses ever manage to get a steak up to their teeth with those tiny arms?), so the meat needs to be either sliced quite thinly or chopped into a multiplicity of chunks.

There are some time-tested models of 'steak in bread' that take this necessary slicing into consideration and which we should initially refer to. Perhaps the most obvious is the hamburger (see page 296). Yes, sure, it's minced (ground) meat and it has been debased in most of its many iterations, but you can't argue that the hamburger is one of the most popular and recognizable foods on the planet – and by the definitions of this book, it's a kind of steak sandwich.

The French dip is an American diner staple which, though it uses sliced roast beef rather than anything we might recognize as a steak, brings with it the astonishing innovation of a meat juice or gravy dip. For fans of British cuisine, the 'stottie cake' – a round, flat loaf from the North of England – offers a similar thing, as it is often enjoyed with a filling of roast beef and gravy. Both of these offer much for us to learn from.

In Philadelphia they have the Philly cheesesteak, which uses cheap steak, cut into finger-sized strips across the grain and browned on a hotplate. It's then combined with equal quantities of stewed onions and melted mystery cheese to create something that looks, frankly, like something that's passed through a dog. Served on a bun, however, it demonstrates much about the clever technique of using cheap cuts for flavour and making them more palatable by manipulation. It also captures and utilizes all the juices of the cooking process.

My favourite steak sandwich combines influences from all these, stealing freely. After some trial and error, I think I've found the ideal combination… at least for now.

As we've identified, a steak sandwich can be a challenging chew, so we should start by finding a suitable bread. Something with enough structural integrity to hold together. I find baguette too narrow to work with sizeable chunks of meat, but you're allowed to disagree. A ciabatta can work, as long as it has a functional crust that can hold it together if things get juicy. For me, however,

it's got to be sourdough – ideally one I can slice to the right sort of thickness (2cm/¾in). Grilling the bread on one side adds to the structural strength and, if you do this in a dry pan, you can leave the outside fabulously soft and fluffy. You can, if you wish, paint the bread with olive oil before you grill it and rub the grilled side with a couple of passes of a raw garlic. Very much a matter of personal taste.

As the steak is going to be cut into what one might term 'munchable' pieces, it's actually a good idea to choose one with longitudinal fibres. You could cook the whole steak as a piece, rest it and then cut it across to serve, but, actually, slicing ahead of cooking means that you'll have twice the surface area of meat and correspondingly double the area of Maillard reaction and crust. By cutting the steak across the grain into slices as wide as the thickness, you also completely transform its behaviour in the pan.

My favourite 'longitudinal' steak is the deckle (see page 110), but flank (at half the price) is just as much of a treat. You could possibly get away with rump cap, though I should warn that this might be moving into the realm of extreme jaw exercise.

With the larger surface area provided by slices, it would be almost criminal not to marinate the meat. My favourite marinade for a sandwich has evolved from the famous 'Bifé Ana' (a riff on the classic *bifana*) served at The Eagle, London's first gastropub. What's clever about it is that the marinade is strongly flavoured but also contains onions. Later, we'll see how that marinade has a superb double use.

The marinade needs a terrifyingly strong and tannic red wine. I used to buy cheap Rioja, until I discovered a shop near the station that was stocking Malbec in tins. They're perfect. They take the enamel off your teeth but they come in useful third-of-a-bottle portions and last forever in the larder.

It's a strong marinade, with a little acid in the form of balsamic vinegar. After it's done its overnight tenderizing job, it is reduced to create a sauce, which will take precisely as long as it takes the meat to rest beautifully. A small dollop of cream brings the sauce to the perfect consistency. Some people find this too much and you can easily leave it out, but for me it's the ideal final touch – partially lifted from the classic steak Diane. Any spare sauce can be served with the sandwich for dipping.

This recipe is a little bit 'extra', but it's not like you'll eat it every day and it tips its hat to so many brilliant traditions of steak cooking and so many classic recipes.

Serves 1

250ml (9fl oz) red wine

100ml (3½fl oz) olive oil

1 tsp balsamic vinegar

1 onion, thickly sliced

1 garlic clove, crushed, plus extra
   for the bread (optional)

3 tbsp dried oregano

Chilli (hot pepper) flakes, to taste

250g (9oz) deckle or flank steak

2 thick slices of white sourdough

1 tsp double cream or crème
   fraîche (optional)

Dijon mustard and/or horseradish
   sauce, to taste

4 leaves of Little Gem lettuce

Sea salt and freshly ground black
   pepper

Pour the wine and oil into a non-reactive bowl and add the balsamic vinegar, onion, garlic and oregano. Season with salt and pepper and chilli flakes.

Cut the steak into thick fingers across the grain and add to the marinade. Cover and leave to marinate overnight in the fridge.

The next day, heat a dry cast-iron frying pan over a high heat until it's as hot as you can get it, and sear one side of each slice of bread. Rub the seared side with a clove of garlic if you like.

Lift the meat out of the marinade and pat dry with paper towels, then sear on all sides in the hot pan, rolling and shaking to ensure an even char, until the a core reaches 54°C (129°F) on a probe thermometer. Remove from the pan and set aside to rest.

Pour the marinade and onions into the hot pan and scrape up any baked-on meat juices. Reduce the heat to a vigorous simmer and cook until everything is well reduced and the onions have softened. Add the cream, if using, and allow to bubble.

Toss the rested meat into the sauce along with any juices.

Spread the grilled sides of the bread with mustard or horseradish (I go for one of each), then spoon the meat and onions on top.

Add a little more of the sauce, spread over the lettuce leaves and nail on the lid with cocktail sticks. Serve with any leftover sauce for dipping.

The Berni Inn
Steak Dinner

The Berni Inn steakhouse dinner was such a key part of their development for so many contemporary food lovers that it needs to be honoured, so I've grouped together the recipes that it requires. For anyone who grew up in the UK, the menu doesn't need repeating but, for others… we start with a prawn cocktail. Chilled from the fridge, the prawns sweet, the lettuce crisp and the sauce… well, it's Marie Rose sauce and is very much unique to its time and location. The steak is a cheap cut that's been made the very best of and should be served with chips. To finish, you're going to want the BFG, the anglicized corruption of the Schwarzwälder Kirschtorte, the Black Forest Gateau.

If I remember correctly, the meal finished with a huge balloon of disgusting 'Cognac' and a slim panatella for the Gentleman and an 'Irish Coffee' for the Lady. There would have been complimentary mints… but honestly, I'm not sure I can stoop to that.

Prawn Cocktail

~

Steak and Chips

~

Black Forest Gateau

Prawn Cocktail

At its very simplest, the prawn (shrimp) cocktail comprises a handful of cold poached prawns tossed in Marie Rose sauce and usually served in some sort of cocktail glass on a bed of shredded iceberg lettuce. It looks classy, takes approximately eighteen seconds to produce and could well be the most lucrative thing ever to be sold in a restaurant. On that basic and utterly beguiling theme can be built a thousand glorious variations.

Unfortunately the prawns usually used for restaurant prawn cocktails are what's known as IQF – individually quick-frozen. The process involves steaming and mechanically peeling the prawns before rolling them around in a very powerful freezer while misting them with water. The benefit of this is that you can grab as many as you need, they defrost in minutes and then they're good to go, ready-chilled for service. They also, however, have absolutely every trace of flavour sucked out of them, which probably explains why they are subsequently dressed in the two bottled sauces guaranteed to make a flip-flop edible – mayo and ketchup.

As with many of the dishes we've ruined in restaurants, the original idea of a prawn cocktail is a lot more appetizing than the version we're left with. Freshly cooked prawns retain all their flavour of the sea and chilling them quickly enhances their gorgeous 'popping' texture. The sauce has all the umami and creaminess of a mayonnaise, but balances with a little sweetness, and chilled, shredded iceberg lettuce is the ideal medium to deliver the prawns. In fact, outside of a wedge salad with blue cheese dressing and crumbled smoky bacon sprinkles, the prawn cocktail is the only excuse for the existence of iceberg.

Steak and Chips

The chip arrives comparatively late in food history. The first recorded use of the word 'chip' to mean fried potatoes appears in Charles Dickens' *A Tale of Two Cities* (1859), when 'husky chips of potato, fried with some reluctant drops of oil' are described in a scene that takes place in a poor district of Paris (thus giving some credibility to the painful American nomenclature, 'French fries'). The dish soon became popular throughout Britain. There had obviously been fried potato preparations before, but this tantalizing combination of the new name with cheap ingredients to create a fast food for the poor is a key point in chip history.

By the 1920s, there were over 25,000 'chippies' in Britain, using an estimated 15 per cent of the national potato crop. Fish and chip shops took in raw potatoes, processed them in-house and passed them hot to the customer – making them, counterintuitively, some of the freshest food most urban dwellers would ever eat.

Today, it's rare for even a purpose-built chip shop to cook chips from raw, so pervasive is the infrastructure for peeling, cutting, blanching, blast-freezing and delivering to the back door of even the most expensive restaurants.

My great-grandfather had his name on the front of a chip shop on Kingsland Road in Bristol. In a fairer world, it wouldn't have been there. My great-grandmother inherited the place from her family, but it was the way of the world back then that they should put her husband's name over the door – John Chillcott, known as Jack. The building has been gone for decades now, and all we have is a single photograph of him, taken in 1913, blinking in the daylight outside the dark little emporium. My nan, his daughter, could still remember sitting up on the counter as a child, eating out of newspaper. She made the best chips I ever tasted – carefully chosen potatoes, washed, cut, mysteriously dried under a dish towel in the fridge, then fried twice in the 'chip pan'.

This was the bottom half of an old aluminium pressure cooker, the size of a bucket, with a wire basket which, to my appalled childish fascination, was usually set in a solid block of flecked ivory fat. I don't think a day ever passed when the chip pan wasn't used, so there was no need for anything as worryingly modern as refrigeration. The fat was boiled up every day and constantly replenished with more melted scraps, so it was a rich, characterful brew of dripping, lard, possibly butter, oils and any fat remaining from the daily breakfast bacon.

My own mum couldn't abide chips. She was of the generation of new women who wanted little to do with unhealthy, heavy, old-fashioned foods. Dad, meanwhile, a diligent young insurance loss adjuster, seemed to come home shellshocked from another chip-pan fire at least twice a week. These happened all the time, in family kitchens just like ours, when the hot fat boiled over, caught on the gas flame, ignited the 100 per cent man-made fibre net curtains and spread to the expanded polystyrene foam ceiling tiles.

Mum feared chips would eventually kill us all and Dad had actuarial figures proving it, so, when it happened – a small flare-up, quickly and correctly suppressed with a damp dish towel – Dad carried the pan straight to the bin. I must have been about eight years old when we became a chipless house and I had to skulk to Nan's for my regular fix. Nan always had chips ready. I never really understood why she kept them in the fridge, lined up on a baking sheet and covered with a clean cloth ('Souvenir of Brean Down') but I knew she fried them twice and that they were sublime. In hindsight, Nan's chips explain my entire life.

If we accept the proposition that the ideal chip is a combination of crisp exterior with fluffy interior, then the cutting of the potato becomes a key part of the process. A thick chip will have proportionally more inside material than surface. It will need longer to get fluffy in the middle but, if such things worry you, there will be proportionately fewer chips per serving and less fat adhering to the surface. The corners and edges of the chip will also brown faster than the flat surfaces (hence crinkle-cut chips). A thinner chip will have proportion-ally more 'edge' to 'flat'.[89] Thin chips, therefore, cook quicker and tend to be crisper. Finally, fatter chips hold their heat on the plate longer than thin ones. Only you can decide how fat you want your chips.

If you'd asked Nan about the dry matter content of potato varieties, she'd have thought you'd lost your marbles, yet, back in the 1970s, she had standing instructions to all her local greengrocers to get her Maris Piper potatoes whenever available.

When you run a chip shop, you can sell all the odd little weird-sized ends of potatoes to drunks at the end of the evening, but when you're making chips for your grandson, it's important that they're all regularly cooked. My nan sliced by hand and discarded any chips that didn't have four clear, flat sides. To make this easier, choose potatoes as close to the same size as possible. Don't bother peeling them, but cut a slice off one long side of each potato so they stand on the table without rolling. Now cut the 'sides' off each potato and the 'top' and you'll be left with square sections of potato flesh with a little skin on either end.

Starting with the smallest potato, cut the ends square, removing as much skin as possible and trimming all the other potatoes to the same length. Pare any remaining corners with a vegetable peeler.

---

[89] If this sounds familiar, it's because it's similar to the logic we applied to cutting and cooking steaks (see pages 128–9). Different shapes offer different surface-to-volume ratios, affecting cooking times and eventual flavours.

Cut the potatoes into thick slices vertically, then lay the slices flat and cut them into chips, keeping as close to a regular-sized, square cross-section as you can.

My nan would then wash the chips carefully, rubbing them in cold water. After this she would spread them out on a baking sheet and transfer them to the fridge to dry. Laid out in rows, they were as pale and chubby as my little fingers.

She fried her chips twice, just like they had in her dad's chip shop. Once at a low temperature to 'blanch' them and a second time to crisp them up for serving. Chefs today take chip cooking a stage further: theirs are steamed to just short of al dente before the first fry. 'Triple cooking' is a high-risk strategy as some chips won't survive the first stage. Chips that are cut fatter to begin with have a better chance. The survivors are carefully dried in the fridge, then blanched at 140°C (275°F) in vegetable oil, cooled again in the fridge, then finished at 185°C (365°F) to brown and crisp.

By now, almost everyone in the UK is used to the great, hench triple-cooked chips that have become the staple at gastropubs and steakhouses. These things are so completely different to the 'fries' that we've also become used to via fast food chains that many good restaurants now offer both styles.

The fries used in the hospitality industry are delicious, but they're an industrially manufactured product. You can try all you like to carve your potatoes down to the right thickness and fiddle with times and temperatures but you're never going to get that Proustian hit unless you do exactly what every restaurant does, from McDonald's to Gordon Ramsay, and grab a bag from the freezer.[90]

McCain has been making chips in the UK for fifty years.[91] In the UK, they're based in Scarborough, where they're investing 100 million pounds in rebuilding their biggest factory. It's fair to say that they make a lot of chips, processing over 15 per cent of our national potato harvest.[92] In a world where domestic deep-fat frying seems to be on the wane, their frozen oven chips have taken over. McCain Home Chips have been the nation's most popular frozen chip since their launch in 1997. They can be found in 27 per cent of UK households and feature in 408 million British meals every year.

On the face of it, nothing could seem further from Nan's chip-pan chips or triple-cooked beef-dripping gastropub chips, so when I called them to ask about their recipes, I was a little wary. I think I was expecting spectacular science, some impressive kit and quite possibly a machine that extruded processed potato paste into tanks of boiling oil. I wanted the full, ghastly details.

---

[90] I love big, gourmet chips with steak and I love a pile of crisp fries with steak, too, but the idea of proper chip shop chips with steak just doesn't work. I was worried it was just me, so I asked my daughter. 'Ach no! Fuck off!' was her answer. It's obviously genetic.

[91] Although actually a Canadian company…

[92] The same percentage of the crop that all the chippies in Britain were using in the 1920s.

'Every oven chip is made from a whole potato, just like you would make it at home,' said Naomi Tinkler, category controller at McCain. This was, to be honest, a bit disappointing.

'We're sourcing the very best-quality potatoes from British growers, some of whom we have worked with for three generations. We use twelve different varieties, including Maris Piper potatoes, for oven chips and continually adjust our recipes to take into account the time of year,' she continued.

So far, so artisanal. But we're talking about the largest manufacturer of potato products in the UK here. With a multitude of variations in shape and packaging, they serve multinational brands, independent operators, pubs and restaurants, hospitals, universities, prisons, Michelin-star restaurants and the military. I reckon if you eat chips more than three times in a year, you are bound to enjoy some that come from their factory.

'Once the potatoes arrive, we take a sample to check the quality, then they're unloaded on to a conveyor belt, washed and then whizzed through a high-pressure steam peeler,' Naomi tells me. 'Then they go through our high-tech cutting system – very sharp blades that ensure the smoothest cut. We again inspect them, and then water-blanch to give the fluffy internal texture.'

I'm still waiting for the lasers and plasma furnaces…

'They're dried, cooked in sunflower oil and then shaken on a vibrating conveyor belt to remove any excess oil. Finally, the chips are packed and sent to the quality control at the end of the line. They're made just like you would make chips at home,' said Tinkler. 'Washed, peeled, cut, lightly cooked in oil and then frozen, ready to be finished in your oven.'

So that's it. Two ingredients: potatoes and oil. With only the addition of a hundred million quid's worth of equipment, it was a process remarkably similar to my nan's. Could my family sue them for millions?

It's up to you, then. Follow my method for my nan's chips or pick up a bag of McCain's fries and create whatever your own perfect steak and chips might be, whether that's a mighty chateaubriand with peppercorn sauce, creamed spinach and thick wedges of fluffy potato, or a perfect French bistro-inspired *steak frites*, with a minute steak and crisp fries.

Me? I'll take both.

Serves 1

3–4 Maris Piper potatoes, all
  a similar size and shape
Vegetable oil, for deep frying
1 x 2cm (¾in) rib eye steak
Knob of butter
1 thyme sprig
1 garlic clove
Sea salt

Cut a slice off one long side of a potato and place it cut-side down on the chopping board. Now cut away the other two long sides, then rotate and slice off the 'top'. Slice both ends off and you should be left with a potato cuboid. Pare any remaining visible skin with a vegetable peeler.

Cut the potatoes into thick slices vertically, then lay the slices flat and cut them into chips, keeping as close to a regular-sized, square cross-section as you can.

Place the chips in a large bowl and rinse them in cold water, rubbing them gently. Drain and place the chips in neat rows on a baking sheet lined with kitchen paper or a clean tea towel. Slide into the fridge to dry overnight, uncovered.

Season the meat all over with salt and place on a wire rack set over a tray. Transfer to the fridge to rest overnight, uncovered next to the chips.

The next day, fill a large, deep pan with vegetable oil no more than two-thirds up the sides of the pan. Heat the oil to 165°C (330°F) on a temperature probe, then fry the chips until just barely changed in colour. Remove from the oil with a slotted spoon and drain the chips on a rack.

Heat a dry cast-iron frying pan over a high heat until it's as hot as you can get it, then sear the steak on both sides. Use a probe thermometer to check the internal temperature and, just before it reaches 56°C (133°F), add the butter, thyme and garlic and baste the steak for a final minute. Remove from the pan and set it aside to rest.

While the steak is resting, increase the temperature of the oil to 185°C (365°F). Add the chips back to the pan and fry until golden, or to your liking. Remove from the oil and toss in salt.

Black Forest Gateau

The recipe for the authentic Schwarzwälder Kirschtorte is, quite rightly, defended by the noble bakers of Baden-Württemberg. It is a glorious confection, light,
creamy and generously soaked with their local sour cherry brandy, kirschwasser.
The Black Forest Gateau of a British Steakhouse in the 1970s was a no less
glorious thing, but adapted for expediency and local tastes. Although BFG looks
like it's been lovingly prepared by a craftsman confectioner, it actually comprises
moist chocolate cake… which can be baked in industrial-sized trays and has a
long fridge life. The cherries come in a jar or a can and the cream can be aerosol
whipped. A good soaking in booze and the syrup the cherries came in will bring
the whole thing together and chocolate, grated over the top will make everything
look classy. It's another of those wonderful 'Chef's Shortcuts'.

Of course… if you're an eight-year-old, being taken for his one 'meal out' in
the year and you're sitting at a big table in a twinkly room with Mum and Dad in
their best finery… it's also the most unbelievably spectacular and memorable
thing a larval foodie's mind could encompass. I'd like to think my tastes have
refined since then, but no. Stick a big plate of BFG in front of me and I'm
transported straight back.

Serves 6–8

For the sponge
260g (9oz) plain (all-purpose) flour
260g (9oz) caster (superfine) sugar
100g (3½oz) light brown soft sugar
50g (2oz) cocoa powder
1½ tsp baking powder
¾ tsp bicarbonate of soda (baking
  soda)
¼ tsp salt
150g (5½oz) sunflower oil
90g (3oz) warm water
90g (3oz) buttermilk
3 eggs
1½ tsp vanilla extract

For assembly
2 jars 'Luxardo' Maraschino cocktail
  cherries, including syrup
  (about 800g/1½lb total weight)
750g (1lb 6oz) double (heavy)
  cream
200g (7oz) dark chocolate

Preheat the oven to 180°C (350°F/gas 4). Grease and line the
bases of two deep, round, 18cm (7in) cake pans.

In a large bowl, combine the flour, sugars, cocoa powder, baking
powder, bicarbonate and salt. In another bowl or jug, combine the oil,
water, buttermilk, eggs and vanilla extract. Mix well, then pour into
the dry ingredients and stir until you have a smooth batter.

Split the mixture between the two pans and then bake the sponges
for 25–30 minutes until a skewer comes out clean (or use your probe
thermometer – it should read 98°C/208°F for sponge perfection).
Allow the cakes to cool completely in the pans before turning out.

Cut each sponge horizontally into two even layers, to give you four
sponge layers (and remove any 'doming' if you have secret ambitions
to go on *Bake Off*). In a large bowl, whip the cream to soft peaks.

Place a sponge layer on a serving plate and drizzle with a quarter
of the syrup from the cherries. Pipe or dollop on a quarter of the
whipped cream, then dot over a quarter of the cherries, ensuring a
few of them will be visible at the edges of the cake.

Repeat until you have four layers – it's worth being a bit more careful
about placement on the top layer to ensure the gateau looks its best.
Finish with a good grating of dark chocolate.

HAWKSMOOR,
LONDON,
ENGLAND

As I've worked my way through this project, it's become increasingly apparent that one of the most important strands in the steak story is the steakhouse. No … it's more than that. The steakhouse is where the whole myth built, grew and expanded. Our steak culture comes from steakhouses. So it seemed appropriate for my last personal adventure into steak to be lunch with Huw Gott and Will Beckett.

They are the founders of Hawksmoor, a group of steakhouses that they grew from scratch, starting in London at the beginning of the British food renaissance in 2006 but now with outposts in New York and Chicago. Few people have spent quite as much time immersed in steak, steakhouses and what they mean today and in the future.

We met for lunch at a branch just off Regent Street in Central London. You could stagger there from Piccadilly Circus in under a minute. It's a beautiful dining room in Art Deco style up a flight of sweeping stairs that wouldn't look out of place in an old Hollywood musical, the sort of room they don't build anymore. The place is quiet as we meet and we take a booth in the back of the dining room.

'I think the Berni Inn probably played as much a part in Hawksmoor as the hallowed steakhouses of New York. Will and I grew up in St Alban's – we were a couple of streets apart – and there was a Berni Inn in The George or The Feathers or something. A really nice old Tudor building where we went occasionally to mark special occasions. I remember having a sip of my grandmother's Irish coffee there.'

What I really want to know is what possessed them to start this exercise. Back in 2006, the British restaurant industry was taking off on a dizzying climb, but steak-and-chips still felt like what we were trying to escape. Steak was what old men ordered, not adventurous new 'foodies'. Yet, after cutting their teeth in a pub, and then an experimental Mexican restaurant, Huw and Will took over a grotty abandoned Turkish restaurant in the then yet-to-be-fashionable Shoreditch, and started grilling meat.

'It was definitely meant to be all about steak. Even now, when we serve a steak on a plate, I think: it's just beef, salt, charcoal … that's all. There's no garnish or sauce or anything around it. Going back to that first room, it felt a bit like that. Perhaps over time, the design has developed and we've grown to enjoy that side of things more, but at heart, it's still just a steak on a plate.'

'Before we got started, we used to ask people, what's your best steak restaurant? And, more specifically, can you remember the first time you were taken there? Can you remember the first time that you paid for the table? And the answer is almost always yes. I can't remember the first time I paid for the table in a French or an Italian restaurant, but I remember the first time I picked up a check for the table in Berni's. That kind of thing really resonates. I've heard people say, "When I turned 16 or 18, my dad took me to a steakhouse." It marks phases of life. It's woven into our culture, the steakhouse as a kind of rite of passage.'

'Someone said to me once: "Oh, yes, 'steak restaurant' is a cheat code for fine dining."'

I love this idea. It seems so clear to me that, throughout our history with steak – sometimes implicitly, sometimes explicitly – it's been all about balancing worlds. Taking the agreed trappings of wealth and luxury, but making them freely available to all. Hawksmoor could easily have gone upscale, foie gras starters and gold leaf on the steaks…

'… but Hawksmoor was never intended to be fine dining. It was the opposite of that. I remember Tim [Chief Operating Officer now, but assistant general manager of the first Hawksmoor restaurant] wore basketball shorts. And his now wife, who was a waitress, wore a fairly loose vest. And they were banging out steaks like it was supposed to be. Fun and accessible. Steakhouses as cheat codes for fine dining? Maybe partly, but partly I think the good – the really good ones – are democratic.'

Huw orders a gigantic steak pie. And we get a porterhouse for the table to share, with anchovy hollandaise on the side. I'm intrigued to know precisely how they cook the meat and Will explains how the original ocakbası grill from the Turkish restaurant has followed them around. They've had a new one made for each restaurant, growing a little in size each time.

Huw won't accept that the kitchen is high-tech: 'the guys come in, in the morning, fill the grill with charcoal and light it. We're so technologically advanced that in the original kitchen they've got a little circular holster thing that holds a hairdryer that they buy every month from Argos when the last one breaks down or melts.'

I've got to admit, that sounds like a pretty lo-fi way to be starting your fires, but Will also talks me through The Thermodyne. This is a piece of American kit: a highly controllable electric holding cabinet with drawers that can be set to temperatures accurate to the degree. Lots of steak restaurants use these to hold steaks at 56°C (133°F) throughout service so they can be finished on the grill. At Hawksmoor, he explains, they sear the steaks first and then hold them at temperature.

I'm obviously fascinated by this. In fact, I spent the next day on the phone to Thermodyne, talking through the process. Perhaps unsurprisingly, they love Hawksmoor, but they're most excited by the way they've chosen to use the kit. The longer, gentler 'hold' keeps the steak in an absolutely premium state but also gives it much longer for fats and juices to render and for the 'cuisson' to stabilize.

Our porterhouse really shows it. The surface of the meat is dark and burnished, but there's no carbonized char. This has been a considered and relaxed process. The interior, as I'd expect from their grass-reared beasts, is strongly beefy in flavour and would be robustly textured had the long holding not given the fibres time to gently separate. I'm not sure I can work out a way to fake up the Thermodyne effect in my own kitchen – no domestic kit is that accurate – but, I promise myself, I'm sure as hell going to give it a go.

There are 13 Hawksmoors now across the British Isles and the US and if you ask most people to recall them, they'd say there was a coherent, Central Casting steakhouse look about them. Closer examination shows that every one is different. They've chosen venues with a kind of gravitas to them: old banking halls, a Victorian courthouse, a nineteenth-century brewery cellar and this spectacular, purpose-built 1930s restaurant, but each interior is completely unique. They've deliberately avoided any overweening corporate design aesthetic in favour of a kind of consensus on how a steakhouse should look: antique restaurant fittings in the Liverpool branch, panelling at the Guildhall made of old doors recycled from a London Museum.

Will understates it: 'We kind of wanted to create the idea of something that's been around for a long time, which I think is very difficult to recreate, but my favourite comment just after opening was when someone walked in and said – you haven't done anything! Why haven't you done anything with the interior?'

With Hawksmoor opening in New York and Chicago, I wondered if there was a strand of 'Britishness' in their design aesthetic.

'It goes back to the old chop houses. I mean, not just steak, but steakhouses come from us, right? Obviously, in part because of our postwar food history. So, yes, Britishness. I think that's definitely part of it.'

Hawksmoor, its food, its ethos and its design is a remarkable exercise in semiotics, but it's also testament to the sheer weight of collective expectation and belief in what makes a steakhouse.

The Perfect Martini

There's a strong case for good red wine being the perfect accompaniment to steak. There's also historical precedent for various beers, ales and stouts. My argument, however, is that even if you don't drink a martini with your steak, you ought to have one in very close temporal proximity. It's a bit of a harder sell than the wine and beer, as it's not that a martini particularly tastes good with steak. You could argue, perhaps, that ferociously chilled clear spirits can clear the palate of fats and rinse away the irony flavour notes of blood and meat juices, but those are mere physical effects and, besides, they'd require you to drink the martini after the steak and that would be the act of a barbarian. No. The truth is that a martini is one of the few things a human can consume that is as laden with lore, myth and symbolism as a steak is and is thus the only drink that can stand up to it in a philosophical and emotional sense.

A martini is also as simple as a steak; as blatantly and directly functional. It is so simple that it should be impossible to screw up, but that doesn't stop millions of people doing it every year. It's just gin and vermouth, mixed and made very cold. Nobody should be able to mess that up, and yet...

Gin is a high-proof white alcohol that can be made from almost anything. Gin, and indeed vodka, can be made from corn, potatoes, barley, wheat or pretty much any vegetation that produces starch or sugar. The process involves the reduction of starch into sugar, then the fermentation of sugar into alcohol and then finally distillation to a high degree of purity. It doesn't matter what is used because the original material is entirely changed by the process. Vodka is just pure alcohol with added water and gin is pure alcohol with water and some additional aromatics, one of which must be juniper. The Dutch were the makers of the original gin and *jenever* is Dutch for juniper.

The only other ingredient in a martini is a splash of vermouth. Vermouth is a class of fortified wine flavoured with lots of aromatics. First produced in Italy, they were patented mixtures, often made by religious orders. But they were too good not to spread throughout Europe. Vermouth is the French pronunciation of *vermut*, which is German for wormwood. The defining characteristic of a vermouth is that it should contain wormwood, a strong bittering agent.

The martini was first mixed in San Francisco, reputedly around the time of prohibition. It's named after the Martinez Hotel, where it was invented. Gin was pretty rough at the time but never less than effective, so the barmen served it as cold as they could, to mitigate its harsh flavour, and added vermouth, which was bitter and distracting. It was probably the cheapest thing in the bar, but it was still added in very small quantities.[93]

---

[93] It's generally agreed that the proportions of the original martini were around 7-1 gin to vermouth.

In truth, then, the martini was never about taste; it was always about effect. Martinis have a very steep learning curve. Nobody can claim to 'like' their first martini, but only an insensitive oaf is not entirely in love by their third. It is an acquired taste, but one that's actually worth acquiring. My favourite slang term for a cocktail is not a 'livener', a 'stiffener' or a 'reviver', it's an 'attitude adjuster'. At the end of a long day, when you've just received bad news, even when you're setting yourself up for an evening ahead, the martini jolts your attitude out of its track and onto another, more agreeable, set of rails. It doesn't have to taste good – it has to do its job with brutal efficiency.[94]

Today, we seem to have entered a new gin age. Every hipster with a brand strategy has 'created' a gin with their own carefully curated recipe of outré aromatics. They've made up stories about finding their grandfather's recipes or travelling the world in search of the wildest of scents, but in reality they are just gilding a perfectly lovely lily. I don't need my gin to smell like perfume; I need just enough smell of juniper to tell me it's not vodka. I favour an authentically robust and uncomplicated gin. Surprisingly, the generic stuff on the rail at the bar is probably OK, but for safety I usually go for Tanqueray Export, which I'm pretty sure Dorothy would have enjoyed.

We are also, suddenly, importing hundreds of vermouths. Sweet ones, dry ones, red ones and white ones. Spanish, Czech and Hungarian variants with origin myths stretching back into an entirely imagined history. With each, the unique flavour twist that makes the brand stand out from its competitors is precisely what's going to fuck up my martini. Even in homeopathic amounts, a fashionably curated vermouth can turn my attitude adjuster into a cheap air-freshener. There are more myths about the dryness of a martini[95] than we have space for here. Of course, it should be dry, but there's no shame in liking a little more vermouth.

I don't mind if you shake or stir. There's a gigantic amount of rubbish talked about which is correct, but both will do the job of chilling the mixture – though, to be honest, you should really have kept your gin in the freezer anyway. Shaking and stirring both mean a certain amount of the ice will melt into the drink, watering down the booze. If that's how you like it, knock yourself out.

A martini is one of the few cocktails that doesn't object to being made in advance and in quantity. Guests should always be indulged, so I'm happy to play along and custom-build any number of martinis to individual requirements – I even made an ex-friend a vodka martini once – but if I'm among people who really trust me, I'll make up the mix in advance, freeze it for at least 24 hours and then serve it from a bottle frozen into an ice block (if I'm being flash) or my dad's old Thermos. This arrangement conforms perfectly to the only rules that matter in martini drinking: they should be immediately available, in quantity, as strong as possible and very, very cold.

---

[94] Everyone I ever idolized knew this. Dorothy Parker, Ernest Hemingway, Hunter Thompson, Joan Didion, Dean Martin, Errol Flynn, Evelyn Waugh, Ava Gardner, Chandler and Hamnett and Tony Bourdain all took martinis like others took drugs.

[95] This is basically how little vermouth you can get into the mixture. My favourite is that you should fill a jug with ice and gin, stir it then lean over it and whisper the word 'Vermouth' once. But I have a friend who loads a shaker with frozen gin and just points it toward Italy.

Tl
Trimr

ne
hings

The Steakhouse Kitchen

Consider for a moment how a traditional steakhouse works. Unlike a full-scale restaurant kitchen, it has a limited repertoire. The grill chef will be the lead individual, simply searing pieces of meat. Accompaniments must be simple: chips, mash or baked potatoes are the usual go-tos. There will be simple vegetables, prepared in advance, and everything else will come from a well-stocked mise-en-place. Compound butters can be made well in advance and sauces have usually evolved to be either recipes that can be made in advance and held, like béarnaise, or which can be finished quickly in the pan, like Madeira, poivre or bordelaise.

These are the best flavours to accompany steaks – simple and robust – but it's important to understand that the repertoire has evolved from the mechanics, even the limitations, of the steakhouse kitchen.

Serving great steak at home invariably means trying to replicate some of the conditions, ingredients and preparations of the traditional steakhouse. But fortunately, the same logic – advance preparation, enabling a focus on the meat and then finishing the dish while it rests – serves the home cook equally well.

Another thing you can be sure of at a steakhouse is a lot of spare beef trim, bones, fat and leftovers – and probably a fair bit of red wine. These are all by-products of a busy restaurant, so it's not surprising that so many of the best sauces rely heavily on beef stock or its better-developed offspring, demi-glace.

Café de Paris Butter

Café de Paris butter is one of those recipes that doesn't have to be adhered to as holy writ but is instead a piece of restaurant cooking history. The Café de Paris was a nightclub on the edge of Leicester Square in London, which, when it opened in 1924, was a glamorous hub of theatreland. It was a place to be seen and not a venue famed for phenomenal cooking. The butter that carries the restaurant's name is not an elegant composition designed to display the skills of a brilliant chef, but rather an expedient use of the ingredients of a well-provided mise-en-place, combined to create a stimulus for appetites jaded by cocktails and cigarettes, or distracted by the glamour and wit of one's dining partner. I probably wouldn't use this butter on an extremely high-quality steak simply because, though it lubricates beautifully, it tends to stamp any subtle flavour out of existence. As you eat it you come to understand that the chefs at the Café de Paris were pretty damn clever. They must have realized that the glittering *jeunesse dorée* – the cocaine-dusted flappers and the cigar-smoking lounge lizards – might not have been the most discerning crowd and that 'CdeP' could make an average steak into an easy crowd-pleaser.

Vary this recipe as much as you like. The ingredients towards the top of the ingredients list add saltiness, sweetness, umami and that all-important lubricating richness. The stuff further down is easier to substitute. I would recommend you keep the curry powder in, though. No half-decent cook would use the stuff to make curry any more but it's the powdered essence of London gentleman's clubs and adds a wonderful sub-note of rakishness.[96]

Makes about 300g (10½oz)

2 anchovy fillets (the canned oily
  type)
1 garlic clove
250g (9oz) butter, softened
30g (1oz) tomato ketchup
1 tbsp English mustard
10g (¼oz) salted nonpareille
  capers, very finely chopped
1 shallot, very finely chopped
1 tbsp lemon juice
1 tbsp Worcestershire sauce
1 bunch parsley, leaves chopped
1 thyme sprig, leaves chopped
3 tarragon sprigs, leaves chopped
1 tsp ground black pepper
Zest of 1 lemon
Pinch of sweet paprika
Pinch of Madras curry powder
Pinch of cayenne pepper

Mash the anchovies and garlic to a paste with the side of a knife.

Put the butter into a bowl and add the anchovy and garlic paste along with all the remaining ingredients. Using a silicone spatula, beat the ingredients into the butter until completely homogenous.

Scrape the butter onto a piece of greaseproof paper, then roll it into a neat log and refrigerate or freeze.

(Pictured overleaf…)

---

[96] Café de Paris butter is also claimed by a restaurant of that name in Geneva. As it's a peculiarly undistinguished concoction, make of this information what you will.

Anchovy Butter

It seems quite recent that we've accepted the notion of fish flavours as an accompaniment to meat. Many cite the 'discovery' of the fish sauce used in all sorts of East Asian cuisine. But in fact the Romans were hot on garum, a sauce made from fermented fish. Anchovies feature in old French and Italian recipes for lamb and are a constituent ingredient in Worcestershire sauce, in which we've been drenching meat for hundreds of years. In fact, it may seem that any perceived objection to combining meat and fish might have been a momentary squeamish aberration. Whatever the cause, we were wrong and anchovy butter is an absolutely unbeatable relish for a good steak.

Makes about 300g (10½oz)

2 cans or jars of average-quality
   anchovy fillets in oil, drained
125g (4½oz) unsalted butter,
   softened
Zest of 1 lemon
Nutmeg, to taste
Black pepper, to taste

Very finely chop the anchovies, then grind them to a paste with the edge of a knife.

Put the butter into a bowl and add the anchovies and lemon zest. Using a silicone spatula, beat the ingredients into the butter until well combined, then season to taste with nutmeg and black pepper.

Scrape the butter onto a piece of greaseproof paper, then roll it into a neat log. Refrigerate for 3 days to allow the flavours to develop before freezing. (*Pictured on pages 268–9.*)

Maître d'Hotel Butter

Maître d'hôtel is a simple, classic, compound butter that works equally well with other meats, fish or vegetables.

Makes about 300g (10½oz)

250g (9oz) butter, softened
Bunch of curly parsley, leaves
   picked and finely chopped
Zest and juice of 1 lemon
2 garlic cloves
Freshly ground black pepper

Put the butter into a bowl. Grate in the garlic and lemon zest, Then add the juice of the lemon, parsley and a few grinds of black pepper.

Using a silicone spatula, beat the ingredients into the butter until well combined.

Scrape the butter onto a piece of greaseproof paper, then roll it into a neat log. Refrigerate overnight to allow the flavours to develop before freezing. (*Pictured on pages 268–9.*)

A Note on Other Butters

The method for compound butters is easily repeatable. They're great to have around and easy to go off piste with. Four that I've personally found extremely interesting with steak are: chilli crisp, sriracha, truffle (grated or paste) and espresso. Simply beat a spoonful of your chosen flavouring into 250g (9oz) softened butter (adjusting to taste) and shape and wrap as above.

Demi-glace

Demi-glace (short for *demi-glaçage*) or 'half glaze' is one of the secret weapons of a classic restaurant's mise-en-place. The good stuff is a thick, smooth gloop, more set even than the usual 'jelly' of stock. It will have been built up with a more developed flavour than stock, too, to the extent that a spoonful of it, let down with some hot liquid, will make a sauce or gravy all by itself. It only needs some pan drippings or maybe some kind of alcohol to be made into any one of a dozen magnificent classic sauces. 'Demi' or 'DG' is not usually found in domestic kitchens, but it's not too complicated to make a simple version at home.

If you're cooking steak, you're going to be concentrating on getting the meat right, so finishing a complex sauce is often out of the question. This means that a good demi-glace, which has had half the work done to it already, is a key element in many of the most respected and loved steak presentations.

The sauce is attributed to Auguste Escoffier, but then again, most things are. I'm sure that similar sauce concentrate shortcuts existed long before the great man donned his toque. But it's Escoffier's recipe, part of the grand interlocking brilliance of his method,[97] that has come to be regarded as the ideal. As far as he was concerned, demi-glace was made by combining one of the basic 'mother' sauces, espagnole, with an equal quantity of veal-rich stock and then reducing the mixture by half.[98]

Espagnole (or 'Spanish') sauce is made from a mirepoix of vegetables and tomatoes, which are browned and then simmered with stock before being thickened with roux, seasoned with herbs and reduced. By itself, it's a great sauce and, with additions, it can be turned into sauces included bigarade, bourguignonne, chasseur, financière and Robert.

Making demi-glace this way takes bloody ages, is fiddly and complicated and requires the kind of bulk of ingredients and large-scale kit that means only the really old-school restaurant kitchens can even dream of making it from scratch these days. Fortunately, there are shortcuts.

I asked my mate Victor Garvey – who's the sort of starred chef who makes 100 litres of 'DG' in his kitchen every week – what he does at home. In his

---

[97] Escoffier's method was brilliantly adapted to the large professional kitchens of the day. A huge number of sub-recipes, tips and tricks could be assembled to make a vast repertoire of finished dishes. A recipe for a historically significant dish was often just a few brief instructions, combining other recipes and adding new ingredients here and there. A modern website designer would recognize the economy of content of the constant cross-linking and internal references.
[98] The first recipe for sauce espagnole was written by French royal chef Marie-Antoine (or Antonin) Carême in the early nineteenth century. Escoffier named it as one of the 'mother' sauces in his system.

(Continued overleaf…)

bones are hard to come by in any quantity, we use more unorthodox methods to achieve the gelatinousness of the traditional stock.

In a strictly traditional kitchen, the wines would be varied depending on the eventual use of the demi-glace but ours is going to have to be more general purpose. I usually go for an inexpensive, easy-drinking red.

The beef stock doesn't need to be something you've spent weeks building and reducing yourself, just the ready-made stuff from the supermarket. Not a stock cube, jelly or canned consommé, though, as there are too many additives in those. I use the plastic pouches.

For some reason, very little collagen or gelatine makes it through the process of commercial stock production. To get that silky mouthfeel into our speedy DG, we'll use xanthan gum. This is a neutral thickening agent used in food manufacture and should be a secret weapon in your cupboard, just as it is for a huge number of professional chefs. You need only a very small amount, whipped into a hot or cold liquid, to thicken something as well as a roux would but without the flouriness or added fat. You won't see the full effect until at least a minute after you've added the xanthan, so wait for two before considering whether to add more.

It's important to keep tasting throughout the cooking. You're after something like strong Bovril or a really intense roast beef gravy. Resist the temptation to add salt to improve it. You can add salt at the very end if you wish, but this is always going to be something you add to other liquids to create sauces so should really only be adjusted just before serving.

Demi-glace will keep for a couple of weeks in a sealed jar in the fridge and can also be conveniently frozen in Ziploc bags. If you freeze these flat, they take up little space in the freezer and you can snap off pieces easily whenever needed.

Makes 800ml–1 litre (24–35fl oz)

1 thyme sprig
1 rosemary sprig
1 bay leaf
½ star anise (optional)
10 black peppercorns
750ml (25fl oz) red wine
1 shallot, roughly chopped
2 litres (4 pints) beef stock
1.25g (pinch) xanthan gum
Sea salt and freshly ground black pepper

Wrap the herbs and spices in a piece of muslin (cheesecloth).

Put the wine, shallot and the muslin-wrapped aromatics into a saucepan and reduce to 100ml (3¼fl oz).

Add the beef stock and reduce to 1 litre (35fl oz). This makes a mathematically correct demi-glace, but, personally, I prefer to reduce mine to about 700ml (24fl oz), making it closer to a *tiers de glaçage*. This offers a really punchy flavour, and you can always dilute it later.

Adjust the seasoning if necessary and then pass the sauce through a sieve while warm.

Transfer back into a pan and whisk in the xanthan gum. Wait at least 2 minutes before deciding whether to add more. You want it to be a pourable or spoonable consistency. (*Pictured overleaf…*)

Madeira Sauce

Once you have some demi-glace in your freezer, Madeira sauce – one of the most traditional steak sauces – becomes an absolute breeze to make. It uses a simple deglazing technique to capture the pan drippings and juices from the meat. This is a useful technique that you can use in lots of other dishes.

Madeira is a fortified wine with a distinctive taste that is sweet, caramel-like, dark and even a bit nutty so, unlike the usual sauce routine in which you boil hard to drive off the alcohol, this process should be a little gentler. You want to preserve the character of the wine – a good Madeira sauce should remain just a little 'boozy'.

Makes about 225ml (8fl oz)

50ml (1¾fl oz) water
100ml (3½fl oz) Madeira
100ml (3½fl oz) Demi-glace
  (opposite)
20g (¾oz) butter, cubed

After cooking a steak, remove it from the pan and pour the water into the hot pan without wiping it out. As the water boils, scrape up all the brown bits on the bottom of the pan. I use a wire whisk for this.

Add the Madeira and continue whisking. Bring everything to a simmer and start sniffing. You should be able to detect the most volatile alcohol boiling off. As soon as it has, add the demi-glace. Once it comes back up to a simmer, take the pan off the heat and whisk in the butter.

When you slice the steak, save any juices and whip them back into the sauce before serving.

(Pictured overleaf...)

Demi-glace
(see page 271)

Madeira Sauce
(see page 273)

Blue Cheese Sauce
(see page 283)

Poivre Sauce
(see page 277)

Bordelaise Sauce
(see page 276)

Béarnaise Sauce
(see page 282)

Bordelaise Sauce

Bordelaise is the sauce of the Bordeaux wine region, and its big claret energy makes it a hoary old favourite of traditional steakhouses. Traditionally, this would be made with a demi-glace that used Bordeaux wine in its base.

The other key ingredient that makes it a bordelaise is bone marrow.[99] You'll occasionally see split marrow bones at your butcher's. Preparing them is easy and the marrow freezes extremely well, so it's worth making a little batch so you've got some in the freezer, next to your demi-glace, ready to make a fast and sophisticated sauce.

To do this, find a couple of bones that have been split vertically and carefully brush away any bone chips or dust. Lift the marrow out in one piece and then slice it into 0.5cm (¼in) cubes.

Drop the cubes into a saucepan of simmering salted water and blanch for 30 seconds, then remove them with a slotted spoon and drain on paper towels.

Lay them out, carefully separated, on a baking sheet lined with greaseproof paper and freeze them. Once they're solid they can be stored in a bag so you can grab a handful to finish a bordelaise at any time.

Makes about 500ml (18fl oz)

*375ml (12½fl oz) Bordeaux red
  wine*
1 shallot, roughly chopped
*200ml (7fl oz) Demi-glace (see
  page 271)*
*75g (2½oz) blanched bone
  marrow, cubed (fresh or frozen)*

Pour the wine into a small saucepan, add the shallots and reduce by two-thirds.

Add the demi-glace and bring to a gentle simmer.

Add the bone marrow and simmer gently for a further 5 minutes to warm through.

Serve in a warmed sauce boat.

(Pictured on pages 274–5.)

---

[99] There's a very similar sauce called marchand de vin which leaves out the bone marrow.

Poivre Sauce

To my mind, this is the best of all the traditional steakhouse sauces. Although it's well known around the world, it doesn't seem to have any deeper roots outside the steakhouse world, which is probably the reason it's my favourite.

In the UK and the US, we grind black pepper over almost anything as a seasoning, and most of the time we don't give it much thought, but pepper actually has a very strong and distinctive fragrance alongside the slightly nutty heat that we've come to expect. In British cooking, we use white pepper in traditional sausages, pork pies and pasties, often accompanied by mace, to give that unique British butchery flavour profile, but the expensive black stuff rarely gets the same attention.

Whole black peppercorns, in heftier amounts than we usually use, offer a superb flavour, slightly reminiscent of allspice but far cleaner and more punchy. There's even a slightly citrus bite to it.

You can use any black peppercorns, but Wayanad or Pondicherry peppercorns, though expensive, provide a lot more fragrance in fewer corns. Green peppercorns usually come pickled or brined in cans or jars and they can be used, too.[100] Red (not pink) peppercorns are rarer and give an interesting colour, but they don't add much distinctive flavour. Cubeb pepper, if you can find it, is quite astonishingly good.

To make the sauce, simply poach the peppercorns in brandy, white wine or even vodka, to infuse the flavours. Reduce the alcohol to a syrup then add demi-glace. I usually add a spot of cream too and reduce further, but not much. The pickled green peppercorns are soft enough in flavour and texture to crunch, but hard-dried black peppercorns might be a challenge to anyone else eating and are often sieved out before serving.

(Pictured on pages 274–5.)

---

[100] Sometimes hard to find in the UK but I often pick them up when I'm in France. Most groceries seem to have them, they have an infinite shelf life and come in tins just the right size for a single batch of sauce.

Mayonnaise

There is a variety of mayonnaise or egg-emulsion-based sauces that can really add to your repertoire, but most of us have experienced the terrifying performance anxiety of making one from scratch.

Fortunately, with the arrival of the cheap hand-held immersion blender, all the mystery has disappeared. Making mayonnaise this way is a game-changer. Genuinely indistinguishable from magic. Once you have this simple mayo as a base, try the variations below.

Makes about 250ml (8¾fl oz)

1 tbsp Dijon mustard
1 egg
Pinch of sugar
Neutral oil (rapeseed/canola, avocado or groundnut are all good), as needed
Fragrant olive oil (optional)
Freshly ground black pepper

Find a jug, cup or jar into which the head of your blender fits right to the bottom. For me, that's a 450ml (15fl oz) Kilner jar. Measure 250ml (8¾fl oz) water into your jar and mark the level with tape or a Sharpie. Pour out the water.

Put the Dijon mustard and egg into the jar along with the sugar and a few grinds of black pepper. Now top up to the line with your chosen oil. You can mix in a portion of olive oil if it's appropriate to the taste you want but don't use olive oil by itself as the flavour is far too pronounced.

Now put the blender head right to the bottom of the jar and hit the button. The mayonnaise will start to form immediately and all you'll need to do is draw the blender slowly up to the top, making sure the everything is properly emulsified.

Variations:

- *Replace the mustard with three completely mashed cloves of garlic. Use the side of a knife and a little coarse salt to grind to a paste. This will make instant aioli.*

- *Add the juice of a lemon as you blend.*

- *Grate fresh horseradish into your mayo once it's finished. Make this the day before and refrigerate overnight to let the flavours really combine.*

- *Or, do the same trick with wasabi. This is amazing with steaks that have been basted in soy butter, such as London Broil (see page 194) or Chaliapin Steak (see page 206).*

- *Replace the regular oil with the oil from a can of tuna. Blend the tuna meat and a couple of anchovies to a paste, then blend this into the finished mayonnaise. This is the sauce you'd use on Veal Chop Tonnato (see page 232). It's incredible with steaks, veal chops and even on slices of tomato. Sprinkle with capers to finish.*

Louisiana Remoulade

Remoulade is a mayonnaise-based sauce of French origin that contains Dijon mustard, tarragon and finely chopped capers and cornichons. It has a lot in common with a tartare sauce and even the noble gribiche. The French serve it with all sorts of meats, fish and charcuterie and a lovely thing it is, but they've also passed it on to Louisiana and Denmark, where it has become more complicated and, frankly, more interesting.

In Cajun and Creole cooking (both influenced deeply by French), they add horseradish, pickled red (bell) peppers and a fantastic local Louisiana mustard that's sweet, hot and seedy. In Denmark, they add a lot of finely chopped vegetables – carrot, cabbage, pickles and red onion – as well as chives and sometimes curry powder.

Recipes vary hugely according to individual tastes and you can even knock out a quick, serviceable Danish remoulade by chopping up some good-quality piccalilli and stirring it into your mayo, but try both traditions and work out which you prefer with your steak

Makes about 400g (14oz)

250g (9oz) Mayonnaise (see page 278, or use shop-bought)
30g (1oz) English mustard
5 pickled red (bell) peppers, very finely chopped
10g (½oz) salted nonpareille capers, very finely chopped
Juice of 1 lemon
1 shallot, very finely chopped
1 garlic clove
Small bunch of flat-leaf parsley, leaves picked and finely chopped
10g (½oz) horseradish sauce
5g (¼oz) garlic powder
5g (¼oz) House Creole Seasoning (see page 291)
Splash of Worcestershire sauce
Sweet paprika, to taste

Combine all the ingredients in a bowl and stir together using a silicone spatula. Transfer to an airtight container and refrigerate overnight to allow the flavours to develop.

Béarnaise Sauce

**Béarnaise used to be as terrifying to prepare as mayonnaise, but now…
it's as preposterously easy.[101]**

Makes about 300ml (10½fl oz)

260g (9½oz) butter or ghee
1 tarragon sprig
1 shallot, roughly chopped
60ml (2fl oz) white wine vinegar
120ml (4fl oz) dry vermouth
10 black peppercorns
*5g (¼oz) chervil, chopped (or a big
  pinch of dried chervil)*
2 large egg yolks
*Sea salt and freshly ground black
  pepper*

Put the butter or ghee into a saucepan over a very low heat. We need
it to melt and sit at around 105°C (220°F).

Separate and reserve a few leaves of the tarragon, then roughly chop
the rest, stalks and all. Place in a saucepan with the shallot and pour
over the vinegar. Heat until the initial pungency of the vinegar has
dissipated, then pour in the vermouth.

Add the peppercorns and chervil, then reduce to about a teaspoonful
of liquid. Strain into your marked 'mayo jar' (see page 278).

Allow the vermouth mixture to cool for a couple of minutes, then add
the egg yolks.

Now, pour the clarified butter into the jar up to the line. Try to keep the
milky liquid in the pan but it doesn't matter if a little splashes in.

Blend with a hand-held blender until emulsified, then taste and adjust
the seasoning if necessary. Finely chop the remaining tarragon leaves
and add to the sauce.

Serve immediately or store the sauce either in a Thermos or in a
squeezy bottle placed in a warm water bath. The egg is cooked by the
hot butter but it's never safe to reheat béarnaise or to hold it for more
than 2 hours.

(Pictured on pages 274–5.)

---

[101] I don't even bother with clarifying butter any more, I just buy
tinned ghee from my local Indian supermarket. It lasts forever and
has a subtly stronger 'brown butter' flavour, which is no bad thing.

Blue Cheese Sauce

I'm not sure what the science is behind the deep connection between blue cheese and steak, but it's undeniably there. I've certainly visited butchers where beef is being aged for long periods and they've pointed out the blue-cheese smell… to be honest, it's not so subtle that you wouldn't notice without help.

You can, of course, finish your meal with something blue and veiny and no-one will object, but it's never wrong to bring it right into contact with the meat.

I've certainly seen chefs just crumble a bit of Stilton over the resting steak, and there's a certain purity in that.[102] The classic in an old-school steakhouse would be a sauce based on the deglazings of the pan, possibly with some alcohol, a big glug of demi-glace, and then the cheese melted into it… almost the same way you'd create a cream sauce. Port works for the deglazing, though I find the sweetness too much. Brandy works. And I once saw a Tuscan chef clean out the pan in which he'd cooked the Fiorentina, with a splash of grappa, and then finish the sauce with a load of creamy Gorgonzola. Blue cheese even adds immense character when melted into a hollandaise.

I wish it wasn't so stereotypical… the stupidly traditional cheese with the most establishment of meats, but honestly, it's the most blessed union and the gift that keeps on giving. Blue cheese crumbled into sour cream has always been what they pour over a wedge of iceberg in a diner. It's a respectable enough side dish, but the dressing isn't half as interesting on tasteless leaves as it might be on your steak. You can't honestly tell me you've never essayed an exploratory dip.

It's a natural, unimpeachable pairing, and perhaps the purest evocation of the theory is demonstrated at Keens Steakhouse in New York (see page 38) where the steak comes, without asking, with a side of lightly sour pickled vegetables and a pot of whipped blue cheese to dip them in. It's not, as far as I could recognize, any particularly distinguished brand of blue, but it's blitzed till it looks like a kind of grey face cream. The combination of salt/dairy fat/ sourness and frankly lip-puckering umami means you can't physically restrain yourself from smearing it on your steak like a kind of savoury butter icing.

However you choose to do it, you need to try blue cheese with your steak.

(Pictured on pages 274–5.)

---

[102] I want you to promise that you never saw this footnote but, if you're in a hurry and there's no one around to be judgemental, you can crack open a packet of Boursin and spoon an ugly great lump of it onto your steak. It melts to form a kind of split, creamy butter/sauce with much of the same flavour profile as the garlic bread from your favourite crappy pizza joint. Now, let's never speak of this again.

Salsa Verde

Salsa verde is one of a family of herby green dressings that can be found all over the world. It's just such a good idea that everyone wanted to have a go. The French have *sauce verte*, which is a green, herby mayonnaise that was originally designed to go with poached eel.[103] The Germans have *Grüne Soße*.[104] The US has the green goddess dressing. You can make a reasonable argument for Ligurian pesto being a green sauce and, of course, the English have mint sauce, which historically was called green sauce and contained lots of other herbs.[105] Versions of salsa verde are found both in Spain and Italy, but the best for grilled meat is the excellent Italian recipe, which contains a bunch of exciting things, including salty tinned fish, vinegar and pickles... truly maximalism at its best.

Makes about 150g (5½oz)

1 bunch flat-leaf parsley
½ bunch basil
2 tbsp salted nonpareille capers
4 anchovy fillets (the canned oily type)
4 garlic cloves
2 tsp Dijon mustard
2 tsp sherry vinegar, plus more to taste
6 cocktail gherkins or cornichons
Red pepper flakes, to taste
Extra virgin olive oil, to taste
Sea salt and freshly ground black pepper

Chop the green herbs very finely with a large knife.

Blitz the rest of the ingredients in a blender, adding the olive oil slowly until you get a texture you like.

Stir in the chopped herbs and adjust the texture with more oil.

Store overnight in a sealed container at room temperature, then taste and adjust the seasoning with red pepper flakes, salt, black pepper, or perhaps a splash more vinegar, just before serving.

(Pictured overleaf...)

---

[103] And therein not a million miles away from the weird and wonderful parsley loaded 'likker' that's the traditional accompaniment to Cockney eels, pie and mash.
[104] Made with a vast variety of fresh herbs – usually at least seven, supplied in mixed bunches for the purpose from food markets. It goes well with eggs, fish, cold meats or potatoes.
[105] One of the most popular was sorrel, a wonderfully sour, acidic herb, almost lemony in a cold dark country with no citrus fruit. One of the archaic names for sorrel in England was 'greensauce'.

Chimichurri

The best green sauces hum with chlorophyll like some sort of health smoothie. But I'm not suggesting this is a penitential liquidized salad – chimichurri is sensational as a clear counterpoint to spicy, fatty meats.

It occurs all over Latin America. Many recipes suggest using flat-leaf parsley, which is all very well, but to me this feels like avoiding the issue of something that tastes a tiny bit like coriander (cilantro) without scaring the horses. For me, it's not chimi if it's not all coriander – and bugger the horses. This is not a hill I'm going to die on, though, so feel free to cut it with as much parsley as you feel you need.

The oregano, by the way, is non-negotiable. And don't try it with the fresh stuff. It has nowhere near the concentrated punch of the dried product, which just needs to be revivified by the vinegar.

Makes about 200g (7oz)

1 tsp dried oregano
2 tbsp sherry vinegar, plus more
* to taste*
1 garlic clove
Juice of ½ lemon
½ tsp red pepper flakes
1 bunch coriander (or a mix of
* coriander and flat-leaf parsley),*
* very finely chopped*
1 shallot, very finely chopped
5 tbsp extra virgin olive oil
Sea salt and freshly ground black
* pepper*

Soak the dried oregano in the vinegar in a small bowl.

Mince the garlic finely, then grind to a paste with the side of your knife and a little coarse salt. Add it to a bowl along with all the other ingredients (including the soaked oregano) and stir well to combine.

If you prefer, you can blitz it in a food processor to a smooth paste, but I prefer a few short blips with a stick blender, which leaves small chunks of interesting stuff in a rich, oily green medium.

Add salt and pepper to taste, and more vinegar to balance if needed. You may also need to add more oil to manage the consistency. I find this is greatly improved if you make it a day ahead and refrigerate it overnight.

(Pictured overleaf…)

Steak Sauce

This is a homemade version of any one of several proprietary steak sauces. It is fruity, hot, sour and garlicky, but you can tweak the recipe according to your own taste. Golden syrup or black treacle are useful for upping the sweetness if that's what you're after. I often add some extra sriracha and a large pinch of House Creole Seasoning (see page 291) to my batch, but you can go as far off piste as you like here. This recipe is a good starting point but, like a Padawan with a lightsaber, you must eventually build your own.

Makes about 400ml (14fl oz)

100g (3½oz) prunes, pitted
3 garlic cloves
2 tbsp chopped onion
Zest of 1 orange
Flesh of 1 lemon
100ml (3½fl oz) Worcestershire sauce
100g (3½oz) tomato ketchup
50g (1¾oz) English mustard
1 tbsp sriracha
2 tsp chilli (hot pepper) flakes
1 tsp garlic powder
2 pickled walnuts
100ml (3½fl oz) vinegar from the jar of pickled walnuts
1 tsp ground white pepper

Combine all the ingredients in a food processor and blend to a smooth paste.

Pour into a non-reactive saucepan and simmer extremely gently until you reach the consistency you'd like. Add water if necessary to loosen.

Rubs

Rubs are aromatic ingredients that are applied to raw meat in order to impart their flavours over time. There are as many recipes for dry rubs as there are barbecuers, pitmasters and celebrity chefs, but many of them are just simple variations on a very basic theme.

We know from our understanding of brining that salting steak early will enhance its flavour, so the main ingredient in a rub is often salt. Woody and oily aromatic herbs can impart flavour a lot better than the green, leafy fresh type, so dried thyme, rosemary, oregano, cumin or fennel are also good additions. There's also an opportunity to impart heat by using ingredients like dried chillies or mustard powder. If sweetness is to your taste, sugar helps to balance out both heat and saltiness. Finally, most rubs include garlic powder, onion powder and even MSG to enhance the umami flavours of the meat. All would probably feature in the house rub of a decent Southern diner – for me, garlic powder is a kind of Proustian thing.

Powdery dry rubs can be combined with oil or fat to make a smearable paste – in fact, all the butters in this book (see pages 268–270) could be applied to a steak before it is left in the fridge overnight, then scraped off before cooking. Nancy Silverton, the American doyenne of Californian-Italian cooking, smears her steak with maple syrup and dredges it in porcini powder before leaving it somewhere quiet overnight to reconsider its behaviour. Some restaurants have evolved a way of ageing meat in an encapsulating layer of bacon fat which, arguably, is a kind of rub.

Rubs are an amazing tool but there's one caveat. If you're going to drop a steak into a searing hot pan, any rub ingredients will scorch and burn in seconds. Dry rubs or butters should be removed before cooking by scraping them off or wiping the steak with paper towels. Butters can then be added back to the pan later, at which point they become bastes (see page 271).

I spent a lot of time cooking in the rural American South, so my go-to house mix (see page 291) is derived from a Creole blend I picked up in Louisiana and have since gently tweaked.[106] Personally, I'm of the opinion that complex spice mixes, be they South American, Asian, North African or otherwise, become quite indistinguishable when used for deep flavouring before cooking. Of course, there are differences between ras el hanout, shichimi togarashi, Chinese five spice, garam masala, Old Bay and your own 'special' recipe, but in practical use as rubs – i.e. for enhancing flavour at the earliest stages of a longer cooking process – they can all be used in similar ways.[107]

---

[106] There is definitely no English mustard powder in an authentic Creole spice mix, and the fennel is pretty questionable, too.

[107] A few years ago, I tried to work out what was actually in Colonel Sanders' blend of eleven secret herbs and spices as part of my research for a newspaper article. I went online and asked as many people as I could reach what they thought might be in it. It was an interesting use of the hive mind and, in the end, we came up with a mix that actually tasted pretty authentic, though we never managed to get KFC to confirm or deny either way.

House Creole Seasoning

I love this stuff immoderately – you will notice that it crops up in several recipes in this book. I sprinkle it into sauces and stews, season my own sausages with it, use an approximate shit-ton of it over barbecue season and, through the winter, it features in the bloody Marys that keep me sane.

Whether or not you include salt will make the difference between whether this works as a seasoning or as a rub. Leave the salt out and you have a highly versatile spice mix that can be used for recipes in which salt is controlled separately. Combined with salt it's a fantastic rub or dry marinade.[108]

This recipe works with proportions, so you can make any quantity from a small spice jar to a full-on bucket if you feel like it. Just choose a measure (teaspoons, tablespoons, tens of grams, cups, etc.) and go from there. The ingredients are already dried so the combination will be stable and have a really good shelf life if kept in an airtight container.

Makes as little or as much as you like

4 parts smoked paprika
3 parts sea salt
2 parts cayenne pepper
2 parts garlic powder
2 parts sweet paprika
1 part dried oregano
1 part dried thyme
1 part black peppercorns
1 part dried onion flakes
1 part chilli (hot pepper) flakes
1 part fennel seeds
1 part English mustard powder

Combine everything in a food processor and blend to powder, then transfer to an airtight container.

---

[108] Roasted nuts tossed in the salty rub mix are also ideal.

Creole Mustard

All mustards go well with steak. There's a place for the ferocious yellow 'English' stuff. Tewkesbury mustard is brilliant if you can get your hands on it. Dijon is a terrific standby and I particularly favour the Japanese stuff that comes in little squeezy tubes. It looks like baby poop but it's fiery enough to torch a kilometre of treeline in an airstrike. There's a special place in my heart though for Zatarain's Creole Mustard, which is difficult to find outside of New Orleans. It's at the other end of the mustard spectrum to the hot stuff, being sweet and spicy and is a peerless accompaniment to a charcoal grilled steak.

Mine is only an approximation but it works well and, of course, uses the 'house' creole spice mix (see page 291) to advantage.

Makes sbout 170g (6oz)

150g (5½oz) wholegrain mustard
10g (½oz) fresh horseradish, very finely grated
1 tsp House Creole Seasoning (see page 291)
1 tsp Worcestershire sauce
1 tsp black treacle (molasses)

Combine all the ingredients in a bowl, mix well, then transfer to an airtight container.

Store in a fridge for at least a week so the flavours can combine and mellow.

Addendum: The Hamburger

Look, I'm sorry, but sooner or later we're going to have to talk about the hamburger. I realize that in many ways, the hamburger is everything that steak is not. It's the anti-steak, you might think. But this connection is much more nuanced than it might first appear.

Because if we're going to talk about cheap or sub-prime steaks, those tougher cuts that have loads more flavour but are more challenging to chew, that we cut more thinly or across the grain, or which we hammer to tenderize or marinate with onions or wine, then we inevitably come to the hamburger.

Once we move away from the filet mignon, every steak becomes an act of balancing flavour with tenderness and, once we go down that route, minced (ground) beef could theoretically lead us to something akin to the 'ultimate steak'.

The hamburger evolved as a way to grind up tough meat that's big on flavour but lacking in texture (let's not be coy here, the meat mincer is simply pre-chewing the stuff so we don't have to) before reassembling it into a steak shape, sometimes with added ingredients. We needn't shirk from the truth that the hamburger is dirt cheap and we don't need to conceal that it sometimes contains some incredibly shabby raw ingredients, but we also should not deny that it's bloody delicious and at least warrants proper examination.

First, though, let's shed some of the myths. It's true that there was a particular tradition in Hamburg, Germany, of manufacturing cured minced beef sausages, but though it's tempting to extend that into a narrative where it travels to America, via Ellis Island, to develop into a Big Mac, it doesn't really stand up logically. If you want the whole story, I urge you to read Josh Ozersky's masterful book *The Hamburger: A History,* but to paraphrase cruelly, the concept of a burger patty served in a bun evolved more as a natural function of ineluctable American business logic and early twentieth-century capitalism than German charcuterie and immigration. Mechanically turning inexpensive offcuts of commodity beef into almost addictively delicious, easy-to-digest portions and serving them quickly and conveniently – it's as good a shorthand representation of the American Dream as you're ever going to see.

One of Ozersky's most brilliant revelations is that the hamburger does not exist without the bun, in any philosophical sense. The patty is never consumed alone. It only functions in synergy with the other elements. Recipes for chopped or ground beef patties have existed for centuries. From the time of eighteenth-century English cook Hannah Glasse onwards, many domestic cookbooks contained recipes for 'Salisbury steak', a type of meatloaf flattened into a steak-like shape and often dressed with a sauce. This wasn't in any sense a 'burger', but rather a direct attempt to build an economical dish for a family.[109]

The hamburger, however, is something designed to be eaten by hand at the wheel of a giant chromed and finned automobile as you barrel down an interstate. It requires that you embrace a vision of convenience and prosperity while trusting that the burger won't drip down your shirt. A hamburger is a patty of minced beef, for sure, but it doesn't taste much of beef. The patty is really there to remind you that you're eating beef, while the sauce, pickles, lettuce and cheese are there to provide flavour. The flavourless bun is there so you don't need crockery, cutlery or even a table to sit at and the brand identity, including 100 per cent reliability from branch to branch, is there to give you a warm fuzzy feeling.

This book can therefore not be considered complete without discussing the Salisbury steak – the quasi-steak – more commonly known as 'the hamburger', humankind's most successful expression of 'steak', in which the meat is the least important thing in the recipe.

Recipes for Salisbury steak rely on similar principles to sausage-making. The meat, with additional fat if necessary, is minced and then combined with a neutral filler, usually breadcrumbs, to ensure that not a drop of flavour or fat remains unabsorbed. The meat is then cooked and served with a pan gravy so that even the seared bits in the pan are picked back up and recombined with the main dish.[110]

For the hamburger, high-fat, tough cuts of beef are used to produce a strong meaty flavour. They are heavily minced (effectively pre-masticated), so will always be tender. However, the key thing to understand about the hamburger is that the meat patty itself doesn't have to be kept 'juicy' and rare at the centre. A high proportion of the flavour in the patty comes from the Maillard reaction that takes place on the outside, so the more surface area you can provide, the better the finished construction will taste. This is why the best

[109] Like 'mock' turtle soup, Salisbury steak is one of the few historical dishes that actually announced itself as a cheaper alternative to the real thing. This could be incredibly useful on boarding house menus or even in steakhouses, flagging up a low-cost alternative for diners on a budget. Under a decent layer of sauce, you could even pass it off as a real steak to anyone watching you across the room.
[110] The French steak haché was originally designed with the same quasi-medical ideas behind it, as was the steak tartare (see page 160). Like steak tartare, health-giving beefsteak was chopped extremely fine to make it more digestible to invalids. Steak haché, though, makes no concessions to economy and, like tartare, is based on the highest-quality steak available.

burgers have thin patties, with cheese, sauce and some salad vegetables included to add back in some of that moistness. It's easy to realize that you can double the tasty surface area of a given weight of meat by making two thin patties rather than one thick one. Then, the really demonically clever idea is to construct the finished burger with three layers of bread, so the patties are both in contact with a thin slice of unadorned bun, which can soak up any fats and juices so no flavour is lost…

Nobody had to invent the double-decker cheeseburger with chop sauce… it was an evolutionary inevitability.

Epilogue

Around the time I began working on *Steak*,[111] there was great public enthusiasm for 'plant-based' eating and an incredible amount of research seemed to go into lab-grown, artificial 'meat'. Food prices were increasing and there was much worry about the environmental impact of intensive cattle rearing. One or two friends pointed out that that to write about the most prestigious and expensive meat on the planet would put me on the wrong side of history. Thank god I didn't listen.

It didn't take much examination of commercial animal rearing practice to realize that, yes, the way most beef is reared for the mass market is dreadful. That we are too used to an abundance of low-quality meat and we don't ask questions about its provenance.

When I started planning the book, I intended to visit Japan for Wagyu, Korea for Hanwoo beef and Argentina for the pampas-reared cattle of the region. What I learned was that each of these great beef cultures has now moved, almost entirely, toward intensive corn fattening and early slaughter. This is how market forces have driven us and will continue to do so.

But somehow, these commodity steaks were not what I was searching for – the steaks around which a culture had grown. And, in fact, as the book developed it became clear that we need a way to separate, in our heads, the markets for good steak – eaten rarely, by keen and discerning enthusiasts – from the millions of tons of commodity beef being processed into our food chain every year.

Steaks have been part of our lives longer than we've been *homo sapiens*. We don't just love to eat them more than almost anything else, but we've imbued them with powers and values. It turns out the scientists are getting quite close to something, in a tank somewhere, that they can make cook, smell, bleed, cut and taste like a steak – but the problem they're coming up against is cultural rather than scientific. You can make the meat, but you can't fake that huge attendant load of history, belief, culture and lore. Nothing could ever come close to replicating the experience of eating a perfectly butchered steak from a humanely-reared, grass-fed animal that has been allowed some length of life.

As I was considering how to end the book, I found myself waiting in a queue for a cab at King's Cross one afternoon, behind a group of around a dozen people. I thought they were maybe some kind of veterans rugby team. Huge men with big hands, strong necks and an alarming variety of broken noses. They were also wearing an interesting selection of tweed. I asked one extraordinarily wide fellow, standing about 6'4", who the team was. In a not unpleasant gust of beery breath, he said they were beef farmers, down from Northumbria, for their annual dinner.

---

[111] Who am I kidding? I've been researching steak since I got my first teeth.

We talked for about 20 minutes and it was an almost magical experience. They cared intensely about their animals and the meat they provided. They talked about the land and the pasture – not of sheds, inputs and units. They were built like that because they spent their days working, physically, with the creatures I wanted to eat. And unlike most farmers I meet in my work, they were, well, cheerful. They were producing healthy animals they were proud of. Prices were going up but more people, they reckoned, understood better what good meat was and that it was worth paying for. Best of all, they were proud of what we're doing with meat as a nation. There is, of course, some intensive beef rearing here, but we also have a small ecosystem of farmers producing meat in sustainable ways and a substantial audience that appreciates this enough to pay.

It's a great story for us in the UK. Beef production around the world continues to industrialise at a bewildering pace, yet here we're doing a world-leading job of protecting an older, slower way … and, as my new best friends pointed out before they stuffed themselves into two cabs, the most important thing is to keep spreading the word.

They were heading to Borough Market, to look at the very heart of the 'British Food Scene' and then, for lunch, they were going to Hawksmoor. As the cabs tootled off to the south, their suspensions visibly challenged by their cargo, it was hard to suppress emotion. Oh! To live in a world that has such heroic giants in it.

The chance encounter, though, also helped me to finally crystallize what I'd learned; that steak has always been uniquely 'special' – it should never become an 'every day' thing. There are fewer and fewer special things in our lives and we need to preserve them where we can. And now, I've grown to believe that the only responsible way to continue to eat steak is to fully understand it – so we can choose it carefully, cook it with respect and consume it with joy. So we can make it more special.

And that required a whole story.

Ind

lex

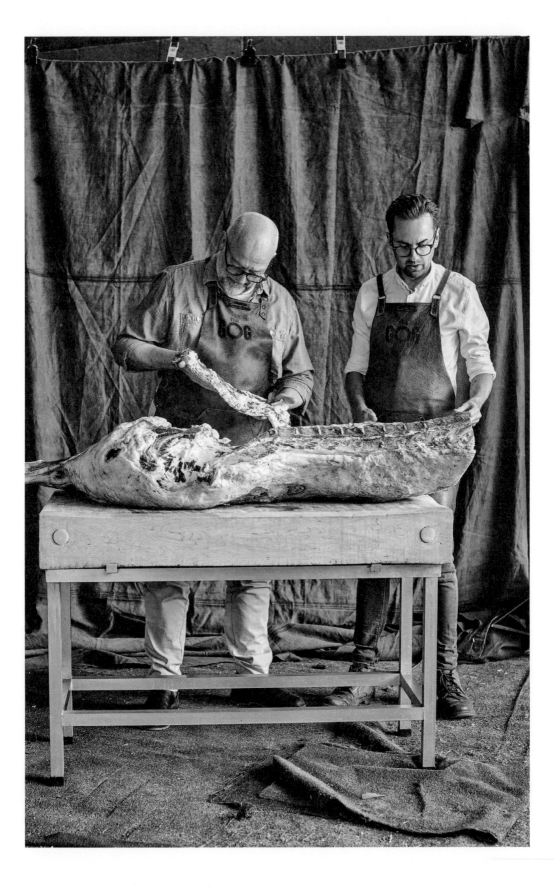

L

lactic acid 46, 83, 85
Lactobacillus acidophilus 83
Lambert, George 22
Leidenfrost, Dr Johann Gottlob 129
Leidenfrost effect 129
lemons: maître d'hotel butter 270
lettuce
  prawn cocktail 249
  steak sandwich 242–5
Limousin 33
Lipton, Sir Thomas 23
London broil 194–6
London broil steak 58–9
Longhorn 32, 36
Louisiana remoulade 281

M

Madeira sauce 273
Maillard reaction 118, 127
maître d'hotel butter 270
maraschino cherries: Black Forest gateau 256
marjaryasana 72–3
marrow bone: steak pie 238–9
Martini, the perfect 261–2
masculinity, steak and 22–3
mayonnaise 278
  Louisiana remoulade 281
Meades, Jonathan 20
Meiji, Emperor 42
Mexico 33
milk: chicken-fried steak 225–6
mince 13, 74
minute steak: chicken-fried steak 225–6
mirin: steak tataki 211
mise-en-place 11–12, 15
monkey gland steak 11, 186–7
The Morgue 23
mozzarella: veal 'parmigiana' sandwich 222
muscle fibres 75
mushrooms: steak Diane 185
mustard
  Café de Paris butter 267
  Creole mustard 292
  London broil 194–6
  Louisiana remoulade 281
  mayonnaise 278
  monkey gland steak 186–7
  steak sauce 288
  steak tartare 8–17

N

National Hanwoo Breeding System 43
New York 22–3, 24, 38–41
New York strip 98
Norfolk Red 32

O

omasum 37
onglet 118–19
onions
  Chaliapin steak 206–7
  steak tartare 8–17
oranges: steak sauce 288
oven finishing 142–5
oyster steak 88
oysters: carpetbagger steak 168–70

P

pans, non-stick 129
Pantaniero 33
papain 85
paprika: house Creole seasoning 291
Parmesan
  veal Milanese 218
  veal 'parmigiana' sandwich 222
parsley
  Café de Paris butter 267
  maître d'hotel butter 270
  salsa verde 284
  steak tartare 8–17
pecorino: veal 'parmigiana' sandwich 222
peppercorns: poivre sauce 277
peppers: Louisiana remoulade 281
Peter Luger Steak House 39
pie, steak 238–9
Pineywoods 33
poivre sauce 277
Pontin's Chophouse 23
pope's eye 88
porterhouse steak 74, 82, 96–7
  bistecca alla Fiorentina 171–2
potato starch: chicken-fried steak 225–6
potatoes
  duchess potatoes 204
  steak and chips 251–5
prawn cocktail 249
primals 82
prunes: steak sauce 288
Puerto Rico 33
pyrolysis 127

Acknowledgements

I'd like to thank Keens Steakhouse, Asador Horma Ondo, Trattoria Sostanza, Brasserie Georges and Plachutta – none of whom asked for my opinion but got it anyway – and Will Beckett and Huw Gott, founders of Hawksmoor. They were encouraging when this book was just an idea and, when I went back to see them at the end, it turned out we agreed on pretty much everything.

Dan Northrop is the sort of butcher I wish everyone could have: a craftsman enthusiast, always willing to pass on his knowledge. We need more Dans. I also thank his colleagues at the Gog Magog Farm Shop for letting us cut up a cow in their barn.

I thank my daughter, Liberty, as always, and also Elliott. Young people like this are the future of food and cooking. It's a privilege to show them stuff, in the certain knowledge that they'll be better than us sooner rather than later. This book should really be dedicated to them.

Creating an illustrated book is as much a team effort as any band making an album and all the members deserve praise. Harry Webster was an incredibly efficient and creative editor. Luke Bird was an art director whose commitment to the project didn't stop at getting his notebook splashed in fat and blood at a butchery day. Sam Folan was the photographer who pulled all of our insane capering into coherent and beautiful imagery. Faye Wears found props to enhance a constantly shifting brief and food stylist Sam Dixon… she can literally make a lump of dead cow look appetising.

Not everyone is present the shoots, so I also thank Laura Willis, Ruth Tewkesbury and the rest of the team at Quadrille. It's profoundly reassuring to know they are there.

Alex Pole, Netherton Foundry and Joel Black handle iron and steel for me. They are my favourite suppliers of knives, pans and utensils and their work appears throughout. If you see something here that makes you think, 'Damn! I have got to get one of those!' get in touch with them, you probably can.

I am indebted to Chef Victor Garvey, Naomi Tinkler at McCain and Craig McNerlin at Thermodyne UK.

Of course, I am enraptured by the work of Len and Alex Deighton, and honoured beyond description that they agreed to work on *Steak*.

Some days, I've looked at this project and wondered why it doesn't look like any other book I've ever seen… and I'm intensely proud. It's all down to the inspiration of people like Len Deighton, to the creativity and flexibility of the whole crew, and to the flat-out genius of my publisher, Sarah Lavelle. No other team could have done this.

About the Author

Tim Hayward is an award-winning food journalist and broadcaster, and the author of *Food DIY* (2013), *Knife* (2016), *The Modern Kitchen* (2017) and *Loaf Story* (2020). He is a regular panelist on BBC Radio 4's *The Kitchen Cabinet*, and has written and presented several documentary series on Radio 4 on subjects ranging from modern craftspeople to bacteria. His three-part documentary on fungi won gold at the 2023 New York Festivals Radio Awards, in the Environment & Ecology category.

Tim is both food writer and restaurant reviewer for the *Financial Times*, and winner of awards including the Fortnum and Mason Food Writer of the Year 2022 and Guild of Food Writers awards for Food Writing and Restaurant Reviews. He is co-owner of Fitzbillies Bakery in Cambridge.

Managing Director and Commissioning Editor Sarah Lavelle
Project Editor Harriet Webster
Copy Editor Lucy Kingett
Designer and Illustrator Luke Bird
Photographer Sam Folan
Food Stylist Sam Dixon
Prop Stylist Faye Wears
Head of Production Stephen Lang
Senior Production Controller Gary Hayes

First published in 2024 by Quadrille,
an imprint of Hardie Grant Publishing

Quadrille
52–54 Southwark Street
London SE1 1UN
quadrille.com

ISBN: 978 1 83783 100 5
Printed in China

ULTIMATE STEAK & CHIPS

COOKSTRIPS

1. TRIM UP peeled potatoes*

LIVE LARGE: keep only the **PERFECT** chips

CUT batons

LAY chips on clean cloth

SALT a 2cm (1 in.) Rib Eye

DRY the steak & the chips in fridge

OVERNIGHT + UNCOVERED

*best spuds: Maris Piper or Yukon Gold

2. FRY the chips in veg. oil

165°C (330°F)

cooked chips will barely change colour

DRAIN the chips on a RACK

FIRE SAFETY: keep the pot lid handy

while steak rests

RE-FRY the chips

small batches

oil temp 185°C (365°F)

get them as **DARK** as you like

TOSS chips in salt

SALT

3. SEAR steak

FLIP regularly

DRY HOT PAN

then, towards the end, **BASTE** with:

butter + thyme + garlic

REST steak @ 56.6°C / 138.9°F core temp

fresh watercress lightly dressed

SERVE with **BEARNAISE** or **PEPPERCORN SAUCE**

… We didn't have DVDs back then. Just very bad VHSs, so I rented one and started 'rock-and-rolling' it backward and forward, trying to hold the frame. It was useless. I got the biggest monitor in the college and shot the sequence from the screen on a motor drive Nikon. Eventually I got one adequate shot and blew it up so I could cut out the blurred smudge on the pillar. You couldn't read it… God. No, nothing was that easy. The grain on the original film, the degradation of 'telecine', the grain on my own film… there was no way to get a clear shot.

What I did know was that every Cookstrip was unique, because the framing was different in every single one. It took days. Drawings from the blurred photo. Matching, narrowing down. Looking at it again. Then finally, I nailed it. It was Cookstrip No. 37 on page 186 of his second book *Ou Est Le Garlic*. It was called 'Braisé – Basic Method' and explained in three panels how to prepare *boeuf mode en gelée*.

I took a photocopy from the page and pinned it up in my crappy student kitchen. And now, 40 years later, the same photocopy is pinned up next to my knives.

At the time I wrote this book, Len Deighton was 94. Still brilliant and productive and, unbelievably, along with his son Alex, prepared to do two new Cookstrips for us.

I don't have words for the honour, honestly. There's just an amazing circularity to this. The brilliance of his communication about food inspired me from the very beginning. First to cook and ultimately to write. And now, thanks to my brilliant crew at Quadrille, I get a chance to try to communicate something too. And Len Deighton is there… just inside the covers… wrapped around the whole thing.

These Cookstrips are designed to be cut out and displayed… God knows they're beautiful enough. Or maybe you could just photocopy them and pin them up in your kitchen like Harry Palmer.

Maybe they'll still be there in 40 years' time.